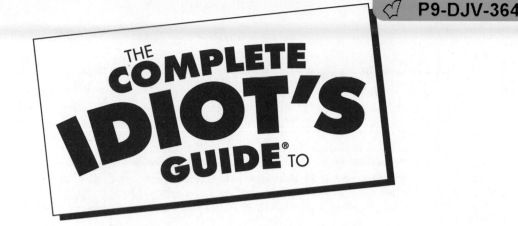

THE COMPLETE IDIOT'S GUIDE® TO

Creative Visualization

by Shari L. Just, Ph.D., and Carolyn Flynn

ALPHA

A member of Penguin Group (USA) Inc.

For Art and our children, Tom, Chris, and Robin
—Shari Just
To my little inspirations, Emerald and Lucas. You are my vision.
—Carolyn Flynn

ALPHA BOOKS

Published by the Penguin Group

Penguin Group (USA) Inc., 375 Hudson Street, New York, New York 10014, U.S.A.

Penguin Group (Canada), 10 Alcorn Avenue, Toronto, Ontario, Canada M4V 3B2 (a division of Pearson Penguin Canada Inc.)

Penguin Books Ltd, 80 Strand, London WC2R 0RL, England

Penguin Ireland, 25 St Stephen's Green, Dublin 2, Ireland (a division of Penguin Books Ltd)

Penguin Group (Australia), 250 Camberwell Road, Camberwell, Victoria 3124, Australia (a division of Pearson Australia Group Pty Ltd)

Penguin Books India Pvt Ltd, 11 Community Centre, Panchsheel Park, New Delhi—110 017, India

Penguin Group (NZ), cnr Airborne and Rosedale Roads, Albany, Auckland 1310, New Zealand (a division of Pearson New Zealand Ltd)

Penguin Books (South Africa) (Pty) Ltd, 24 Sturdee Avenue, Rosebank, Johannesburg 2196, South Africa

Penguin Books Ltd, Registered Offices: 80 Strand, London WC2R 0RL, England

Copyright © 2005 by Amaranth Illuminare

International Standard Book Number: 1-59257-398-3
Library of Congress Catalog Card Number: 2005929443

08 07 06 05   8 7 6 5 4 3 2 1

Interpretation of the printing code: The rightmost number of the first series of numbers is the year of the book's printing; the rightmost number of the second series of numbers is the number of the book's printing. For example, a printing code of 05-1 shows that the first printing occurred in 2005.

Printed in the United States of America

Note: This publication contains the opinions and ideas of its authors. It is intended to provide helpful and informative material on the subject matter covered. It is sold with the understanding that the authors, book producer, and publisher are not engaged in rendering professional services in the book. If the reader requires personal assistance or advice, a competent professional should be consulted.

The authorS, book producer, and publisher specifically disclaim any responsibility for any liability, loss, or risk, personal or otherwise, which is incurred as a consequence, directly or indirectly, of the use and application of any of the contents of this book.

Most Alpha books are available at special quantity discounts for bulk purchases for sales promotions, premiums, fund-raising, or educational use. Special books, or book excerpts, can also be created to fit specific needs.

For details, write: Special Markets, Alpha Books, 375 Hudson Street, New York, NY 10014.

Publisher: *Marie Butler-Knight*
Editorial Director: *Mike Sanders*
Senior Managing Editor: *Jennifer Bowles*
Senior Acquisitions Editor: *Randy Ladenheim-Gil*
Book Producer: *Lee Ann Chearney/Amaranth Illuminare*
Development Editor: *Lynn Northrup*
Production Editor: *Megan Douglass*
Copy Editor: *Emily Bell*

Cartoonist: *Shannon Wheeler*
Cover/Book Designer: *Trina Wurst*
Indexer: *Julie Bess*
Layout: *Ayanna Lacey*
Proofreading: *Mary Hunt*

Contents at a Glance

Contents

22 Healing Visualizations   279

23 Imagine the World You Want to Live In   291

Appendixes

Foreword

I'm a huge fan of visualization. How could it be otherwise? My entire business, Intuitive Consulting, Inc., began as the result of using the affirmation and visualization techniques that authors Shari Just and Carolyn Flynn so compellingly write about in this life-changing book. Here's how it happened.

In 1987, I was the Operations Manager of a small software company near Boston. I really disliked being there and I dreamed of developing my own business. I had taken classes on intuition development and discovered that I had a wealth of natural talent in this area. My main concern: could I develop such an exotic skill into a business? I quipped that if God posted a "Psychic Wanted" ad in the employment section of the Boston Globe, I'd apply. Barring that, I wasn't sure where to begin. So I decided to try using my newfound tools of affirming, visualizing, and asking the Universe for help.

About a month later, a friend who had been sick for a long time died. As I walked into the room for his funeral service I felt a strong inclination to sit next to a woman I hadn't met before. I briefly questioned why I should sit there when the room was full of people I knew. But the feeling was strong, and so I sat.

At the end of the service the woman and I exchanged pleasantries and she asked me what I did for a living. Despite the fact that in my current job I was an Operations Manager, I answered, "I'm a psychic." I was immediately stricken with alarm. "Why had I answered this way?" "What would she think?!" I had done a few readings for friends, but I had never defined my career that way!

I felt flustered by my answer. To my surprise she was quite open and receptive. She then told me that she was a writer for the *Boston Globe* and would love to have a reading so she could write about it in her column.

To make a long story short, I gave her a reading, she wrote the article, and in a very few months, more than 400 people called to schedule appointments. Suddenly, I was running my own business!

I attribute this amazing synchronicity and coincidence to having used the tools of visualization and affirmation. It led me to the exact path I needed to travel in order to create a full-time business virtually overnight.

Since then, I've also used these same techniques to become a bestselling author of four books on intuition. For example, when I received the opportunity to write *The Complete Idiot's Guide to Psychic Awareness*, the opportunity seemed to have appeared out of the blue! But I knew it had more to do with writing down my goals, affirming them with positive statements, visualizing clear results and trusting my intuition.

If any of this intrigues you, then you must own and read the book you hold in your hands. The authors, Shari Just and Carolyn Flynn, seem to me to have gotten it just right. This book is not just a fun-to-read guide to a better life. It's also a wonderfully wise and engaging primer on how to lead one's life with confidence and creativity.

Perhaps it was best summed up by writer Shakti Gawain who said, "Creative visualization is magic in the truest and highest meaning of the word." I've certainly experienced that magic. And with the help provided so skillfully and generously by the authors of this book, you will, too.

Dream big. Enjoy the journey.

—Lynn Robinson

Lynn Robinson, M.Ed., is one of the nation's leading experts on the topic of intuition. Through her work as an intuitive coach she's helped thousands of people discover their life passion and achieve their goals. She's a best-selling author whose books include *Real Prosperity, Compass of the Soul, Divine Intuition,* and *The Complete Idiot's Guide to Psychic Awareness.* Her free Intuition Newsletter is available at www.LynnRobinson.com.

Introduction

This book is about realizing your most heartfelt desires. We all want to live our lives to the fullest. We want to achieve that state of continual contentment, and at the same time, we want to attain fulfillment of our wildest and dearest dreams.

Creative visualization is a powerful technique that can help you manifest your best life. The techniques that we will explain in this book are tools you can use again and again. You may apply them in all areas of your life to achieve deep and lasting happiness.

Why would you need an entire book to learn these simple techniques? After all, isn't it just about visualizing what you want and thinking positively about it? We asked ourselves the same question. But it's so much more than that, as we learned, and as we were writing together, our own dreams unfolded right before our eyes.

Practice, practice, practice … will get you where you want to go, whether it's Carnegie Hall or Mount Everest. In the practicing, you perfect the techniques. In living it, as you manifest the dreams you have always desired, you find contentment. Thus rewarded, you practice again.

The central tenets of creative visualization became popularized about 25 years ago in a slim volume written by Shakti Gawain. But since then, as many people like Shari and Carolyn have put the techniques into practice, we have discovered so much more. This book pulls all that together and carries it forward into the now—and the future. Read on and find out about how you can use creative visualization. You'll wonder how you lived without it.

How to Use This Book

This book is divided into a six-part exploration of how to create visualizations and use them to manifest what you want in life.

Part 1, "What Creative Visualization Is All About," introduces you to the building blocks of creative visualization. Creative visualization is equal parts imagination, desire, belief, and focus.

Part 2, "Learning to Visualize, Creatively!" gets you set up for the most effective creative visualizations possible. Once you get going, you'll find it's more than a practice, more than just a few techniques—it's a way of living and manifesting.

Part 3, "Know What You Want, Set Your Intent," takes a deeper look at intention. Learn how to use this immeasurable, infinite quality to manifest changes on the outer and inner paths. And learn how to use the power of the present moment to create your future.

Part 4, "You've Got to See It to Be It," draws upon various techniques to strengthen your imagination and belief. Here, you'll learn about the layers of energy and the way ideas and creativity work through them. You'll also learn about ways to use creative visualization with life-affirming results.

Part 5, "Manifest Creative Ways to Visualize," shows you that there is a personal style of visualizing for everyone. Build on the foundation of techniques introduced in early chapters to invent new techniques that enhance your imagination and summon stronger belief.

Part 6, "More Visualizations You Can Do," offers four chapters full of ways to practice techniques of creative visualization. Apply creative visualization to loving relationships, health, prosperity, or global concerns—you name it!

Following these parts you'll find three useful appendixes: a guide to setting up your Creative Visualization Journal, a list of resources if you want to delve deeper into this topic, and a glossary of terms.

Extras

Throughout each chapter of this book, we've added five types of extra information in boxes, to help you learn even more about manifesting your vision:

 Deeper Meaning
These definitions will provide more illumination on a term central to creative visualization.

Affirmations
You'll discover ways to write affirmations and create some of your own through the examples we drop into each chapter.

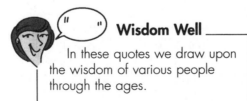 **Wisdom Well**
In these quotes we draw upon the wisdom of various people through the ages.

Imagine, See, Do

These boxes contain practical tips and tidbits to help bring forth your visualization techniques and reach your inspired goals.

Don't Panic, *Focus!*

Don't let doubts and obstacles hold you back from creating your vision and manifesting it. Use these tips to work through them.

Acknowledgments

From Shari:

I wish to thank my book producer Lee Ann Chearney, Creative Director of Amaranth, who continues to think I have something to say, and my co-author Carolyn Flynn who gave me the support and encouragement to not only write with her but to reveal some of my deeply personal experiences in the pages of this book.

I thank the many courageous people I have worked with in my practice who have allowed me to accompany them to the edges of spiritual growth and shown me the wonder of being there.

I thank my friend and colleague Dr. Marya Barey for simply being who she is.

I also thank my grandchildren, Ashley, Ben, Owen, Connor, and Aubrey who show me each day that anything is possible, and my parents Bert and Virginia Wheeler who set me on my spiritual pathway.

To Art: Thanks for 44 years of love and light.

From Carolyn:

I would like to acknowledge the calm assurance and wisdom of my co-author, Shari Just. Many thanks go to book producer Lee Ann Chearney for her role in sending me creative work that's good for my soul and assuring that every chapter and every word strike just the right chord. Thanks also to Alpha Books for its commitment to publishing books like this that enrich people's lives. Mostly, though, I would like to thank you, the reader, and encourage you to believe that you can live your best life.

Finally, I'd like to thank my twins, who are a continuing source of inspiration and imagination. Because my Creator has entrusted me with such a gift, I do truly believe all things are possible.

A Special Thanks to the Many Who Contributed Their Knowledge, Power, and Unique Style

The publication of this book benefits from the collaboration of many talented people who lent their special focus and talent to this book. At Alpha Books, we thank Alpha publisher Marie Butler-Knight, Senior Acquisitions Editor Randy Ladenheim-Gil, Development Editor Lynn Northrup, and Senior Managing Editor Jen Bowles. At Amaranth, we thank Creative Director Lee Ann Chearney for her wisdom and strength.

Trademarks

Part 1

What Creative Visualization Is All About

Seeing *is* believing. Great visionaries of the ages have started their paths to wisdom with just that—an unmistakable vision that guided them.

Creative visualization starts with the power of your imagination. When you create a vivid picture in your mind, you can create what you want to happen in your life. Creative visualization is equal parts imagination, desire, belief, and focus. What infuses these techniques with power is your intent.

Creative visualization *can* be a spiritual journey, and it most certainly *is* a personal journey. The journey ahead will take you from a state of wishing to a state of believing. Along the way, you will gain a sense of your power to create what you want and need in your life, gaining a deeper understanding of your best self.

Seeing Beyond: The Potential of Creative Visualization

In This Chapter

◆ What creative visualization is all about

◆ How do you use creative visualization?

◆ A modern history of creative visualization

◆ The five essential components: imagination, focus, belief, conscious-ness, affirmation

◆ How affirmations work

Nearly every story of great achievement begins with a vision. Magellan saw a vast sea that led to a new world, and he set off to chart it. Galileo imagined a round world and a vast universe, and he held fast to his vision. Think also of Moses hearing the voice of Yahweh in the burning bush, the apostle Paul and the blinding light on the road to Damascus, Jesus Christ and the doves that ascended from heaven, Buddha and the bodhi tree,

Mohammad and his visions in the desert, or the Virgin Mary getting a visit from Archangel Michael. In legends, ancient and modern, from King Arthur to Luke Skywalker to Harry Potter, heroes receive a vision and answer the call.

Throughout history, that's also true for ordinary people—that is, those of us who are not deities or legends—who see a vision for how they can make a difference and heed the call to duty—from Harriet Tubman to Sacagawea to Florence Nightingale to Eleanor Roosevelt.

What is your vision for your life? What is your *most heartfelt* dream? Can you see it clearly, as Michelangelo saw the form of youthful masculine beauty in the white marble that became *David?* In this book, we know that seeing is believing. When you can see it, you can make it happen. That's what creative visualization is all about.

What Is Creative Visualization?

"I have a dream, that one day ..."

As the words of Martin Luther King Jr. rang out from the steps of the Lincoln Memorial in Washington, D.C., that day in 1963, he created a picture so vivid it became a shared vision for our society. Line by line, in this famous speech, King created a picture of a society where all men and women were free. We may not have the complete picture in our society today, but because of his vision, we can picture it.

Creative visualization is the technique of using *your* imagination to manifest what you want your life to be. At its simplest, it's a way to identify your goals and make them reality—but it's so much more than a goal-setting and problem-solving technique. Creative visualization goes beyond wishing and dreaming to make something you want happen. Creative visualization goes above using sheer willpower or drive to bring what you desire into your life. Both of those methods require great effort, and you may have accomplished much in your life through tireless hard work. But creative visualization is much more powerful because it works in harmony with the positive energy of the universe.

Deeper Meaning

Creative visualization is the technique of using your imagination to envision what you want your life to be. By directing positive energy to that mental picture, you can make that vision a reality.

In your imagination lies an ally. About 30 years ago, a writer and workshop leader named Shakti Gawain realized the power of using mental pictures to help people reach their dreams. Her book, *Creative Visualization: Use the Power of Your Imagination to Create What You Want in Your Life*, developed a set of techniques that guided a whole generation in ways to think, visualize, and realize personal objectives. (Gawain's book, like many others to which we will refer in this book, is listed in Appendix B.)

Since then, others have lent their voices and visions to the field, honing different techniques. In this book, we'll provide a guide to incorporating those techniques into realizing your best and brightest life.

By using your creative imagination in a conscious way and directing your focus on that vision, you can create what you truly want in life. That can be:

- ◆ Love
- ◆ Fulfillment
- ◆ Meaningful and rewarding work
- ◆ Thriving and satisfying relationships
- ◆ Creative self-expression
- ◆ Health and well-being
- ◆ Harmony and beauty
- ◆ Prosperity
- ◆ Inner peace

The possibilities are limited only by what you can imagine!

Introducing Ourselves

In the upcoming chapters, you'll learn the basic principles of creative visualization, and we will guide you in visualizations and techniques that you can apply in your life. But before we take you on our journey, we'd like to introduce ourselves and tell you a little bit about how we have used creative visualization personally, in our own lives.

Meet Shari

When Shari was an undergraduate studying clinical psychology, she began to form an image in her mind of where she wanted to go. She saw herself going in and out of an office that had her name and credentials on the door—*Shari Just, Ph.D.* She envisioned herself escorting clients in and out and doing therapy in the quiet of her office.

She made a list of the steps that she would need to take to meet this goal. Sometimes she had to change the specific steps, but she kept the list current. Often her goal was just to pass a test—or sometimes, just to get through the day.

What stood in the way of Shari realizing her dream were two more degrees, some analytical training, internships, licensing tests—and *a lot* of money. But she found it became critical that she had formed a vision of her goal early on. This vision took her through some rough times (such as three children who came down with chicken pox simultaneously). Shari points to that picture in her mind—*Shari Just, Ph.D.*—as the crucial component in meeting her goal. For Shari, it was a joyful moment to escort her first client into an office with *Shari Just, Ph.D.* posted on the entrance.

Shari has practiced as a psychologist now for 24 years, where she focuses on adult and older adolescent analytical insight therapy. With Marci Pliskin, CSW, ACSW, Shari is the co-author of *The Complete Idiot's Guide to Interpreting Your Dreams, Second Edition*, (Alpha Books, 2003). She has written a column on dream interpretation for *YM* magazine, as well as a question-and-answer dream column for the Internet.

Meet Carolyn

Carolyn has known since she was eight years old that she was going to be a writer. She imagined herself living in a two-story house with hardwood floors, sitting at a typewriter (this visualization predates the laptop!), writing most of the day and looking out the window each afternoon to see her children come off the bus. She could picture the details of this scene down to the maple finish of the staircase and the royal blue dress she was wearing.

The vision has modified over the years. She lives in an adobe home in the Southwest. It's one story—so, no staircase—but it has a flagstone fireplace and a sunken living room, two architectural features that resonate for her and provide comforting, creative energy. It's the twenty-first century now, so she types on a computer and sends her work via e-mail. She *does* have those two beautiful children—boy/girl twins.

What strikes Carolyn now about that vision is how vivid it was. She knew absolutely that she was going to be a writer, and that vision has carried her through a 23-year career as a journalist, book author, and literary fiction writer.

How You Can Use Creative Visualization

Creative visualization can have many applications. It can work in every area of your life: health, work, family, love, money, creativity. You may direct creative visualization toward getting a job, finding your calling, manifesting more money, manifesting a relationship, deepening a relationship, healing a relationship. You may seek immediate, tangible results such as finding work or learning a new skill. Or you may have broader goals, such as creating more harmony in your life or cultivating inner peace. You may use it for virtually anything you desire.

Creative visualization works on several planes—physical, emotional, mental, and spiritual. A physical goal could be improving your stamina or muscle tone, or it could be for a healing of an illness or chronic condition. An emotional goal could be creating more serenity in your life. A mental goal could be to acquire knowledge about something you'd like to pursue, or it could simply be to improve your mental capacities, such as to improve your vocabulary. A spiritual goal could be to bring forgiveness to a situation. The possibilities are endless.

You might use creative visualization for an immediate situation, for an ongoing challenge or the big picture. Most often, we think of it as a way to reach a big picture goal—those five-year goals. Maybe it's that you want to play jazz piano in a nightclub or you want to live in a beautiful home in the mountains with your soul mate. (That last one encompasses several areas of life!)

Creative visualization may also be used to meet an ongoing challenge in a more directed way. That might include an effort to be more patient with your children, more empathetic with your spouse, or more fulfilled at work. Creative visualization can be very effective in these examples because creative visualization calls upon us to consciously direct our focus on an issue that can seem pervasive—and sometimes overwhelming.

Creative visualization, too, can be used for an immediate situation, such as a confrontation with a boss or ex-spouse, negotiation of a tricky business deal or performing for the first time. It can be used on the big scale or the small scale. It's up to you!

Creative visualization can also be used to shape a vision. Let's say you know you want to use creative visualization to find meaningful work you are passionate about and you want to do that within five years. Once you develop a vision, you may use creative visualization to identify the small steps you must take to explore and define the type of work you are seeking. Or you may use it to invite the needed influences and/or resources into your life so that you can realize your vision. Maybe you

> **CAUTION**
>
> **Don't Panic, *Focus!***
>
> So you don't know exactly what you want yet? Don't worry. If all you know at the beginning is that you want meaningful work, you can use creative visualization to sort it out. As you practice, you can begin to fill in the picture.

know where you want to go—maybe you know you need to go to school or you need to develop a business plan. Maybe you know in the larger sense the area you want to pursue—let's say film making—but you are not certain if you want to do documentaries, write screenplays, or produce films. Creative visualization can help you get clearer on your dream and fine-tune it.

Meet Your Innermost Dreams and Visions

No doubt before you picked up this book, you already developed dreams for areas of your life and visions to go with them, just as Carolyn did in her vision as a writer, without knowing the term *creative visualization* or understanding that she was using the principle of intention. Take a few moments before we begin to write about visions you have had in your life, and reflect on how you used them to reach your goals. Think of a picture that came to you through inspiration, and write about how it guided you in bringing that picture into the reality of your daily life.

Imagine, See, Be

To get the most out of this book, you may want to start a Creative Visualization Journal. You can use it to develop your vision and mark your progress. Choose a notebook that symbolizes your intent, with an image on the cover that speaks to you or in a color that signifies the kind of energy you want to direct to your vision. For more guidance on how to set it up, turn to Appendix A.

We start there, because we want you to realize that you probably have already done creative visualization many times in your life! And you have probably had success with it. With this book, you will learn how to become conscious of a process.

You may already have tried visualization in some areas of your life but not others. For many of us, it's easier to be clear and direct in reaching goals in the area of work but not as natural or comfortable to do it in the area of relationships. This book will help you sharpen your skills so you can apply creative visualization to all areas of your life.

Nine and a Half Lives: Your Life Arenas

Let's start off by assessing your Life Arenas—those areas in which you live, dream, and function. We call this section Nine and a Half Lives because while we will list 10 Life Arenas, we know there is work to do: the arena where you need to work the most is the one that is only half a life. Now, we say this tongue-in-cheek because we know that if you charted your 10 Life Arenas on a bar graph, measuring fulfillment against potential, not every one would depict 100 percent fulfillment. In some arenas, you might come close—85 to 90 percent. In others, you might be functioning only at 50 percent, or, if you are honest with yourself, maybe even less than 50 percent.

For each arena listed below, write a sentence or two assessing what fulfills you in this forum of living and what might be missing. If you were to measure fulfillment against potential, what would the percentage be? Which arenas need more focus and development?

It's also important to evaluate each arena as a center of power in your life. Which arenas are strong? Which arenas provide structure, stability, and security in your life? Think about how these arenas supplement the other arenas. You'll want to keep your centers of power in mind as you develop the arenas that are "half-lives." We've listed the Life Arenas in no particular order; each one is important and holds deep meaning for your optimal experience of life, that is, your happiness and success!

Love _____

_____

_____

Family _____

_____

_____

Work _____

_____

_____

Money _____

_____

_____

Health _____

_____

_____

Home _____

_____

_____

Personal growth _____

_____

_____

Spirituality _____

_____

_____

Leisure/rejuvenation _____

_____

_____

Creative self-expression _____

_____

_____

Now, graph it by filling in the bars in the illustration to match the percentage of fulfillment you feel in each Life Arena. Take a look at your measure of fulfillment against potential, to see a visual map of where you believe your strengths are, and where there are areas for improvement.

Your Life Arenas

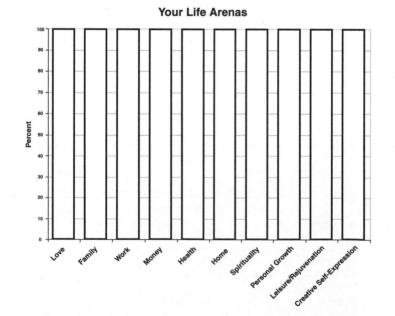

Looking More Deeply

When you look over the arenas of your life that form its foundation, which arena seems to need the most attention? What arena do you feel most passionate about right now? In which arena do you currently place the most energy?

Considering the goals you wrote for your Life Arenas, what talents, skills, and personal qualities would you like to start cultivating to achieve those goals? What jumps out at you as the one quality or skill you'd like to start cultivating. What quality that you already have would you like to continue to hone and fine-tune to precision?

Don't Panic, *Focus!*

In her book *Wishcraft* (Ballantine Books, 1979), Barbara Sher urges readers not to set their sights too low when developing a vision and moving toward a goal. She cautions that her techniques don't work unless you bring your highest hopes and deepest dreams to the process. So it's important to look at what you really want—even if it seems impractical or impossible. Your desire to achieve your dream is the surge of energy that makes the techniques of creative visualization work.

A Guided Tour: A Modern History of Creative Visualization

In 1978, Shakti Gawain wrote a book, *Creative Visualization: Use the Power of Your Imagination to Create What You Want in Your Life*, that birthed the term "creative visualization." Her very simple techniques became the basis for a new field of personal growth and self-actualization. Others have added nuances, deepened the concept, and developed practical ways to apply it. We will weave in their philosophies and techniques throughout this book, and add a few insights and techniques of our own!

What Gawain recognized in her simple book was the power of the imagination to get results in our lives. If you can conceive it, you can believe it. If you can believe it, you can make it happen. Gawain's book originates from the New Age movement, but its techniques transcend the philosophies of New Age. In other words, you don't have to be New Age to practice creative visualization.

Many writers from many traditions have recognized the power of our thoughts to change our lives. In the nineteenth century book *As a Man Thinketh*, James Allen, writing in Victorian England, emerging from the legacy of the Age of Reason and not a small amount of Calvinism, says, "They themselves are makers of themselves by virtue of the thoughts they choose and encourage." He refers to the mind as the "master weaver, both of the inner garment of character and the outer garment of circumstance."

Contemporary writers such as Barbara Sher in *Wishcraft* guide readers in practical goal-setting, brainstorming, and action steps. So, too, with Lynn Grabhorn, who wrote *Excuse Me, Your Life is Waiting*. Incorporating practical techniques into the visualization process is a decidedly twentieth-century application of mental muscle in pursuit of pragmatic results. It is a kind of life coaching, perhaps emerging and evolving from the growing field of psychotherapy, which prompts individuals to look more deeply at their psyche and how it informs their life experiences.

Two writers who have recently deepened some of the central concepts that make creative visualization so effective are Eckhart Tolle (*The Power of Now, Stillness Speaks*) and Wayne W. Dyer (*The Power of Intention* and many other books).

Tolle emphasizes the power of the present moment to bring serenity and discipline to our thoughts, and we'll talk more about his ideas in Chapter 11. His take on it is that staying in the now puts us in the place where we are in harmony with ourselves, each other, and the deeper forces of the universe. This inner work, and the discipline of staying in the present instead of running from the past and fleeing toward the future, can illuminate the techniques of creative visualization.

Dyer added to the dialogue with *The Power of Intention*, which was featured in a Public Broadcasting Service special. Dyer does not equate intention with determination. Instead, he defines it as the source of creation in the universe—a force we can access, trust, and let work in our lives. Intention guides the techniques of creative visualization, and as you'll see, forms the backbone of its success.

So as you see, Gawain was really on to something. In the introduction to her twenty-fifth anniversary edition, her publisher remembers issuing only 2,000 copies in the first printing. With no promotion and no review copies, the book kept selling out, printing after printing, through word of mouth. People bought the book and came back to the bookstore a few days later to buy a copy for a friend. Clearly, then, creative visualization works, and it can work for *you*.

Essential Components

Creative visualization uses five essential components:

- ◆ Imagination
- ◆ Focus
- ◆ Belief
- ◆ Consciousness
- ◆ Affirmation

Deeper Meaning

Affirmations are simple, declarative statements that something good you want in your life is already so. They are always positive. Affirmations serve to "make firm" your vision and your intention.

Let's take a closer look at each of these.

Imagination

Imagination is the first and most essential component, the one that you always have at the ready. With creative visualization, you start with an idea and create a mental picture around it. Your imagination takes you beyond the limitations of your everyday mind; it takes you to the place where new possibilities lie. It takes you to where your passions reside —to what you really, really care about.

Focus

To cultivate focus, you must relax into a quiet, meditative state of mind. This creates the state in which you can begin to fill in the details of your vision. It also creates the intention that you will bring your vision into focus. You are giving positive energy to the development of your vision. Meditation serves to sharpen the focus.

Belief

Once you create your vision, you act as if what you envision has already happened. You don't just hope it will. You believe it *will* happen, with the same conviction that Martin Luther King Jr. had on the steps of the Lincoln Memorial, with the same conviction that launched Christopher Columbus across the Atlantic. You take the belief that it will happen and you direct your meditative focus to expand the feeling of how possible what you envision *is*. You direct your focus to what it feels like to experience your vision as if it were already happening.

Consciousness

Once you have begun the practice of visioning and focusing on your goal, you continue to remain conscious. You stay aware of the feelings, expectations, and doubts that come up around it. Through consciousness, you keep clarifying your desire and your intentions.

Affirmation

Finally, a vital technique in creative visualization is affirmation. To *affirm* is to "declare positively" or to "make valid." It means to make firm. When you are using an affirmation in creative visualization, you are making the image you have created firm. Gawain defines an affirmation as a "strong, positive statement that something is *already* so."

Affirmations can bring about dramatic changes in your life. In one positive statement lies immense power. Affirmations are simple, yet they can affect you on a deep level.

Building Affirmations

How do you create affirmations? It's really quite easy. Affirmations are declarative statements and are always positive. In an affirmation, the good that you want to bring into your life already *is*.

In Chapter 4, we'll discuss some of the building blocks of affirmations, and you'll see examples throughout this book. But some fundamental ways to begin are "I love …" "I accept …" "I appreciate …." Another technique is to say it is happening now: "I am giving …" "I am seeing …" or "I am experiencing …" love, for instance. Some affirmations make broader statements, such as "Everything I need is coming" or "Everything I need is already within me."

A good example might be the way you would encourage a friend who is building his or her own home. Maybe the process takes a while and a few things go wrong. Saying what you would say to a good friend is a good way to get accustomed to writing affirmations for yourself, which might not seem natural at first.

Let's make a list of affirmations you might use:

- ◆ This builder has a good reputation; I know the builder is doing a good job for you.

◆ I know you trust this builder will honor his or her contractual commitment to you.

◆ You have plenty of money for this home and I know you are using it wisely.

◆ I know you can just picture it! I know you have images in your mind that show you how everything will be right about this house.

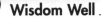
Wisdom Well

If we go down into ourselves we find that we possess exactly what we desire.

—Simone Weil, French philosopher, writer, and humanitarian, *Gravity and Grace*, 1947

Affirmations create an ever-replenishing cycle of positive energy. In this case, your affirmations reassure your friend that the process will go well. His (or her) confidence in the builder comes through when he (or she) discusses concerns, and that helps the builder carry the project through the way he (or she) envisioned. Affirmations carry you through the rough spots and return you to your vision. We'll go into affirmations a bit more in Chapter 4.

A Visualization to Build On

So let's try another simple creative visualization, applying it to your Life Arenas. Go back to the earlier exercise in which you examined your Life Arenas. Choose one arena and set a specific goal for it. For this first exercise, choose something simple, something you might do in the next three months.

Sit comfortably in a quiet place where you will be free of distractions and no one will disturb you. Take three deep cleansing breaths. Bring your awareness to your body, starting at your feet and moving to your crown, gradually and consciously relaxing each muscle. Use your breath to cleanse all the tension out of your body.

When you feel completely relaxed, direct your imagination to your goal and what you would like to happen. Create a vivid mental picture. Imagine yourself holding an object that represents your goal or in a setting where you have already reached your goal. Now bring your picture alive by animating it with people speaking and moving about. The objective is to make your vision as real as possible.

Say out loud or to yourself, "I want this to happen in my life." Then, "I believe I will make this happen in my life."

Holding your mental picture clearly in focus, repeat three or four affirmations, either out loud or to yourself, that are specific to your goal. The following sample affirmations use specific goals.

I love the view <u>from my beautiful home in the mountains</u>.

When I am in <u>my beautiful home in the mountains</u>, I feel whole and complete.

I am now attracting a <u>loving, meaningful relationship</u> into my life.

When I am <u>with my lover in my new meaningful relationship</u>, I am content, and my life is enriched.

I love and appreciate <u>the passionate, creative work I have brought into my life</u>.

I trust that <u>perfect wisdom is in my heart and that I am whole and complete</u>.

Now, you may use these affirmations as a guide, now filling in the blank with your own, unique and specific visions.

Close your meditation with this affirmation:

I trust that what I am envisioning for my life is manifesting in a way that brings about my highest good.

It's that simple. And practice makes perfect. In the coming chapters, we'll provide lots of techniques that can help you sharpen your skills, and realize your visions. We'll also explore the principles behind creative visualization that make these simple techniques so effective.

The Least You Need to Know

- Creative visualization techniques recognize that the imagination is a great ally in reaching our dreams.

- You may apply creative visualization to any life arena. You may use it for an immediate situation, for an ongoing challenge or the big picture.

- The five essential components of creative visualization are imagination, focus, belief, consciousness, and affirmation.

- Affirmations keep you invested and believing in your goal. Affirmations create a circle of positive energy.

Where Does Religion Come In?

In This Chapter

◆ What is spirituality?

◆ Developing spiritual self-knowledge

◆ Belief: the crux of it all

◆ Proof positive: the energy of attraction

◆ Asking and receiving: the role of prayer

The simple techniques of creative visualization transcend any one belief system. You do not have to be a *this* or a *that* to practice creative visualization.

Creative visualization is not theologically based, but some people incorporate their understanding of a Creator into the use of it. Creative visualization is not wedded to any sort of religion. But it *is* spiritual.

What lies at the heart of creative visualization is the belief that it can work for you. In this chapter, we will examine how, no matter your cosmic belief system, you can nurture that belief.

Spiritual: What's That?

What comes to mind when you read the word *spiritual?* And what about the word *religion?* Plenty, you might say.

Shari has asked people to talk about these terms and has found that one person's definition can be radically different from the next. Put 10 people in a room and ask them the distinction between these words and you're certain to get a "spirited" discussion going. Then ask them what it means to experience *spiritualization*, and you will get not 10 but 15 or 20 answers as the discussion evolves. That's because our experience of these concepts is so uniquely personal.

But let's start with *Webster's New Revised University Dictionary.* Webster's defines *spirituality* as "the quality or condition of being spiritual." That doesn't give us much to work with, so let's break the term down further and look at the definition of *spirit.* Webster's defines it as:

1. The vital principle or animating force traditionally believed to be within living beings.

2. Breath.

3. The part of a human being associated with the mind and feelings as distinguished from the body.

These three definitions can be combined into one workable concept:

> **Spirituality is part of all of us, just as the air we breathe. It is the part of us associated with mind and feelings rather than with the physical. It is our principal animating force.**

Spirituality, then, unites all of creation. So it is a part of creative visualization whether we recognize it or not. Think how much deeper the experiences of our life would be if we recognized our spirituality and that of others, and could tap into it on a conscious level, adding beauty and joy to all that we do.

We may use the terms Goddess, God, Higher Power or not call any name at all. Or we may call this higher being Great Spirit, life force energy, or ch'i. We may not even agree with the concept of anything other than what is firmly in the realm of the human. No matter what name we find familiar, spirituality is there for us to discover. It is the essence of being.

That we are spiritual beings is a given. To what level and understanding we use spirituality in creative visualization is up to each of us, individually.

But Is Spirituality *Religion?*

Let's differentiate between the concept of spirituality and religion. Religion is a belief and thought system built on the study of God; organized religion is a group of like-minded people who decide to live out their spirituality in community. They agree on certain principles for living, and they agree to express that shared code of principles together. They provide support for each other's beliefs and agree on certain principles for living. They usually profess a common view of a Creator or God. For them, spirituality is the underpinning, and religion is the expression of that spirituality.

But is spirituality the same as knowing more about a Creator or God? Yes, and no. For some, the experience of spirituality may contain an element of God/Creator/Divine Mind. For others, spirituality is not linked to anything but the understanding of self. But it still remains the principal animating force of the universe. It is the creative energy of everything, human or not.

Wisdom Well

We shall find peace. We shall hear angels. We shall see the sky sparkling with diamonds.
—Anton Chekov, Russian playwright

Some people find they arrive inevitably to the knowing of Creator when they explore spirituality. Still others have difficulty arriving there because they have experienced negative messages in religious settings; they may have scars there, and it may be a challenge to extend belief into a new spiritual setting. People injured in this way may have closed off awareness of spirituality. If that description fits you, try to have an open heart about learning the belief that is the underpinning of creative visualization. We bid you to use creative visualization as a gentle and respectful way to reopen those closed-off feelings. It starts with just being aware the feelings are there and allowing yourself to be open to experiencing belief in a new way. It may take a little time, but it's worth it.

Spiritual Self-Knowledge

We will use our *spiritual self-knowledge* as part of learning creative visualization and for deepening our experiences of it. We must understand ourselves on every level—physical, mental, emotional, and spiritual—to experience the full range of what creative visualization can do to enrich our lives. Understanding yourself will be vital to getting clear on your dreams and desires—and knowing in which area to invest time, energy, and focus.

Introspection helps us gain self-knowledge, so it is a tool that we will use throughout this book. Begin now to commit to time for introspection. At first, if you are primarily an extrovert, it may not seem natural or worthwhile to spend time noticing your thoughts. That's all introspection is—noticing your thoughts and feelings. You may at first not be able to identify exactly what you are feeling. Start by noticing your reactions in certain situations. What is your body language? What are you saying? Does it match what you are thinking?

Deeper Meaning

Spiritual self-knowledge is the awareness of how we fit into the larger picture of life.

Introspection can be defined as:

◆ Examining what dominates your thoughts

◆ Examining your attitudes about yourself, others, the world

◆ Examining what you really want—and why you want it

Committing to more introspection in your life is to acknowledge the power of your thoughts. We may believe that what we think but do not express in words does not matter that much, but the opposite is often true. Later in this chapter, we'll talk about the role of positive thoughts in creative visualization.

Incorporating spiritual self-knowledge into our lives, we see how we fit with others, with nature, and with the animating force of the universe. If you are religious, you try to explain your existence in the context of a Higher Being or Creator. But belief in a deity or not, self-knowledge is an awareness of a purpose for our lives. That awareness connects us with creation. It unites us with others. We begin to see more meaning in our lives.

Self-Actualization

Many of us want to continue learning all of our lives. We want fulfillment and harmony for ourselves and we want to contribute positive energy to the rest of the world. Humanistic psychologist Abraham Maslow identified this desire as self-actualization. He defined a hierarchy of needs for each individual, using a pyramid as a symbol of how the individual progresses through each need. At the bottom of the hierarchy are physiological needs—pure survival. When those needs are met, we progress to safety needs—the need to know that we are sheltered, protected from war, disease or imminent death, protected from financial instability. The next need is to belong—to know we are loved. Fourth are prestige and self-esteem needs.

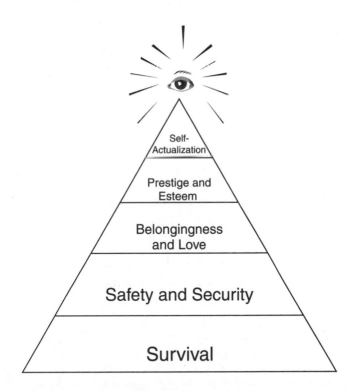

At the top of the pyramid is self-actualization. Self-actualization can be defined, to borrow a phrase from the Army, as "Be all you can be." Self-actualization is about creating what you want in your life. It takes time, work, dedication—and introspection. Creative visualization is one of the most powerful ways in which we may use imagination, introspection, and dedication to move toward self-actualization.

Belief: The Common Ground

A good place to begin learning creative visualization is by investing mental images of success associated with the process. In other words, the belief that we *can* and *will* learn to use it is the central factor in learning creative visualization.

Wisdom Well

Ask, and it shall be given you; seek, and ye shall find; knock, and it shall be opened unto you. For every one that asketh, receiveth; and he that seeketh, findeth; and to him that knocketh it shall be opened.

—Matthew 7:7,8

When an artist begins to paint she must believe that something good or useful or beautiful will result from using her energy in this way. It may be a learning experience more than a finished painting, but she will still gain from the process if she takes the time to recognize what she has learned. When you picked up this book you believed you would gain something from it: information, a good laugh, or even confirmation of your skepticism of "New Age" material.

We believe in physical matter all of the time. That a certain chair will hold us, our car will start, or perhaps that we can do our work the way we are supposed to on any given day. Belief is at the crux of everyday life.

We learn to believe early, before we are aware that we are learning. We have experiences that reinforce belief before we are able to understand or verbalize them. We know that a chair is for sitting a long time before we can say the word. It's the same with dog for barking, spoon for eating. These are material examples of our self-knowledge.

If we are going to use creative visualization spiritually we must approach the process with an open heart and the belief that it will work for us. We would never try anything new if belief in possibility had not formed in us at an early age. Our belief and understanding of the spiritual part of us is formed the same way. We try something and find it to be rewarding to our mind and reason (spirituality) so we continue doing it and we are willing to try something new again.

Belief goes hand in hand with moving beyond rationalism. We must believe, when we are using creative visualization, that something that does not yet exist—our dream— does already exist. It means transcending the limits the rational mind puts on what is possible. In plain words: It's easy to believe in a chair. We have experienced sitting down in a chair many times, and it has held us up. It's harder to believe in something that hasn't happened yet. Yet the artist who puts brush to canvas believes that a painting will exist. She can see it.

CAUTION

Don't Panic, Focus!

When practicing belief, it's inevitable to encounter doubt. As you are doing a creative visualization meditation, doubts may arise. It's important not to try to resist them—or blast through them as though they don't exist. Both approaches tend to give doubts a power they don't otherwise have. Acknowledge them. Be aware of them. Let them float on past. Then direct your mind once again to your desire and focus on positive images.

The Role of Positive Energy

The universe is made up of energy. Everything around us is energy, whether it's matter or ether, solid or liquid, physical or emotional, chemical or nuclear, rock, paper, or scissors.

Energy vibrates at different speeds, some fast, some slow, some fine, some dense. Rocks have energy. Trees have energy. Furniture has energy. Thoughts are a fine, light form of energy, which means they are quick and easy to change. Matter is dense, slow-moving energy. Think about it: your outlook can change in an instant. If you are having a bad day, your mind filled with negative thoughts about the heavy traffic on the way to work or how badly you need a trip to your hair stylist, it can all change with a compliment. One thought can cause a near-instantaneous shift in your perceptions. Though thoughts are light energy, they are powerful.

Have your thoughts ever created an energy that attracted something into your life? Have you ever just been thinking of someone, and that someone calls you out of the blue? Have you ever heard about a good restaurant from a friend, decided to go out to dinner there, and run into a key business contact? This is the positive energy of thought at work.

You attract into your life whatever you think about the most often. Think about your most dominant thoughts, your strongest beliefs, and your underlying expectations. Think about what you can imagine the most vividly. These are the places where you direct the most thought energy. This is what will come into you.

Synchronicity: The Hidden Energy

A kind word. A solution to a problem. A helpful person. When these come to you at serendipitous moments, it's called *synchronicity*—a moment when you are receptive intersects with a moment when someone has the answer.

Deeper Meaning

A **synchronicity** is a meaningful coincidence. Two events occur by different causes at the same moment in time. When you perceive a meaningful coincidence, you allow yourself to see a transcendent truth.

Psychologist Carl Jung was the one to identify the principle of synchronicity. A synchronicity is when two events, each enacted by a different cause, occur at the same moment in time. Because of our awareness of their coincidence, we perceive a new truth. Jung called this a transcendent truth. An example would be when two sisters, separated by miles, have the same thought at the same moment.

Shari refers to synchronicity as the hidden energy because we don't recognize it or understand it. We have to watch for evidence of it in our lives and learn to trust it.

Once Shari was giving a workshop on dreams when a woman asked her about recurring dreams in which bad events happened to her in groups of three. She had had several dreams like that and found them disturbing. Without missing a beat, Shari asked the woman if she had three children. The woman gasped and said yes. She revealed that lately she had been thinking a lot about what she considered her failings as a parent.

One might say that it was intuition that made Shari ask the question, but she says what it felt like at the time was a synchronicity. The woman was putting emotionally charged energy in her words—and about the number three—into the room. Shari's subconscious picked up on that energy and she knew without knowing what the answer was. The synchronicity was that Shari was open to being aware of this highly charged energy and asking about it.

When Shari was asked to write *The Complete Idiot's Guide to Interpreting Your Dreams*, she was very excited. Yet she wasn't sure how to boil down all that she knew about dreams into a manageable text. Just at that time, *Newsweek* published an issue devoted to dreams. Right after that Shari came across several books in her own library that had meaning for her. Then she started remembering her own dreams, and memories of her clients' dream experiences came to her more vividly.

Carolyn, too, has had many experiences with synchronicity and has found it a useful tool as a single mother creating a support system. She will find that merely asking for a solution and being receptive to hearing the answer can bring it in for her in a short amount of time. One example was when she moved into her new house and she needed to find someone to do some earth-moving work. But she didn't have time to jump on it and do the research to find someone with the right expertise. Within a few days, she hosted a dinner party at her home, and one of the guests started analyzing the kind of work that needed to be done in her back yard. She was impressed with how he envisioned the work that needed to be done, because he saw it the way she had imagined it. "Do you know someone who does that type of work?" she asked. "Yes," he said. "My brother."

Imagine, See, Be

Think of meaningful coincidences that have affected important choices you have made in your life. Make a list in your Creative Visualization Journal.

This is synchronicity, and the way we believe it works is this: Shari was putting out the positive spiritual energy of the dream book, just as Carolyn was about the earth work. Wonderful resources were coming back. Some people call this the principle of "like attracting like." It's based on the theory that the energy of the universe is magnetic.

Energy Changes

Think about an experience in your life when you were sending out a lot of highly charged energy. How did it come back to you? Spend some time writing about it in your Creative Visualization Journal. Try to define the negative energy and identify some of the beliefs that were guiding your thoughts at that time in your life. Think about what was manifesting in your life. Did you have experiences that seemed to reinforce those beliefs?

Now think about a time when you were happy and cheerful and good things kept happening to you. It's helpful to examine not just the span of a day but a week, a month, or three months. What were some of your attitudes at that time? How did experiences come to you? Think about whether there were any synchronicities in your life then. Were there any meaningful coincidences that occurred to bring those good things in your life?

Goodness Me! Examining Your Beliefs

Let's try this exercise to see how your beliefs and experiences mesh. It's helpful to do this in a quiet place, free of distractions, a place where you are comfortable. You may want to make it more inviting by playing soft music, burning scented oil, or lighting a candle. Many people find such rituals a good way to quiet the mind and sink into introspection.

Take a few minutes to contemplate each of the following questions:

1. What do you believe about goodness? Is goodness stronger than evil? Is there more goodness in the universe than evil?

2. Where do you see goodness around you?

3. What do you believe about your worth? What do you have to contribute to the world?

4. What do you believe about abundance? Do you believe there is enough for everyone on the planet to thrive, to be happy, to be self-actualized?

5. When you see abundance in other people's lives, do you believe that the same can come to you, or do you believe there is only so much to go around? If you feel envy at others' successes, this might indicate a strain of this belief. It may be you believe only a few are chosen to experience the benefits you see in others' lives.

After you complete this exercise, notice whether your positive energy flow has increased. If not, what do you think that means?

Contact: Prayer and Guidance

Wait a minute! We said this wasn't about religion! What are we doing talking about prayer?

When we discuss the techniques of creative visualization, a lot of what we talk about can mirror the process of prayer. After all, we are imagining what we want in vivid detail, then devoting positive focus to it. Then we wait for it to happen with a belief that something unseen has already occurred.

The central difference between what happens in creative visualization and prayer is that prayer is passive supplication made before a Higher Being. Creative visualization is an active process, requiring belief only in ourselves. We are more likely to think ahead about what we want our goals to be with creative visualization—and take the next steps—and less likely to depend on the concept of "other." In other words, we are not looking for what we want to create in our lives to come from outside.

That said, there are some similarities:

♦ Both involve the belief that we can get what we want or accomplish our goals.

♦ Both require concentration and focus.

♦ Both require an attitude of listening, to being receptive at what is coming back to us.

Still, we probably don't picture what we are praying about with as much care and detail as we do when we visualize it. It's a different, more active level of energy.

Prayer is likely to be a deeper experience, one that leads us to understanding and knowing our Higher Power. Creative visualization leads us to knowing ourselves.

> **Affirmations**
>
> I am listening with an open heart and mind, and I am receptive to all the good that is coming to me.

Where the two overlap is that, with both, the intention is for good to be done. Both prayer and creative visualization require committing time to focus on our spirituality. Both activate a part of our subconscious minds and allow us to bring up material that is meaningful to us.

Working Hand in Hand

Prayer and creative visualization can work together, and many people find that it enhances their experience of creative visualization. Creative visualization can give us knowledge of conditions in our lives that we want to bring to a deeper spiritual place—and perhaps to prayer. Prayer, and the response from the Creator of the universe, can highlight desires and dreams that we can use in creative visualization. So for many people, a spirituality based on a belief in a Higher Being is a necessary and central part of living their lives in a meaningful way.

Practice, Practice

Commitment and practice are integral parts of learning any spiritual habit. It's just like learning to play the piano. Carolyn grew up with practice demonstrated live in her home on a daily basis. Her mother is a piano teacher and would devote hours to practicing her talent. Carolyn grew up in a home filled with the sonatas of Beethoven and concertos of Chopin coming from her mother's Steinway grand. To master a skill or become competitive in a sport, we must practice.

In this case, we use the word *practice* in two ways. One means to continue or maintain an activity to achieve a certain level of skill. The other meaning is more like ritual or devotion. When we engage in a spiritual activity, such as yoga or Zen meditation, on an ongoing basis, we also call that *practice*. First we practice creative visualization to learn how to do it; then, if we keep it up, it becomes a devotion. With devotion, you are continually receiving rewards.

Making Contact

Creative visualization ultimately leads us to making contact with ourselves. Some people define this as the higher self. What we mean by "higher self" is that expression of you that is you operating at optimum—in alignment with your highest values.

This is where spiritual self-knowledge comes into play with creative visualization. By being aware and open to developing ourselves on all levels—including the spiritual level—we open ourselves to functioning at optimum, to reaching the top of the pyramid that Maslow defined as self-actualization.

Some people find it useful to imagine a guide that will help them develop a creative visualization process. Again, some people may define it as God, Goddess, Creator, or Source. Others prefer to think of it as Inner Wisdom, a guide that comes from the higher self. This guide can take the role of counselor, friend, teacher. In some cultures, such as Native American, it can take the form of an animal guide. For other people, it can take the form of an angel. Generally, this guide is a mental picture that takes some form—man, woman, animal, angel, God—and takes on certain attributes that we want to emphasize in our journey. To explore this concept further, we suggest an excellent new book, *Empowering Your Life with Angels* by Rita Berkowitz with Deborah Romaine (Alpha Books, 2004).

If you find the concept of a guide or angel useful for you, take a few moments, using this exercise, to meditate on your inner guide, visualize, and connect with it.

Seated comfortably in a quiet place, close your eyes and take three deep cleansing breaths. With each inhale, imagine taking in the good. With each exhale, imagine releasing limitations and doubts. Let your brow relax. Feel yourself filling up with purifying breath. Let that flow over you, moving down through your neck, your shoulders and down through your body, relaxing each part as you go.

When you feel completely relaxed, visualize a path before you. Visualize summoning strength and wisdom in the form of your guide. Repeat these affirmations:

I am now connected with the source of strength in my life.

I am now connected with the source of wisdom in my life.

I am now receiving the goodness and abundance that my Source is bringing to me.

I am now filled with light.

I feel peace.

As you continue hold in your body the feeling of strength and wisdom, keep your focus on your breathing. Allow your inner guide to appear before you on the path. Visualize this form approaching you. Greet your guide.

I welcome you on my journey.

Continue to meditate on your guide. Continue to take in details. Notice the color of his or her eyes. Notice whether your guide has wings. Notice the light and color that surrounds him or her.

The Connection

Creative visualization is a great way to send positive energy into the universe. You are focusing on your desires, as well as other people's desires and needs. It can't help but come back to you in a positive way. You may not recognize the fruits of creative visualization at first. But when you continue to use it as a tool, you will increasingly recognize the connection between what you put out and what comes back.

Each success will deepen your belief in the process and move you further into self-knowledge—and deepen your spiritual experience.

The Least You Need to Know

- ◆ Spirituality is the part of us associated with mind and feelings rather than with the physical. It is our principal animating force.

- ◆ Spiritual self-knowledge can deepen the experience of creative visualization.

- ◆ In creative visualization, you must believe that something that does not yet exist—your dream—*can* and *will* happen.

- ◆ Positive energy attracts the energy and ideas to us that help us realize our dreams.

- ◆ Commitment to introspection and a positive attitude are vital to learning creative visualization.

What About Wishing?

In This Chapter

- ◆ The difference between wishing and creative visualization
- ◆ How to use intention to get there
- ◆ Why intention is vital
- ◆ The natural energy flow of intention
- ◆ How to nurture intention

Wish I may, wish I might, first star I see tonight … goes the rhyme. Wishing on the first star you see might just work—but it's not the same as creative visualization. Making a distinction between wishing and visualizing is an essential step for effective creative visualization.

Wishing keeps us in a realm where we never can quite see the vision. It's somewhere out there in the night sky, twinkling like a star. It might seem as remote and transitory as starlight. It might seem light years away.

How do you move from wish to creative visualization? And how do you know the difference? In this chapter, we'll guide you in working through it.

Wishing Mode

When it comes to realizing our most heartfelt dreams, we might actually stay in wishing for many years without recognizing it as such. It might be a dream we cherish. We might talk about it a lot with others. It might be ever present, just below the surface of our lives. We might buy books with the aim of learning about the subject. We might take seminars. We might talk all around it, focusing on the obstacles, feeling it just out of reach, feeling the struggle, only to wilt when some kind other says, "If you could do anything in the world, have the life you want, what would it look like?" The answer may be right on the tip of your tongue.

Chances are, you know what you have been wishing for. Chances are, you are giving it a lot of energy—maybe just not the *right* energy.

Creative visualization is the process of moving from a wish that might be the object of much effort and energy, but lacks focus and effectiveness. So the first question you must ask yourself—and that you may not be able to answer right away—is why your wish is not effective. Ask yourself that question right now. Park the question in your psyche and let it stay there as you work through this chapter.

The key differences between wishing and creative visualization are:

- Creative visualization is active.

- Creative visualization is both external and internal.

- Creative visualization is focused.

- Creative visualization is conscious.

- Creative visualization always has clarity.

Let's look at each of these in more depth.

Creative Visualization Is Active

Moving into creative visualization is to take a wish and make it active. It's the difference between *yin* and *yang* energy.

Yin and yang is a concept that has its origin in traditional Chinese medicine and forms the backbone of Chinese philosophy. Most of us are familiar with yin and yang as the dynamic of feminine and masculine energies. We can think of yang energies as acting or releasing and yin energies as receiving or holding. Yang is the rain; yin is the cloud that holds the rain. The two energies are complementary, interdependent, and ever-changing.

Deeper Meaning

Yin and **yang** are the Chinese principles of the interplay of the opposing energies of activity and receptivity. From the "make-it-happen" energy of yang flows the "embrace-it" energy of yin. Yin energy creates a space for something new to materialize. When yin energy reaches its fullest point, it becomes yang, the energy of creation. Yang needs to flow into yin to recharge and regroup. It's the interplay of action with contemplation. Both are necessary.

Yang energy is the energy of creation, of getting things done, making things happen. Behind this energy, when it comes to creative visualization, is the belief that the goal will be realized.

Creative visualization is not all yang energy. It would run counter to the natural law of yin and yang for it to be separate. The two forces are mutually dependent, opposing yet complementary, one flowing into the other. It's just that the first step of moving from wish to creative visualization begins with action. We'll get to the yin part later.

One of the underlying concepts of creative visualization is intention. The process begins with an act—a decision that this goal is where you will put your focus. You decide that when ideas and opportunities that will help you realize this vision come to you, you will act upon them.

Creative Visualization Is Both External and Internal

Wishing is internal. We are told when we blow out the candles on the birthday cake or toss the penny into the well to keep our wish a secret so it will come true. If we do share our wish with others, our family and friends may instinctively know it's just a wish and treat it that way. You may notice they are supportive but don't invest a lot of energy in your wish. Notice when this is happening so that you can gauge when you are merely wishing. The people around you won't put much energy into encouraging your wish if they sense *you* won't.

Wishing is a passive act, though we can seem to be taking actions in pursuit of it. This can take the form of attending seminars or reading books to prepare us for our wish. We're not saying everyone who takes a seminar or reads a book is just wishing; on the contrary, both can be part of a very active, directed effort. But in some cases, filling up our lives with activities that circumscribe our wish are just ways to avoid being faced with the picture of what would really need to be done, if we wanted to achieve our dream.

Creative visualization does begin with the internal, by creating a mental picture of what we want to create in our lives. But the difference is that the internal picture becomes so real to us that we act *as if* it has already happened. When we do this, we create opportunities for ourselves to act upon our dream or desire.

Creative Visualization Is Focused

Wishes come and go. Wishes are plentiful in our lives. Some wishes keep coming back. Some wishes are with us forever. But some are just a pleasant thought in the moment. We could not possibly in one lifetime make all of our wishes happen.

Sometimes our dreams and desires are too diffuse. This diffuseness can sometimes be a defense against having to truly pursue that which we might cherish and might enthrall us, but also might require us to change. This leads to ambivalence and lack of attention to our wish.

Don't Panic, *Focus!*

What if you realize that your fear is not that you will *fail* to reach your goal—but that you *will reach your goal*? Don't worry. If that's the case, it's an important break-through. Turn around and use creative visualization again, creating a mental picture of exactly the change you fear would happen should you reach your goal. Devote a time of positive focus to it. Use some affirmations that are directed at bringing peaceful energy to it. If it works, the goal was meant to be. If, after some effort, the fear grows stronger, consider re-evaluating your goal.

In creative visualization, we bring a focus to our desire that tests this diffusion. The process of creative visualization is the beginning of a test, like the alchemist's challenge to change lead to gold. We might start out as lead at the beginning of the creative visualization process, only to learn that we need to become, and are becoming, gold.

We can create the focus that is true creative visualization through sheer willpower, or we can submit to the process, trust in natural positive energy, and allow it to work its magic. When we do the latter, we can achieve a true focus that can be sustained over time. It stands up to the test. We test our dream against our ambivalence. We ask the tough questions. What would you be willing to change? Think about the ways you identify yourself. Wouldn't the preconceived or long-held beliefs about how you identify yourself *have* to grow, evolve, and change if you were to reach your goal?

Creative Visualization Is Conscious

You might previously have used creative visualization without knowing the term, or used your power of creative visualization in an unconscious way. When you tapped into this power in an unconscious way, with-out examining the deep-seated negative beliefs that we all have, you might have imag-ined what you wished for without acknowl-edging that you are unconsciously expecting lack, limits, difficulties, or challenges. When we fail to acknowledge that this negative *conscious-ness* is present, we unconsciously create limits and difficulties. This is what people mean when they say, "You are you are own worst enemy" or "Be careful what you wish for."

Deeper Meaning

Consciousness is a key element in creative visualization. By examining your motivations in a deep and conscious way, you clarify your vision. By examining deep-seated beliefs that may undermine your vision, you can move forward more quickly.

Creative Visualization Always Moves to Clarity

The dream is not always clear right away, but when the process is allowed to unfold, clarity is always the result. When it's not becoming clear, creative visualization techniques themselves can be used to achieve that clarity. The clarity may lead to redefining the goal or re-evaluating your commitment to the goal.

Another quality that creative visualization has is devotion. You are consistently devoting positive energy to it. Devotion is integral to two vital components of creative visualization: clarifying the vision and moving from desire to belief to intention. Devotion is the practice you will be able to fall back on when you doubt, or when you can't see the way to your goal because you are in the middle of it.

Remember Shari's visualization of seeing "Ph.D." on her office door? One of the most difficult aspects of that process was getting through her last semester. It was her third degree. She had analytical training and lots of tests. She still had two years of internship and her dissertation ahead, but there would be no more tests until her licensing exams. She almost couldn't study. Her study energy was all used up. She says that her devotion to obtaining her degree was the driving force that got her through this difficult time. She kept the vision of *Shari Just, Ph.D.*, on her door firmly in mind, and she was able to finish that last set of tests.

Imagine, See, Be

Creative visualization is a process where you move from desire to belief to intent. Keeping your mental picture before you, you continue to maintain your focus as you move through these key steps.

Devotion brings about the clarity of vision, filling in the colors of your picture, sharpening the details. Devotion brings the clarity that starts to appear in the shape of business cards from people who will help you, phone numbers of people with just the right expertise for realizing your vision.

Intention: Getting There

What guides this movement from wish to creative visualization? Is it belief, as we discussed in Chapter 2? Is it the force within us that creates or motivates the belief? This process begins with a strong desire, we know. But what forms the energy that guides you forward—keeps you moving forward? In other words, now that we know the difference between wishing and creative visualization, how do you get from here to there.

The answer is intention. Intention is what makes strong desire become the belief that what you want to create in your life *has already happened.* You want it. You are devoted to it. Believing that it has already happened, you act *as if* it already has. By acting as if this ambition has already been realized, you strengthen the positive energy surrounding your vision. As we go along, we'll continue the discussion of what intention is and where it comes from. It's the magic that transforms. It's the magic that makes simple visualization techniques so powerful.

> **Affirmations**
>
> I am becoming clearer and clearer every day on what I desire. I feel an assurance that this is good and right for me.

Intention is an annunciation to yourself—and to the universe—that you want it. And because you want it, you see it—right before your eyes.

What makes intention so powerful is that it's a two-way conversation. It's the universe coming back and saying, "Because you want it, I want it for you." This is what *Power of Intention* author Wayne D. Dyer means when he says intention is an energy you are already part of; you simply have to access it. It's an act of choice. Carlos Castaneda, a teacher and author of books about Toltec wisdom, the pursuit of self-knowledge by the ancient shamans of Mexico, defines intent this way: "Intent is a force that exists in the universe when sorcerers (those who live of the Source) beckon intent, it comes to them and sets up the path for attainment, which means that sorcerers always accomplish what they set out to do."

The Yin of Intention

With intention, then, creative visualization has a yin component. Through your visualization, you state your intention that this is what you want to bring into your life, and you wait with the assurance that your request has already been met. You wait to receive. No, you act as though you have *already received.*

It's a little bit like the starlight that inspires our wishes—only wishing is focused on the beguiling and unattainable twinkling light, while creative visualization is focused on a steady light and purpose of intent. You beam the light out to the universe, it becomes a star, and the light is reflected back. The "as if" part of creative visualization is evident in the metaphor of starlight. By the time we see the light of a star in the sky, it has traveled light years to reach us. But it already *is*, from the moment you beam it out.

Star Light, Star Bright

Use the following creative visualization to deepen your understanding of the process of intent. Sit comfortably in a quiet place free of distractions. Close your eyes. Take in a deep breath, expanding your rib cage as you fill your lungs. Relax your shoulders. Let your shoulder blades move down your back. Take in another deep breath. As you exhale, lower your chin to your chest. Roll your head clockwise, bending your right ear to your right shoulder, tilting your head back, bending your left ear to your left shoulder. Relax into it. Take another deep breath, and repeat, going counter-clockwise. With your next deep breath, relax your jaw line, letting it fall open.

Now that you are relaxed, visualize a benevolent figure—your inner guide (from Chapter 2), if you will, or your Creator/Divine Source—standing at the edge of the universe holding your dream cupped in the palms of his/her hands. Imagine it as a golden sphere of light. See the golden rays of light emanating through his/her fingers. Sit with this vision a moment, taking in the glorious light. See how potent your dream is. Feel the warmth of the swirling light in warming your face.

With your next breath, visualize the figure releasing this sphere of light into the universe. Visualize it gliding peacefully toward you. Visualize it as effortless, with no exertion on your part to bring it toward you. As you visualize it moving toward you, imagine opening your heart to receive it.

On your next breath, move your thoughts to how you would go about your life as you see this golden sphere of light gliding toward you. Imagine that it is just a matter of waiting until the light illumines all that you are, and that you do. Meanwhile, how do you move through your day? How do you speak with others? Imagine the calmness in your voice and your movements because you have the assurance that what is good for you is coming.

Imagine, See, Be

No doubt you have heard the phrase, "intent on a goal." Intention is a complex, magical mix of determination, strong desire, belief and clarity. Intention is "I want it!"—and because you want it, you can see it right before your eyes.

Spend another few moments just breathing in and out, taking in the nourishing breaths, releasing old, stale breath. Just sit for a few moments in this vision of light. When it feels complete, end the session.

Yin and Yang Flow: The Natural Energy Flow of Intention

Before a creative visualization session, do an energy assessment to see whether you are in yin energy or yang energy. Not only will it help you see when you are wishing vs. believing, it will help you know where to put your focus. Look at our list of keywords for yin/yang energy. Which words define your energy of the moment? Are you open to possibilities? Do you just want to take action? Is your mind receptive to it being another way? Is it a time for leading, or is it a time for following—of listening within for wisdom?

Yin Intent	Yang Intent
Stillness	Movement
Descending	Ascending
Dark	Bright
At rest	Alert
Earth	Heaven
Moon	Sun
Nighttime	Daytime
Passivity	Activity
Following	Leading
Contracting	Expanding
Conceiving	Fertilizing

Knowing where your energy is at any given point in the intention cycle is key to knowing where to focus your energy during a creative visualization session. Is it a day for imagining—creating a new scene? Or is it a day for listening and waiting with assurance? Is it a day to actively put positive focus on your goal? Or is it a day to practice affirmations that reinforce your assurance?

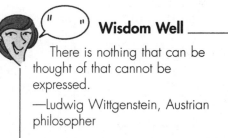

Wisdom Well

There is nothing that can be thought of that cannot be expressed.

—Ludwig Wittgenstein, Austrian philosopher

Summoning Intent

Use the following exercise to summon intention every step of the way. You may use it throughout this book, as you develop creative visualizations for different goals you want for your life. Many people find it helpful to say their goals aloud. Many people find voicing their goals aloud moves them from wish to intent. The sound of your own voice—a physical expression of your desire—strengthens your commitment.

First, state your goal, as clearly as possible.

I want _____

_____

_____

Then, each step of the way, use these affirming statements:

I want to be clear on what my heart desires.

I want to imagine it.

I want to see it happening clearly in my mind's eye.

I want to believe it will happen.

I want to spend (fill in a time frame) _____ *focusing on it.*

I want to give positive energy to it.

I want to affirm it.

I want to believe it is already so.

I want to see it as already so.

I want to receive it.

I want to know how I must open in order to receive it.

I want the assurance that this is right for me.

I want the assurance that all is good.

I want the assurance that what I radiate is good.

I want the assurance that what I attract is good.

I want this. *I want all of it.*

Nurturing Intent

Author Wayne D. Dyer has captured the popular imagination through a PBS series with his concepts about intent. He defines intention as a force in the universe that allows the act of creation to take place. Dyer says everything in the universe has intention built into it. As an example, he gives an acorn. It is wired into the design of an acorn to become a giant oak tree. And so, too, with an apple blossom. The intention begins with the apple seed that becomes the trunk of the tree, which brings forth the buds that become the leaves, which shade the blossoms that become the fruit.

When we are conceived, the raw DNA material of our mother and our father become an embryo. The embryo implants in the uterus and begins to grow. At that point in creation, millions of transactions already have taken place, with millions more ahead. There is an intention that is guiding the growth of that embryo.

Many scientists of the twenty-first century are searching for what is called the "observer." Where is it in the body? Does it lie in the folds of the cerebral cortex, in the neurons and the chemicals that fire through our brains? Is it in the red blood cells that bring nourishment to every cell in our bodies? Is it in the DNA that made us? What forms the intention that allows something organic to be created, to grow into an apple blossom and become a fruit? Who, or what, is directing the process?

We don't need to answer those questions here. (Did we hear a big sigh of relief?) It will be up to you to design your own theory about that observer, whether you call it God or Goddess, Allah, Divine Source, Creator, or just smart DNA. But what will be vital as you practice creative visualization is to trust in the natural process that science has identified but cannot yet name. Using intention is to trust that an intelligent entity or force is guiding your growth.

Yet a lot can happen on the journey from apple seed to apple blossom to ripe fruit, from embryo to fetus to the birth of a living human being. Let's look at why you must nurture your intention along the way:

- ◆ **Intention gives you an ally.** Dyer defines intention as an energy you are part of. It's not outside you. It's not something you do; it's something you access.

- ◆ **Intention gives your vision staying power.** As an ally, intention gives your vision a fortitude that will allow you to weather the ebb and flow of emotions as you move ahead on your vision path. It will allow you to weather what you perceive as disappointments and triumphs along the way.

- ◆ **Intention strengthens your vision.** Think of this as determination + ally. It goes beyond willpower. You are not bringing your dream into your life out of sheer will. Intention is your ally in giving you a clearer vision. The vision becomes clearer because you ask for it. Ask, and you receive. Seek, and you find. Knock, and the door opens.

◆ **Intention clarifies your desire.** How badly do you want it? Will you survive if you don't have it? Intention tests you with these questions.

◆ **Intention clarifies your values.** Let's say that you want to build your dream house. You can visualize where the living room would be. You can see the clean lines, the south-facing windows and the wood beams. You can see the view of the trees from your courtyard. You can see the details of your home right down to the brushed-metal window frames.

But let's say you set up your dream house in a visualization, begin to practice these techniques, and in the meantime, the circumstances of your life begin to shift.

This is where intention plays a role in clarifying your values. Your visualization of this dream may have been very vivid, and you may have given a lot of positive energy to it. The intention is still real.

This is the time to let intention distill your vision down to the values that created it. What did you want when you visualized a beautiful home? Better livability? A space to share with a soul mate? A hearth-and-home family setting? The pride of accomplishing the dream? The values behind that vision are still real. Let intention redirect you to those values. Let intention keep you focused on the true desire that formed the intent.

◆ **Intention gives you self-knowledge.** Intention teaches you. It forms you. It shows you who you are, what you are capable of. It teaches you trust. It teaches you empowerment. It shows you your doubts, your fears, your flaws.

Your Subconscious

Is intention the subconscious? Here's an example we know everyone can relate to. One night when writing this chapter, Carolyn found it nearly complete. Five nights later, though, the gaps seemed glaring. What had changed? One answer could be her subconscious intent. Her deep, underlying motivation had shifted from "get it done" to "get it right." This affected what she saw. The first night, she wanted to see a complete chapter. Five nights later, she wanted to see good work.

The intention you bring to a creative visualization session—indeed, any situation in life—can influence the information you are willing to take in, and the quality of the effort you are willing to put out. It colors your vision, prompts your attention, and urges your nurturing care.

Becoming conscious of what you truly intend to allow yourself to be and see—is an essential step in committing to the process of creative visualization.

What about the question *Is intention really the subconscious?* We think the answer is this: intention *resides* in the subconscious, just as much as the conscious mind, because it resides everywhere. We have described intention as a force in the universe that is part of creation. Intention, then, guides the thoughts we form in both our conscious minds and our subconscious minds.

Become conscious of:

- What you will allow yourself to see
- What you want to see
- What you want the outcome to be
- What you are giving the most energy to

It's helpful to start each creative visualization session by getting clear on these questions. Ask yourself: What do I hope to gain today? What am I willing to see today? What am I not willing to see? Where is my energy today?

Not Just Positive Thinking

The techniques outlined in this book go far beyond mere positive thinking, which is often simply an act of will and transpires on a superficial level. Positive thinking has limitations that do not allow you to explore on the deepest level the motivations and beliefs that guide you. Going that deep and getting that clear are the techniques that are the difference between small wishes and magnificent, transforming shifts in your life.

So the process of this book is to move from wish to desire to belief to intention. Assurance is the ultimate result of intention. You believe you already have received that dream you hold dear. You act *as if.* Assurance is the silent, calm knowing that what you envision has already come to you.

The Least You Need to Know

- Creative visualization is active, focused, conscious, and always has clarity.
- Devotion is integral to creative visualization because it helps clarify the vision and it moves you into intent.

◆ Intention is a two-way commitment. It is you announcing to the universe that you desire to reach a goal, and hearing the universe answer back, "Because you want it, I want it for you."

◆ The intention you bring to a creative visualization session—both conscious and subconscious—influences the information you take in.

Chapter 4

You Have the Power: Create What You Want and Need

In This Chapter

◆ The powers that be—in you

◆ Letting your imagination go

◆ How much do you *really* want it?

◆ Desire becomes intent

◆ Making a contract with yourself

We'll say it in the plainest language possible: everything starts with you. If you want it, you can envision it. Your desire is the flame that activates the techniques of creative visualization.

The potential for creative visualization to work in your life is limited only by your belief in your own power. This, too, is an evolving process. You don't start out with it right away. It's the hero's journey. It's a journey of discovery.

Trusting the Gift of Imagination

Your own sense of empowerment is key to what you will allow yourself to imagine. If you believe that you can make things happen in your life, you can imagine the goal. Conversely, in your imagination, you will find your own power. To imagine what you want and tap into your deep desire for it is to move into a proactive state. So your imagination is central to opening you to your sense of power.

The Kabbalah, the book of Jewish mysticism, defines "the fierce power of the imagination" as a gift from God. To call the imagination fierce is to be in awe of its wildness. Truly letting your imagination go free is a bit scary. But that is the place we must go to reach into ourselves through the most powerful techniques of creative visualization. To get there, we must learn to trust our imaginations, to see the imagination as a gift.

The imagination is the place of revelation, of unveiling, of telling the truth. In all ways, then, the imagination is trying to bring forth a new creation. When you imagine something, you bring your desire to the light. You may only have an intention, or you may only have a wish, or just a question. But when this desire, wish or question marries up with your imagination—and becomes a mental picture—it takes form. Even Albert Einstein acknowledged that "imagination is more important than knowledge."

The Mystery of the Imagination

In his book *Creativity: Where the Divine and Human Meet* (see Appendix B), Matthew Fox tells us that the Celts equated the imagination with the soul. Fox says, "The imagination operates at a threshold where light and dark, visible and invisible, possibility and fact come together."

The imagination is mysterious. We don't have to understand its mystery; we just have to trust it. Our linear, logical minds don't quite trust what we can't explain immediately. When we are in a linear, logical mindset, we only allow our imaginations to crack open a little. We only get a glimpse of what's possible.

French philosopher Gaston Bachelard says of the imagination that, "The imagination is ceaselessly imagining and enriching itself with new images." What we think this means for creative visualization is that the first vision you create begins an auto-unfolding process, activating the imagination to devise more and more images. We only need to push open the crack a little more to allow the imagination to do its work—more work.

Power of Intention author Dyer says, "Your willpower is so much less effective than your imagination." That's because imagination is linked to the power of intention. He describes the imagination as the movement of "universal mind" within you. In this context, universal mind means Infinite Creator, Infinite Wisdom, your Source—or, as we defined in Chapter 2, the vital animating force in all living beings.

The imagination is inherently about possibilities, about expansion, about immensity. The goal of the imagination is nothing less than liberation itself, Fox says. "It takes us to the space of elsewhere," Bachelard says. Fox adds that imagination takes us to the space of nothingness—the place where we have yet to create. It is the place of *what is not yet*, he says, and therefore *"what might still be."* That, precisely, is what is so scary about it.

> **Wisdom Well**
>
> The real voyage of discovery consists not in seeking new landscapes, but in having new eyes.
> —Marcel Proust, French novelist

What If ...? Unleashing the Imagination

Let's put this into action with an exercise. Take a few moments to calm your breathing, expanding your lungs with three deep cleansing breaths. Direct your mind's eye to the image of you liberating your imagination. Imagine someone lifting open the top of your head, pulling the top of your skull back like the lid of a box. Imagine sparks of color shooting out like fireworks. As you breathe, visualize the air from your lungs rising out of your head. Your thoughts are light, riding this magic carpet of fresh air.

Now, with your Creative Visualization Journal at hand, take a few of these prompts and write your answers. Let your pen flow across the page without stopping. Don't stop to cross out a letter or word if it does not come out quite right. Just keep the pen moving. Let it flow. Don't stop until you absolutely can't think of another thought.

What if I lived ...

- ◆ In Paris?
- ◆ On a pig farm?
- ◆ In the rain forest?
- ◆ On the plains of Africa?

- In the 1940s?

- On an island?

- In the projects?

- In a teepee?

- In Tokyo?

- On a houseboat?

- In a cave?

- During Shakespearean times?

What if I knew ...

- How to paint?

- French?

- Martin Luther King Jr.?

- Where the lost city of Atlantis is?

- Biotech engineering?

- How to cook?

- The cure for AIDS?

- Plato?

What if the world ...

- Were upside down?

- Were going to end in one year?

- Had another Ice Age?

- Were 90 percent rain forest?

What if I had been born ...

- Another ethnicity?

- To different parents?

- Taller?
- 30 years earlier?
- In Europe?
- The opposite gender?
- An only child (or if an only child, with seven siblings)?

Now that you're warmed up, let's apply your imagination to the needs in your life. Following are some examples to get you thinking, but what we'd like for you to do is brainstorm some that are personal for you.

I wish my relationship with my teenage daughter felt less fractious.

I do not find my line of work meaningful, but I don't know what else I can do to make a living. I want to do more networking so I can meet someone who can help me figure it out.

I want to manifest a beautiful soul mate relationship in my life.

I wish I had a stronger, leaner body.

I wish I had more leisure time.

I don't like worrying about money so much.

Take a few moments to come up with a few of your own. Now ask, for each one on the list, what would it look like if you had this in your life? What would it feel like to live this life? Imagine it.

I Really, Really Want It

The success of creative visualization lies in the answer to this question: How much do you *really* want it? If you believe what you desire will make your life better, you will imagine it, see it, do it. It *will* happen.

Do you want this more than anything in the world? Or are you inconsistent? Some days do you think, "I'd better get on that"? "The shoulds" are the same as wishing. They are not quite yet desire; they are a "have to." Other days, are you filled with joy as you are working toward the goal, putting in the time, paying your dues? Still other days, do you think that you are just as content with the way things are? Or do you think something else will be better? Summoning a strong desire that becomes the intent that fires creative visualization is a process.

Imagine, See, Be _____

Think of your imagination as the threshold that allows you to enter the space of elsewhere. It allows you to picture what you have yet to create. Activating your imagination begins a naturally unfolding process, where one picture begets the next possibility.

Use this simple "this or that" exercise to distill the vision down to a sharp focus when you need to strengthen your desire. This is a good one if you have a wealth of ideas and talents and any direction you go would be fulfilling—an embarrassment of riches, if you will. This exercise will help you hone in on the one thing that matters the most to you. Getting this clear is particularly helpful if the road to your most heartfelt desire is a long haul.

Let's revisit the list from Chapter 1 of your 10 Life Arenas. Remember that in Chapter 1 you wrote about your strengths and weaknesses and identified your level of fulfillment in each arena.

Now, as you consider each Life Arena, we want you to evaluate whether this arena of your life is satisfactory or needs more attention. Rank each area in relation to the others by assigning each a number. Which arena do you believe needs your most careful attention and focus? Mark that Life Arena with the number 1 (use the following chart). Continue on until you've marked the Life Arena with which you are most satisfied with the number 10. Where do you see the most significant changes? (This may not be in the Life Arena you've marked as number 1.) Place an asterisk next to this arena. Which arena, if you focused on it, would result in broadest improvement in all arenas? Circle this arena and highlight it. Now, write in a specific goal for each Life Arena.

Rank	Goals for Life Arenas
_____	Love: _____
_____	Family: _____
_____	Work: _____
_____	Money: _____
_____	Health: _____

Rank	Goals for Life Arenas
_____	Home: _____
	_____
_____	Personal growth: _____
	_____
_____	Spirituality: _____
	_____
_____	Leisure/rejuvenation: _____
	_____
_____	Creative self-expression: _____
	_____

Compare the goals on your list using this guiding question: "If you could do *this*, or you could do *that*, which would you do first?" Use these questions to explore your goals further: Which is more urgent? Which is more important? Which seems more doable? Which seems utterly impossible? Which one do you talk about more? Which one are you afraid to talk about? Or, which one makes you uncomfortable when you talk about it?

Let's use the goal at the top of the list for a directed creative visualization. Create a mental picture of your life with this goal achieved. Take a few moments to sit with this vision in your mind's eye, making sure you are in a comfortable place, free of distractions. Spend about 10 minutes focusing on this picture, observing all of its nuances and potential.

Repeat these affirmations:

As this becomes part of my life, I know that I want it. I know it is good.

I feel gratitude as this unfolds in my life. I know that I can trust this will come to me, and that it will be for my highest good.

Now say:

This, or something even better, now manifests for me.

As this unfolds in my life, I feel harmonious and whole.

 Don't Panic, *Focus!*

Don't be hard on yourself if it's easier to use creative visualization in one Life Arena but a little trickier than in another. Many people, for instance, find it easy to visualize creating meaningful work but find manifesting a fulfilling relationship more challenging. Don't worry. With time and practice, all will become clearer.

Gaining Power: Desire Becomes Intent

Desire becomes intent when you get clear on how much you *really* want it and you direct your focus to that goal. Intention then informs the way you direct your meditations on the goal and directs the way you move through your life. What's happening in the background as you do this is you are gaining power. You begin to be confident of your goal because you are confident of your desire for it.

The necessary elements, then, for empowerment are:

1. Unleashing your imagination

2. Trusting your imagination

3. Clarifying your desire

4. Trusting your desire

5. Desire becoming intent

6. Acceptance

Acceptance is a two-fold achievement. The empowerment piece of acceptance is accepting yourself. You accept that you have this magnificent power of imagination to create what you want in your life.

The second part is to accept that gift that is unfolding in your life. Sometimes it's hard to accept the good, as much as we might devote ourselves to manifesting it in our lives. On the cognitive level, our first thoughts might be, "Well of course I want that. That's good." But as you work through the techniques of creative visualization, you may find that you don't quite believe this with your whole body, mind, and soul. You may remember too many failures, see too many obstacles. You may not quite believe you deserve it. You may think that you have to struggle to get it.

> **Wisdom Well**
>
> Belief consists in accepting the affirmations of the soul; unbelief, in denying them.
>
> —Ralph Waldo Emerson, nineteenth-century American lecturer, poet, and essayist

None of this is so, but that's easy for us to tell you—not so easy to accept. Affirmations are a vital component in the acceptance process.

Your Power: Affirmations

Even though you have already tried affirmations with these exercises, they might still seem a bit forced to you. It's hard to say out loud a statement such as, "I am whole and complete within myself," or "I love and appreciate myself just as I am." Our first human instinct is to contradict (or perhaps even to snicker). The skeptic rises in us. Our minds jump to evaluate whether the statement is true. Do I *really* appreciate myself just as I am? Immediately, our flaws present themselves.

Affirmations at first may seem egotistical, even narcissistic. But they are a key component in directing the positive energy to your creative visualization. In truth, practice is the best way to understand the power of affirmations. True believing is seeing them as truth in action.

The reason affirmations are so powerful is that most of us fill our minds with negative, critical, evaluative, or analytical thoughts. Some of this is necessary to function in the world. We must evaluate and analyze when we buy a week's worth of groceries, comparing quality and price. We must think critically, looking at the down side, in order to make sure our business succeeds. *What's the bottom line?* We want to know. Some of this is basic survival. If the hunter didn't enter the woods with his senses sharply tuned to watch for danger, the hunter would get nabbed by the bear.

In our achievement-oriented world, we are focused on what we are doing, what we are getting, what we are accomplishing. It's not in our nature to acknowledge what we already have. After all, we already have it. So why think about it?

Affirmations are the practice by which we begin crowding out the negative thoughts that dominate our minds. Affirmations cut through our ongoing daily commentary, our stream of consciousness. Over time, it becomes more natural to appreciate, to accept, to see the good, to trust our own wisdom. We build a reservoir of positive thoughts, replacing the old, negative thoughts. Affirmations are a conscious commitment to do this.

Affirmations work through repetition. The negative thoughts that we are so accustomed to become deeply ingrained in us through years of repetition. After a while, they seem to be the most natural thoughts. When we start a practice of affirmations, we turn that pattern around. We are training our minds to think in new patterns.

Affirmations are the method by which you gain the assurance that your dream has already been realized. They form the backbone of creative visualization. Affirmations give voice to the intention to realize your dream. Affirmations ultimately bring to you the calm, silent knowing that what you imagine will be born.

Principles of Affirmations

There are an infinite number of affirmations—only limited by your imagination. The most important thing is they must always be phrased in the most positive way possible. And, they must work for you. If the core message of an affirmation doesn't seem right *to* you, it won't work *for* you.

Beyond that basic truth, follow these guidelines:

◆ Keep affirmations short and simple.

◆ Keep affirmations in the present tense.

Remember that you are always acting *as if* your dream is already realized. That means you don't say, "I want"; instead, you say, "I accept." You might want to put affirmations in present progressive (grammar *is* important!), reflecting that your ambition is an ongoing project: "I am now attracting …" or "I am now becoming …"

Affirmations might make broad, sweeping statements, or they might be very specific. They might be very abstract, such as, "Perfect wisdom is in my heart." Or they might pinpoint a certain area, as in "I have meaningful work with rewarding pay." They might even name someone who is vital to your creative vision, as in "My relationship with _____ is becoming more fulfilling every day." Some affirmations strike a universal spiritual chord, such as "All things are working together for good in my life."

All kinds of affirmations serve to bring the positive focus toward your goal. You may want to mix it up with each session, so that your positive energy is working on all levels.

Creating Affirmations

It's important to keep your affirmations fresh and original. It's less effective to compile a set of affirmations and use the same ones from session to session. You may have affirmations that are mainstays, but in general, tailor your affirmations to the specific purpose of your session. Take into account where you are with your ambition, directing your affirmation to the next step. Take into account your attitude today toward your ambition. Are you feeling optimistic? Disappointed? Fatigued? Formulate your affirmations for that day's session with these considerations in mind.

Take a few moments to create some affirmations for your Creative Visualization Journal from our list of prompts.

Starts:

Everything I need is

I love and appreciate

I accept

I now give and receive

I am now attracting

I now have enough

I am growing

I am becoming

I am now enjoying

I am open

I deserve

Positive words:

More fulfilling

Satisfying

In every way

Whole and complete

Perfect wisdom

Easily and effortlessly

Prosperous

Happy

Healthy

Beautiful

Infinite creative power

Divine love

Talented

Intelligent

Creative

Attractive

Successful

Fill in the blank:

_____ *is my natural state of being.*

_____ *is coming to me.*

Symbols as Affirmations

Once, Shari had a client we'll call Jennifer who was a freshman in college, and she was distraught at the thought of speaking in public. Jennifer faced a deadline at the

> **Affirmations**
>
> Everything I need is right here.

end of the semester in which she would have to speak in front of the class. That day loomed 16 weeks away, but in Jennifer's mind, it was approaching fast.

Shari saw that creative visualization provided an opportunity for the client to reduce her fear. In the first session, Jennifer examined her past to see if there were any blocks. Nothing significant surfaced. In the next session, Shari instructed Jennifer in progressive relaxation techniques. Jennifer decided to make a tape of Shari leading her through the techniques so she could work on relaxation at home, too. By the third session, Jennifer reported she had memorized some of the tape and was using it when she was nervous.

Here's where creative visualization kicked in. Shari helped Jennifer envision in great detail what it would be like to speak, and speak successfully. Jennifer envisioned herself standing in her dorm room and walking through each step of the day of her speech until Jennifer found herself standing at the podium. Shari asked her to choose someone in the front row who would give Jennifer a present to calm her fears just before she started speaking. Jennifer envisioned opening the present. She was delighted with the contents, but she was not allowed to tell Shari what was in the box.

The next time Jennifer came, she was excited. She had spoken twice in different classes. She had been a little nervous, but not like before.

So what was in the box? The box held a book on public speaking, written by Jennifer.

A Sacred Contract

Affirmations are the line items in a *contract*. Each affirmation represents a transaction—an exchange of negative thoughts for positive ones. Affirmations are the enunciation of your intention, as expressed in your sacred contract.

In any kind of contract when you exchange one thing, another is given. In this case, we want you to make a contract with yourself— a *sacred* contract. You make a promise. The exchange is this: You visualize your dream and you devote your focus and energy to it. The payoff is you realize your dream. To get the most out of this book, make a contract with yourself to believe in your dream and commit to using creative visualization to attain it. Write your contract—complete with terms—in your Creative Visualization Journal.

Deeper Meaning

A **contract** is an agreement between two parties to honor a goal. A sacred contract is a contract you make with yourself to serve your highest desires.

There are five stages in a sacred contract, according to Caroline Myss, a teacher and author (*Anatomy of the Spirit, Sacred Contracts, Invisible Acts of Power*; see Appendix B) on the topic of holistic health. She defines them as:

♦ **Contact.** Contact is when your dream appears before you. It's the inspiration. Myss defines it as a moment of connection between you and the Divine. It's the flash of blinding white light. It's the burning bush. It's the angel bearing a message wrapped in assurance. It's when you first start to believe in the happiness and harmony your dream can bring into your life. And when you first start to believe it's possible.

♦ **Heeding the call.** We don't always start off on the journey from the moment of the first vision. We might stay in wishing mode for many years. But at a certain point, having made contact with our dream—when the image in our minds becomes clear—we decide to heed the call. Myss defines heeding the call as the awakening. It's a moment when new wisdom descends upon us and we make the decision to apply it to our lives. This is intent.

♦ **Renaming.** We'll get to this aspect in later chapters, when we look at how creative visualization can make us grow. The quest for your vision brings changes into your life.

◆ **Assignments.** Once you have made the contract with yourself to use creative visualization to bring changes into your life, assignments will come to you. This is the process of intent at work. It brings you the vision for the next steps you must take. Some of these assignments mean encountering extraordinary opportunities—some you might never have conceived.

◆ **Surrender.** You are tested as you work through the creative visualization techniques to manifest your dream in your life. You clarify your values. You are called upon to choose whether you would follow the easy path or the path to attain your highest good. Again, in later chapters, we'll delve into the inner changes that unfold through creative visualization.

The Path to Success

Trusting in the gift of your imagination is the first step in trusting your power. Strengthening your desire with the fire of intent is to strengthen yourself with a most magnificent power. Using affirmations and making a sacred contract with yourself are vital acts of empowerment. All of these are choices you can make. All are available to you. All set you on the path of success with creative visualization.

The Least You Need to Know

◆ Trusting in the mystery of your imagination is key to getting the maximum out of creative visualization.

◆ An essential step to becoming confident of your goal is to become confident of your desire for it.

◆ Accepting yourself and accepting that good things will come to you are part of getting in touch with your sense of empowerment.

◆ Affirmations are a mechanism to bring forth the positive energy you need.

◆ Look upon moving toward your dream as a contract you are keeping with yourself, and hold it sacred.

Part 2

Learning to Visualize, Creatively!

Let's get practical. Where do you do creative visualization, and how?

In the chapters that follow, we'll give you advice about how to prepare body, mind, and spirit for powerful creative visualizations. We'll help you get everything in order—from your space to your beautiful mind to the way you live your life. So you see … it's not just about visualizing. It's about living life creatively.

Chapter 5

Get in the Flow: Preparing

In This Chapter

◆ How change on the outside generates change on the inside

◆ Getting the most out of your Creative Visualization Journal

◆ Preparing a sanctuary

◆ The right frame of mind

◆ Connecting with your inner spiritual guide

◆ Setting parameters for each creative visualization session

In the first part of this book, we gave you some tools to help you examine, explore, and build a good infrastructure of beliefs and practices in your life. The fullest experience of creative visualization, one rich with insight and best results, lies before you as you continue to deepen your understanding.

We know you have the desire—that's surely why you picked up this book. Now with an open mind and heart, and hopefully, a willingness to go on a spectacular journey, it's time to get down to the details. Now it's time to go into it—to visualize creatively, body and soul.

Open Space, Open Mind

When you want change on the inside, bring about change on the outside. This simple step is one of the basic principles of creative visualization, and so it's vital to your preparation ritual.

Many of us have practiced this same principle before in ordinary daily life. It's the dieter who nears the goal of a healthy, comfortable weight … but sees her resolve wavering. So she motivates herself by bringing out a favorite outfit that hasn't fit in a long time and hanging it on the bedroom mirror. It's the day before you have a big meeting and you carefully design and print the agenda and meeting materials, so you'll project the perfect image of confidence, professionalism, and bold success for the company and for your team's work. It's the way you prepare your house when a special someone is coming for the first time. You light candles. You set a fire in the fireplace. You want the environment to be welcoming and comforting.

The steps you'll take in this chapter are:

- Gather your tools
- Prepare your space
- Get in the right frame of mind
- Prepare your spirit
- Set up your parameters

All of these steps are infused with intention. By taking these steps, you declare your intention that you will be committed to putting your best effort into, and getting the best possible results from, your practice of creative visualization.

Tools of the Trade: Using Your Journal

You'll find a Creative Visualization Journal to be an essential companion for this book. Here are some specific ways you can use it. (You'll find more details about setting up your journal in Appendix A.)

- **Visioning.** Your imagination and self-knowledge are vital components in forming your vision. Your journal will provide a record of both. It can be a record of your enthusiasm at the outset of your vision making, a good reference point to which you might return during times of doubt.

◆ **Affirmations.** Use your journal to record affirmations. Develop these affirmations as you go. Over time, your collection of affirmations will become a vital resource. In fact, you may find you'll have a separate journal just for affirmations, arranged by subject or purpose.

◆ **Bearing witness.** Have you ever noticed that after you share your goals with another person, it strengthens your resolve? The reason is this: what you receive from the other person is enthusiasm, positive feedback, perhaps a refinement of your vision, perhaps a resource or helpful person for your vision. Use your Creative Visualization Journal the same way. Your journal can bear witness to your intention. It is the equivalent of sharing your vision with another person and taking a vow together to support that vision.

◆ **Keeping your vision.** Let your Creative Visualization Journal help you refine your vision. Let it be a vital record, keeping your goal alive, cherishing it, and holding it sacred.

"But why write it down?" you might ask. Details make the difference. Details keep it real. Think about when a friend tells you a story about something that happened to him. Some storytellers can make a scene come to life, and you can picture events unfolding as though you were there, too, in that place at that time. That's the power of detail. Details keep your vision memorable. They make it palpable. As you add more detail to your vision, you strengthen your intention.

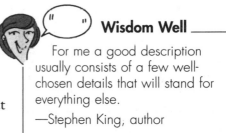

Wisdom Well

For me a good description usually consists of a few well-chosen details that will stand for everything else.

—Stephen King, author

Writing it down moves you to the next step. It calls upon your imagination to be more creative, to imagine the next solution. Your mind no longer has to hold the first vision, and it can be free to imagine the next step.

Writing it down is like taking a vow. It cements your intention to paper. It provides a record. It's something you can come back to for encouragement and for clarifying your vision. We encourage you to review your Creative Visualization Journal regularly.

Writing it down also allows you to fine-tune. Writing in a stream of consciousness, with no stopping, no evaluating, no editing, no crossing out, is a good way to move through a block or clarify your vision when it becomes cloudy.

So write everything down, all of it—even if you don't think of yourself as the "writer type." You may be surprised at how motivating seeing your goals on paper can be. It's good for your mind. Think of it as fitness for the mind. Don't make your head remember all the details. Empty the tank and let your imagination go forth and multiply your vision.

A Sanctuary: Preparing Your Space

Why does the right place matter? Can't you imagine your life as you want it to be anywhere, anytime? Yes, indeed. One of the most wonderful abilities human beings have is the ability to daydream, to transport themselves into a beautiful scene for their lives while in line at the bank or sitting through a boring lecture.

Deeper Meaning

A **sanctuary** is a place of refuge or protection. In a religious context, it's a building set aside for worship, a holy place. Make the place where you practice creative visualization a sanctuary—a safe, holy place.

But setting up a place for regular creative visualization practice, a *sanctuary* in your home or garden, is a way of making a conscious commitment to the process. We have more about outdoor sanctuaries in Chapter 6.

A comfortable, relaxing environment allows your imagination to flourish. A regular place to practice meditations on your vision and repeat affirmations is a commitment. You are telling yourself this is important. In preparing to go to that place to practice creative visualization, you are preparing your mind and heart.

The value of a creative visualization sanctuary in your home is that you have the ability to add objects and symbols there that reinforce your creative vision, and your intention. You set up a devotion station for yourself, and you commit to tending to that place. This, ultimately, is tending to your vision.

Creating a Devotion Station

To prepare your sanctuary, create a devotion station for your intentions. This may be a candle that you burn during your meditations. Or it may be a collage, painting, or sketch you create to symbolize your dream. (We'll come back to this idea in subsequent chapters.)

Some people like to bring symbols that represent components of themselves or the positive energy they want to bring into their lives. Here are some ideas to get you started:

- The clock from your father's desk
- Your grandmother's brooch
- A ceramic rose that reminds you of your mother, who loves roses
- A piece of fabric that represents your softness—or how you shimmer
- A photo from a vacation that changed your life
- A locket or case with tender words from a lover
- A stone in the shape of a heart
- Bark from a tree in your favorite forest

Don't Panic, *Focus!*

Does your creative visualization sanctuary *have* to be a place? Absolutely not. That's the beauty of creative visualization. It is a construct of your mental picture. Your "sanctuary" could be your Creative Visualization Journal, which you carry around with you throughout the day—or anything that has a safe meaning for you. Either way, you'll find that creating a "home" for your creative visualization practice is invaluable.

Creating an Inner Sanctuary

In addition to a physical sanctuary, it may be useful to you to create a mental picture of a sanctuary you can go to during your creative visualizations. This could be a mountain, a beach, a Greco-Roman ruin, a cathedral, a star—anything you imagine. Some people find it empowering to envision their Creator or Source. What matters most is that when you think of this picture, you can transport yourself there in your imagination—and that going to this place in your mind *gives you peace*.

Take a few moments to do this meditation, to create your inner sanctuary. Seated comfortably, close your eyes and take three deep cleansing breaths.

Now imagine your sanctuary, whether it be mountain or ocean, cathedral or star. Sit with this image in your mind, allowing it to come into full focus. As you breathe in and out, breathe life into it. If it is a mountain, add the breeze rustling through the trees. If it is an ocean, add the crashing of the waves. Envision yourself bringing a tribute or offering to your sanctuary—a twig or stone or flower. This honors the intention you have to create this vivid mental picture as a place of peace within your mind.

Preparing Your Mind

Before a creative visualization session, it's important to clear your mind. This will ensure your creative visualization session is the most effective it can be.

Getting Grounded: Heaven and Earth Meditation

Getting grounded can be an important first step before a session because you are exploring your imagination to the fullest. As exhilarating as this can be, it also can leave you with a feeling of being untethered.

Use the following tree meditation before any creative visualization session when you need to get grounded. Use it for a time when you are seeking powerful results. The basis of this exercise is that our feet are the connection between heaven and Earth. By being more aware of where your feet are planted, you can feel less diffuse—fully in your body and clear of mind. Focusing on your feet can help you bring your emotional and spiritual energy into body.

Wisdom Well

To see the world in a grain of sand and heaven in a wild flower, to hold infinity in the palm of your hand and eternity in an hour.

—William Blake, English romantic poet

This is a powerful meditation to do outside, in bare feet, touching the grass or the soil. But it can be just as effective inside, with your bare feet in contact with the carpet, rug, or floor.

With your feet about 12 inches apart and your knees slightly bent, focus on the warmth in the soles of your feet. Spread your toes across the floor or the ground. Feel the vitality of the earth vibrating against the soles of your feet. Take a few deep, calming breaths. In your mind's eye, picture roots moving down through your body and taking hold in the earth. Feel those roots stretch into the earth. Stretch tall, extending through your body, reaching with both arms toward the sky or ceiling.

In your mind's eye, picture the earth's energy rising up from the roots through your body. Feel its warmth. Feel its vitality. Feel your body taking in its sustenance, envisioning it slowly moving up through your legs, your belly, your shoulders, your neck. Stretch a little more, connecting to the vitality of the sky. Envision now that you are the link between heaven and earth. Stay in this vision a little longer, breathing deeply and calmly through six cycles of breath.

Imagine, See, Be

Nature is a wonderful reminder to us of the power of creation. Getting in touch with nature through a heaven-and-earth meditation or by creating an outer sanctuary is a good way to reconnect with your own creativity. Can you think of other ways to incorporate nature into your creative visualization practice?

Tracking Thought Pathways

Think of the negative thoughts and experiences you have had in the last week. Do they keep cycling through your mind? Try to remember whether the negative energy came first in the form of a thought or an action. Write about it in your Creative Visualization Journal.

Next, follow the same pathway with positive energy and experiences. Explore in your Creative Visualization Journal how you arrived at these positive thoughts. It's a good idea to end your journaling with a positive memory or idea. It's a form of affirmation. You can use it to set yourself up the next day to be positive because you are focusing on the good.

You may also use your sleep—and your dreams—to revitalize your positive thoughts. By focusing on the positive thought on which you ended your journaling just before you go to sleep, you may influence your dreams in a positive way.

Why Meditation Is Vital

Creative visualization recognizes the power our thoughts can have in changing our lives. Change your thoughts; change your life.

Why, you may ask? A thought is just a thought. It may be something we keep to ourselves. It may not be something we act upon. We can have thousands of thoughts in a day. Singer/songwriter Jackson Browne wrote in "The Only Child," a song dedicated to his son, not to put too much meaning into the thoughts that crowd your mind, saying there would not be many thoughts that ever really mattered.

But our thoughts *do* matter. To a psychologist, a thought is never just a thought. Thoughts are doorways into our subconscious or comments on our conscious lives. If you tell yourself to write down anything important that crosses your mind, you might end up with a list that surprises you. Where your thoughts go, energy closely follows.

Thoughts form the beliefs that begin to structure our lives and our actions. Thoughts move from the mental plane to the physical plane when an idea becomes an action. Thoughts become material, they gain substance. One, what this tells us is that thoughts can have great power to manifest in our lives. Two, this means we must be ever conscious of what negative thoughts attract into our lives. Negative thoughts, even if not acted upon, draw energy of that quality to us. Think of the term "self-fulfilling prophecy." This is a negative thought ("My partner will leave me" or "I'm going to get ill") that comes to fruition. A person who has the persistent thought that his or her life partner is not in love and will someday leave, begins to act in such a way that the partner eventually *may* actually leave, or at least begin to reconsider the relationship.

Meditation not only relaxes the mind, it disciplines the mind. It's more, then, than just a relaxation technique. We do not let our minds run amok with any thought from the highest to the lowest. When we meditate, we do so with the intention that we will free the negative thoughts that crowd near the surface, dominating the chatter in our heads. Let them go and create the empty, fertile space that allows positive thoughts to flourish. We will go into more depth about meditation as we move through the next six chapters, and we'll show you how to develop the discipline that makes creative visualization so effective.

Preparing Your Spirit

Getting into the right state of spirit is an important part of preparing for creative visualization. Energy moves through us in a progression—from the physical plane to the mental, from mental to emotional, from emotional to spiritual. Part of preparing yourself for creative visualization is preparing yourself to receive information on all levels. You may already have practices in place in your life. They may take the form of religion or spirituality, as we discussed in Chapter 2. They may be body, mind, and spirit practices such as yoga or tai chi, or they may be hobbies (painting, playing piano) or sports that provide you with leisure and rejuvenation. Many people find it useful to draw upon these practices in their approach to creative visualization. We encourage you to continue them or to seek them out if you have not developed them in your life. In fact, one of your creative visualizations might be to make all of your efforts work in synch!

A vital step is to connect with your inner spiritual guide, if you have chosen to do that in Chapter 2. Many people do find that making this contract with their Source at the outset of creative visualization is a powerful ritual. They find their session is not so much a matter of effort and struggle, but intention and allowance. By connecting with their inner source of wisdom, they find their highest wisdom within. By connecting with infinite love, they find the place within to access great compassion as they pursue their goal. By connecting with the source of their strength, they connect with that place where their goal unfolds with grace. Notice we didn't say with ease. It may not be easy, but you can be assured you will be equipped with the strength to do it with grace.

We caution you not to get too hung up on feeling you must shift the focus of your visualization practice to an expression of spiritual principles first and foremost. You don't need to put spiritual principles first in order to make the creative visualization process work. All you need to be successful in your creative visualization practice is a fertile imagination, a strong desire to create a meaningful life, and some trust in the process.

> **Wisdom Well**
>
> Language is the oxygen of thinking; it allows thoughts to breathe and live, to become full-bodied.
>
> —Caterina Rando, motivational coach and author

Your Highest Self

Spiritual teacher and author Marianne Williamson (*Return to Love*, *Everyday Grace*, and other books; see Appendix B) once said, "Our deepest fear is not that we are inadequate. Our deepest fear is that we are powerful beyond measure." South African president Nelson Mandela used this quote in his 1994 inauguration speech.

What do you think of when someone says to you, "You are powerful beyond measure?" Are you tempted at first to laugh? This thought is so grand it's hardly something you can hold in your mind, much less apply to yourself. It just seems impossible that something like that might be true.

But this potential lies within us all. The power of creative visualization rests on this belief that we can realize our highest potential by using these simple techniques of seeing. The process of creative visualization is a gradual chipping away at the resistance to believing in that potential. That's where affirmations come in. Affirmations are like an ice pick, chipping away at the ice that has formed around our highest potential, the higher self within.

> **Affirmations**
>
> I am now connected to the source of my power, my wisdom and my strength.

What does it mean to say that we connecting with our higher selves? It sounds quite grand, really, but most of us know this feeling. Shakti Gawain describes it at its most elementary—it's when we feel "on top of the world" or "able to move mountains." Anytime we fall in love—with another person, with a book, with the mountains, with a beautiful idea—we are experiencing that connection.

What defines that feeling? Here, we have made a list:

- **Clarity**. We can see the possibilities for our lives. We know our true purpose.

- **Alignment**. We are living in alignment with our values. What we are experiencing on the outside matches the hopes and dreams and desires on the inside. The picture of who we are on the outside matches with the picture on the inside of the person we want to be.

- **Flow**. We are in synch with the universe. We are connected to those around us and to nature. We are connected with our Source. We do not feel separated.

- **Receptivity**. Falling in love, essentially, is about being open. Suddenly, the armor falls away and we are no longer protecting ourselves from the possibility of hurt. We allow ourselves to be vulnerable, and we see in the other the possibility that we can open up and be safe.

Mirror, Mirror: Contacting Your Higher Self

For this visualization, get comfortable in your sanctuary. You will need a mirror. But first, close your eyes. Take in three deep cleansing breaths. Form in your mind's eye the picture of yourself when you are acting from your higher self. Hold the picture in your mind of your higher self. Repeat these affirmations:

I can now see all the possibilities that lie within me.

God/Goddess/Source/Creator [use your own word] *is working through me now.*

God/Goddess/Source/Creator [use your own word] *is working through me on all planes— physical, mental, emotional, and spiritual.*

The light within me is creating harmony and peace.

I am receiving infinite love now.

The universe is unfolding perfectly.

I am connected to the flow of all life.

Now, open your eyes and look in the mirror. See yourself with the eyes of your higher self. Take in your posture. Notice the details of your face. Repeat these affirmations, listening to the strength of your voice. Hear the confidence. We want you to experience your highest self on all levels, with all senses. Repeat these affirmations as necessary until you have worked through all levels and all senses.

Setting Up Parameters

How often should you do a creative visualization session? And how long should each one be? What will be most effective for you might not be the most effective for another person. However, we can recommend some parameters that work for maximum effectiveness. You might start off this way, then fine-tune as you get used to the techniques, customizing the practice length for yourself.

- **Set up a regular time.** Some people find morning is best, others find evenings work better for them. At the outset, commit to a regular time. Bringing a discipline to the practice of creative visualization is an important component of the intentionality that makes it work.

- **Commit to at least 10 to 12 minutes per session.** We recommend starting off with short sessions, but over time, as you grow more comfortable with the techniques, you will find that shorter or longer times may work better for you.

- **Commit to frequent sessions.** At first, it's important to practice frequently. Some people find three to five times a week works initially. Starting off with more frequency will help you gain the focus and practice you'll need to incorporate the techniques into your life. It also will help you get the results you are looking for—and that may be the best positive reinforcement of all.

Doing a creative visualization daily can make your sessions very powerful. But we caution you that there is no right or wrong. Some people find, once they have gotten the techniques down, that sessions can be just as effective if they practice once a week, once a month, even occasionally. The most important consideration is what works for you. If creative visualization works for you, you'll devote time to it regularly. And that's the bottom line. It's just human nature: We do the things we *want* to do.

Prepare for Takeoff

We have taken the time to walk you through the preparations for your sessions because we believe the intention you bring to preparing is vital to the results of creative visualization. Now that you have the tools, the place, the right frame of mind, a clear and open heart, and a schedule, let's go.

The Least You Need to Know

- ♦ A basic principle of creative visualization is that change on the outside brings about change on the inside.

- ♦ Using your Creative Visualization Journal to record the details of your vision will help you keep your vision memorable, fresh, and alive.

- ♦ Setting up a regular place in your home as a sanctuary is a way of keeping your creative visualization practice conscious.

- ♦ Creating an inner sanctuary—a peace within—can be a vital component of creative visualization.

- ♦ If you change your thoughts, you can change your life.

- ♦ To get the most from your creative visualization sessions, it's best to set up some parameters.

Chapter 6

Stay With the Flow: Believing

In This Chapter

◆ What it means to stay in the flow

◆ Staying with your desire

◆ An exercise for getting in touch with your goal

◆ Letting go of control

◆ Getting aligned with your higher self

Okay, got vision, got desire. Now you have the essential components of creative visualization, right down to the practicalities of the place to do it and the place to record it. So what's next? Do you just wait?

Remember, you must live *as if* what you desire has already happened. You don't *expect* something that has already happened; you *enjoy* it. In this chapter, we'll talk about how you stay in the flow. We'll show you how to make a believer of yourself.

Flow: Riding the Magic Carpet

Staying in the *flow* means staying in that state of believing your dream is coming. It means staying focused on your dream—and not letting rough waters or other undercurrents knock you off course. You stay in alignment with your most heartfelt desire, the desire that you have tested and become clear on and know to be true for your life. You believe, ahead of time, that what you desire is meant to be. It means staying firm, and using your affirmations to do that.

This might sound really hard. It may sound like something only for the most determined or most spiritually enlightened among us. But it's not. It's not about struggling and striving. We'll repeat: *it's not a struggle.*

Learning to Trust

The most effective way to use creative visualization is to trust the flow and just go with it. The way Shakti Gawain puts it is that you don't have to exert effort to get where you want to go. She says, "You simply keep clearly in mind where you would like to go, and then patiently and harmoniously follow the flow of the river of life until it takes you there." It's more like Aladdin's magic carpet. You just get on and glide.

Deeper Meaning

Flow is to move gently, smoothly, easily; to glide. Flow is to tap into the positive energy of the universe, your truest desires and your highest self. Flow is the way to stay the course.

At the same time you hold your vision firm in your mind's eye and in your heart, you hold on to it lightly. You have to let go. You have to trust. This is the paradox.

Begin at the Beginning

In this chapter, we'll use the story of "Marianne," who represents a composite of clients Shari has seen over the years—women who feel the tug of demands others place on them and lose sight of their own visions. Shari has worked with clients like Marianne to create, refine, and achieve a personal vision. So while there is no one real Marianne, the truth behind the story and the techniques Shari used are real.

Marianne came to Shari because her wheelchair-bound mother wanted to move in. Marianne's husband, Tim, was adamant that he would not live with his mother-in-law. He liked her and they were on friendly terms, but Marianne and Tim had a small house. Tim was semi-retired, and he was home a lot. He wanted the freedom to spend time with his wife. He did not want to take care of Marianne's mother, Liz. Liz was equally adamant, insisting it was a daughter's duty to take care of her mother. Liz had done it, taking care of her own mother, and she expected the same of Marianne. Marianne found herself caught in the middle.

In the first session, Marianne came with her mother, who had suggested the counseling. Liz was paying, hoping a therapist would talk her daughter into taking her in. Marianne spoke in an anxious, defeated voice. "Whatever I do, it seems I will make someone unhappy," Marianne said. "My mother is not young anymore. She has had a light stroke, and she wants me to take care of her. She says it's my duty. Tim says, 'No way.' He won't even talk about it. I don't really know what I want."

Shari focused on moving Marianne toward the goal of making her own decisions. Shari wanted Marianne to get in touch with her true desires. She instructed her to meditate and begin to listen to her heart. She advised Marianne to come to the next session alone. At that session, Shari and Marianne decided to use creative visualization to help her work through the conflict. Marianne decided she had been pulled between Tim and Liz for too long. That week she decided to visualize what being happy would look like for her.

We'll pick up Marianne's story throughout this chapter to show you how to use the different steps of creative visualization to open yourself up to new possibilities for your life. It starts, as in Marianne's case, with getting in touch with what you really want.

Strong Desire Becomes Belief

Another way of saying "stay in the flow" might be "keep your eye on the ball." Whether you're a lifelong athlete or still the same awkward kid who could never quite absorb the barrage of instructions from your elementary school P.E. coach, you'll be familiar with this simple advice. If your bat is going to make contact with the ball, you have to know where the ball *is* at any given moment. Keeping your eye on the ball means knowing its velocity, its direction, and its trajectory.

So, too, it is with creative visualization. In this respect, "the ball" is your desire. Keeping your focus on your heart's desire means connecting to the truest essence of *why* you want your dream to come true. So again, it's not a matter of willpower so much as it is self-knowledge.

It didn't take long for Marianne to see in her mind's eye what would make her happy. It jelled by her third session with Shari: Liz would move into assisted living, Tim and Marianne would go into counseling. Marianne's creative visualization had led her to question whether she wanted to be married to Tim.

This is a good example of the way creative visualization can bring about surprising responses. There may be something we have desired for a long time, but we just sort of go along, not willing to rock the boat, and we don't ask for it. We may even lose our awareness of our desire for it. But when we focus on our true desire for happiness, we may decide to respond in a different way than before.

CAUTION **Don't Panic, *Focus!***

What if you know that you will rock the boat if you seek what you truly want? When you start to make changes—even positive changes—you will shake up some of the people around you. But the way through it is to keep a vision in the forefront of your mind for something better than what you have now. Return again and again to that vision. You will see the shining light of the new possibility contrasted with the way things have been. Keep your eye on the prize, and there is no going back.

Marianne's assignment was simple: just keep doing what she was doing with creative visualization. She stayed with the vision she had formed, continued her meditation, and spent time alone with it, giving it her focus. She stayed with the flow.

By staying with it, Marianne's desire solidified. Three weeks later, she became firm in her original plan. She wanted Liz in assisted living. She would visit often and take her places, but she wanted to be a daughter, not a caretaker. Liz mostly accepted Marianne's decision.

Marianne's misgivings about Tim were another story. The more they talked about the issue—the intrusion of the mother-in-law—the more Marianne realized Tim was depressed about life in general and she wasn't happy in the marriage. Marianne engaged in firm persuasion to get him to go to counseling. In doing so, Marianne announced she would no longer be in the middle, pulled between her mother and her husband.

When Shari asked Marianne what part of creative visualization was most effective, she said "the middle." When she was meditating and staying true to her goals, she was in the flow. She was affirming that her true desires had been met before she knew exactly how things would work out. It was this part that gave her the strongest sense of peace.

It's About You and Your Goal

Use this candle-gazing exercise to get yourself in touch with *your* goal. Returning to your Creative Visualization Journal, pick one of the Life Arenas from Chapter 1. What goals, dreams, or desires come to mind for that arena? Choose a candle in a color that symbolizes your dream. Sit comfortably in front of your candle. As you light it, say:

I am now seeing vast possibilities for my life.

Spend a few moments gazing into the candle. Repeat the following affirmations:

I am filled with light.

The light within me is creating miracles in my life in the here and now.

I am filled with peace.

The peace within me is allowing new possibilities to unfold in my life.

I am living in harmony with the people in my life.

I am now attuned to my higher purpose in life.

With each statement, focus on the glow of the flame. Imagine storing the flame within you. Imagine it burning brightly within.

The Mental Plane: New Thoughts, New Possibilities

Marianne realized she was stuck thinking she only had two alternatives—choose her mother or choose her husband! It was that black and white for her. At least, it seemed that way at the outset, when she had buried her sense of self and saw her existence only in terms of others. She had lost sight of her own decision-making power.

But creative visualization opened her up to new thoughts that showed Marianne a range of possibilities. Some of them might involve her mother, some of them might involve her husband, but some of them might not involve anyone but herself.

When Marianne held that belief and kept her thoughts on it 24 hours a day, it became strong enough for her to act on it. No longer was there room for hurtful, negative, or unrealistic thoughts.

Filtering Your Thoughts

You can do the same thing. Start with a meditation in which you allow yourself to listen to the stream of words and phrases in your mind. Some may repeat over and over. Some you may like, and some you may not. At first, when you become aware of negative thoughts, don't resist them. Just be mindful of them. It's only by being aware of negative thoughts that we can begin to filter them and open up to new, more positive possibilities.

You may not even be able at first to label certain thoughts as self-defeating, fearful, or shameful. You may not see them as thoughts that come from low self-esteem. You may simply know they just don't feel good to think about. Imagine how Marianne felt when she thought she only had two choices, neither of them pleasant. That feeling is the product of a negative thought: I don't have any say in what happens in my life.

Know that when a negative thought begins to manifest in this state of mindfulness, it's not going to thrive. It's the beginning of the end of that thought—because now, being mindful, *you are not going to keep this thought.*

Repeat instead what you want to hear from yourself. Add this positive thought, in a declarative sentence—an affirmation—to the mix:

I have the power to decide what happens to me in this situation.

I am deciding that I will respond to this situation with inner peace, clarity, and grace.

Start now to make this shift in your thoughts a daily practice, something you can do 24/7 as you are walking around. Over time, you'll find the ratio of positive thoughts to negative thoughts shifts in favor of positive thoughts.

The Power of Stillness

What lies in the power of moments alone is stillness. Stillness brings to us a deep sense of lasting peace, contentment, and serenity. Stillness does not have the need to go forward in time, nor does it need to reach back into the past. It just *is*.

Stillness invites us to drop out of active mind, dropping away from emotions that form our thoughts and perceptions, freeing ourselves of them. When you free yourself of those old patterns of emotions and thoughts, you allow something new to be. You allow the imagination to open up, to create a space to receive new possibilities.

In his book *Stillness Speaks* (see Appendix B), Eckhart Tolle urges us in our daily lives to pay as much attention to the gap between the sounds as to the sounds themselves.

He urges us to listen to the spaces between words in a conversation, between the notes played on a piano, between the in-breath and the out-breath. Suddenly you will notice how much more time there is to simply exist. You will notice how much more time there is for your imagination to be fertile. You will see how much time there is to create new possibilities.

Breath is a tremendous instrument for creating this inner stillness. It anchors you in the now. Breath creates the expansion of possibilities. When you breathe in the space between an emotion or an old thought, you stop the immediate reaction. You open a new dimension of time where a new possibility resides.

The Emotional Plane: Trusting

When you are aware of the flow of the river of life, it can be a powerful sensation. Some days, as you move toward your goal, you may get glimpses of the unfolding of forces that move you toward your goal. This can be exhilarating as you see events and opportunities unfold before you that begin, step by step, day by day, to make your goal more possible—even steps that you had not yet imagined. It is indeed a beautiful process, because each step is a little dose of encouragement.

As you become aware of the flow, you will gradually learn to trust in it. You will gradually learn to let go of control.

There, we said it: control. To truly let the flow take you toward your goal, you must let go of control. Though you hold your vision clearly in your mind, you hold on to it lightly. Sometimes flow sweeps you in a different direction than you think you should be going. Maybe it brings changes, and without being conscious of it, you struggle against the changes.

No doubt you have heard the saying, "What you resist, persists." Another way of saying it is, "What you resist is trying to get your attention." So pay attention to what *you* are resisting. It's telling you to let go, to trust the process. It's bidding you to change.

No More Control

Shari's client, Marianne, felt on a very deep level that the only control she had was over who to please first. In addition, pleasing herself simply did not exist as an option! As Marianne began to meditate, to visualize her goals, her subconscious mind began to surface. She had thoughts and feelings about being free of being controlled by anyone. She realized she was an adult. When she accepted the idea that she was a separate being from those who wanted her attention, Marianne's first emotion to surface, not surprisingly, was resentment. In therapy she talked about her resentment and began to understand that she was angry at herself for relinquishing her power. Shari asked her to practice between sessions saying: "I am an adult woman and I am powerful!"

After a week of keeping this thought in her mind, she began to feel it on a deeply emotional level. She had let the genie out of the bottle—and boy was he mad! One afternoon she was so overcome with rage at how she had given her life to her husband and her mother that she stopped her car at the edge of the road and ran into the woods screaming—not even real words, just screams of rage. Afterward she struggled back to her car, spent physically. But in the peace and calmness that followed that episode, acknowledgment of her personal power became a part of her conscious mind—no longer repressed or subconscious. Marianne later told Shari that running screaming into the woods was both scary and fun. The episode gave her the first hint that she could really trust what was happening to her, that she could believe that it would all work out. One simple phrase had opened the way for all of that repressed power and energy to surface: "I am an adult woman and I am powerful."

After that, Marianne had great faith in her ability to continue the creative visualization process, and confidence that the resolution of her situation would be one that also both acknowledged and accomplished her deepest desire.

Nature and Flow

Nature can be an immediate way to reconnect with the flow of the river of life. When we meditate on the beauty of creation, we contemplate its inherent wisdom. We see the wisdom of the snow geese as they fly in formation, migrating south to their winter habitat. *They know how to get there.* We see the wisdom in the bud of an apple tree that will become the branch that bears the fruit. *The bud knows how to become fruit.* We see the wisdom in the way snow melts from the mountaintop, flows into a river, carves its way into the earth, carrying water to the sea. *The river knows where it must go.*

In nature, all has a purpose. Creativity and wisdom are built into nature. A baby knows how to be born. Any woman who has waited ... and waited ... and waited for those first pangs of labor will tell you that her baby knew when it needed to be born.

Forget Chinese food, a walk around the block, a mighty thunderstorm, or any other old wives' tale technique for inducing labor. A baby comes when it comes.

In his book *Creativity* (see Appendix B), Matthew Fox says when we contemplate nature, "we are drawn into transformation ourselves." Nature reminds us to create. It reminds us of our capacity to create. We regain a sense of wonder and restore our sense of gratitude for life. Nature reminds us of our own inherent wisdom, of the intention that forms the matrix of our being. It inspires us to give birth to what is within us.

Nature also bids us to trust once again in the positive energy flow of life. Nature reminds us, in the words of Jesus, that we are well taken care of: "Consider the lilies of the field, how they grow. They neither toil nor spin, yet I tell you, even Solomon in all his glory was not arrayed like one of these." (Matthew 6:28)

> **Affirmations**
>
> I am inspired to give birth to what is within me. I am powerful.

Your Outdoor Sanctuary

In Chapter 5, we encouraged you to create a sanctuary, a place in your home for creative visualization, and we guided you in creating an inner sanctuary to use during meditation. Now we will create an outdoor sanctuary. This is a place near your home where you can get in touch with nature—the mountains, a hiking trail, a nature preserve, a park, a beautiful garden.

Get some comfortable clothes and sturdy walking shoes and head to your outdoor sanctuary. As you walk, give mindful attention to the way your body feels as you move. Be aware of each step. Notice the way your feet move. Follow through on each stroke, noticing the way your leg muscles feel. Feel the ground beneath your feet.

Now notice the fresh air as you breathe. Let it fill your lungs. Match your breath to the rhythm of your steps, inhaling a certain number of steps, then exhaling the same number of steps.

As you walk, turn your attention to your surroundings, noticing the trees and flowers. Take in the scents around you. Are those lilacs on the breeze? Is that a whiff of pine? Take in the shapes of the oak leaves against the azure sky. Note the precise pattern of striations on the lilies. Notice the spin of the hummingbird's wings.

Now notice the serenity you feel, with the movement, the fresh air, and the scene around you. Make a commitment to return to your outdoor sanctuary soon—very soon.

Imagine, See, Be

The next time you go to your outdoor sanctuary, bring an offering. Choose something that symbolizes your intention for the day, or that represents the vision you want to focus on bringing into your life. Leave the symbol on the stump of a tree or on top of a rock, perhaps at the beginning and end point of your walk. Use it to check in with your intention at the beginning and to anchor yourself when you return.

A Powerful Connection

Next, Shari invited Marianne to participate in an exercise that would make the powerful woman more permanent in Marianne's mind and in her actions. She agreed.

They began with a progressive muscle relaxation exercise. A progressive relaxation session is a good way to train yourself to know what it feels like when you are relaxed. First, you tighten areas, one by one, then release. In order to know what it feels like to release and relax, you must tighten. There are many good audiotapes on the market that can lead you through this.

Shari then asked Marianne to draw a picture in her mind and describe it, directing her to imagine herself in a situation of being and acting out her most powerful self— the strongest image she could imagine. Marianne chose a memory from her childhood: "It's me, and I'm 12 years old. I have on a red shirt and my favorite pair of jeans and red sneakers. I am scrambling up an enormous, old oak tree that grew in our front yard. It is summer, and the tree is full of leaves. I have a book stashed there that I like to sit in the tree and read—away from everyone. My mother is screaming at me to get down because I might hurt myself. I ignore her. I climb the tree and reach for my book. I know she won't follow. She can't. I read for a long time, like I am trying to show her that she can't keep me from doing what I want."

Marianne opened her eyes. "I forgot that I ever felt that way! I can't get these things out of my mind. The woods, the tree, they just tumble around and around."

Clearly nature represented a certain freedom and peace for Marianne, as it does for many women who discover that for a time they have buried their sense of self. Shari ended the session with the idea that it was time for Marianne to visualize a picture of her grown up self on her own and tell Shari about it the next week.

The Spiritual Plane: Alignment with Your Higher Self

Remember when we assured you this was easy? Right, you said. Manifesting what you desire in your life isn't about striving; it's about alignment. When seen that way, it's not a big long to-do list of things that must be accomplished. It's not daunting. It's really quite simple. It's about getting in line with what you desire, what you believe, and what is meant for you. You are aligned with life, with truth. It's only a few steps away.

Alignment means that as you ride on the river of life, holding lightly to your goal; you can float. You are not floating alone. You are connected to your truth. You have examined your values and you know your aim is true—on target with what you believe in and what you want to manifest in your life.

You are also connected with your highest self. You are clear on your Source and what is meant to be for you. You know your purpose.

The River That Refreshes

Meister Eckhart, a fourteenth-century Christian mystic (not to be confused with Eckhart Tolle), equated the river of life-giving flow with the Holy Spirit. Again, we leave room for you to define your Source in your own terms. But what holds fast and true, across many spiritual belief systems, is a belief in the replenishing power of the Source. When rock-and-roll artist and visionary Bruce Springsteen raises a concert crowd to its feet with the fervor of an old-fashioned tent revival, he often invites his listeners to wash themselves with the water of the holy river of life. The cleansing power of the river is a theme that runs through many of his songs, from "The River" era to "The Rising" era. Springsteen is not off the mark from the words of David in Psalm 46, which says, "There is a river whose streams refresh the city of God, and it sanctifies the dwelling of the Most High."

This is the highest alignment, with your Source. This is where you find replenishment when you need a clearer vision, when you need to trust. This, ultimately, is where you can trust in the good work and good intentions of the

Wisdom Well

Every man is a channel through which heaven floweth.

—Ralph Waldo Emerson, nineteenth-century American lecturer, poet, and essayist universe—and let go. So you don't wait. You don't expect. You are not anxious. You are here in the now, nourished and replenished, because you have committed to allow that which you desire within yourself to be.

The River Deepens

When Marianne got to the essence of what she wanted, she realized she had deeper needs than not being caught in the middle between her mother and her husband. Other desires surfaced from her deeper self. College. Travel. Honoring her self more. Listening to her deeper self. Marianne realized that to be who she wanted to be for the people in her life, she had to honor those needs. When she focused on their needs only, it deprived them, too, of her best self.

So how did Shari know that Marianne had found the river that refreshes?

◆ **By her crisis in the woods.** Marianne had abandoned desire to life a false life and threw it off like it was an old coat—screaming while she did it.

◆ **By her creation of a picture of direct defiance.** In this case, it was defiance of her mother in her childhood, someone Marianne also found herself clashing with in the present.

◆ **By her enthusiasm at her next session.** Marianne wanted to experience more and more of her powerful self.

◆ **By her willingness to create another picture of a powerful self in the now.** Marianne had slipped easily into the flow of belief, trust, and readiness to go forward in obtaining her goal. She was no longer afraid. She was excited about moving forward.

◆ **By her trust.** Marianne initially placed most of her trust in Shari, but through creative visualization, she transferred that trust to herself. Positive experiences—going through these difficult episodes and coming out just fine—formed the basis for her trust in herself and the creative visualization process.

While Marianne started making choices that included herself, she did not go to the other extreme—putting herself first, to the exclusion of considering the needs of others. Having discovered her own need to express her highest good, she still maintained a healthy respect for the highest good in others. Her mother settled in to the assisted living home and made new friends. All was good on that front. But through Marianne's visualization practice, she increasingly realized she had little in common with Tim. They separated, and Marianne continued seeing Shari for about a year. By then she felt peaceful and able to work through any problems or issues on her own using the tools that she had learned in therapy. She and Tim agreed to divorce. Marianne has not remarried, but Tim has struggled, expressing dissatisfaction that Marianne was not there to take care of him, as expected, at retirement. He returned to his hometown, where his parents still lived, and rekindled a relationship with a high school sweetheart, eventually moving in with her.

Self-Knowledge

Ultimately, what solidifies your ability to stay in the flow is self-knowledge. The process is an ever-replenishing cycle. You stay in the flow simply by keeping a powerful image in your mind. When you stay there, you know yourself. You trust yourself. You connect to your Higher Self. Then, you don't want to ever leave.

The Least You Need to Know

- Keep your vision firmly in your mind, yet hold on lightly.

- Stay focused not just on the thing itself (on what you desire), but on the value behind it.

- Stillness is a way to drop out of active mind and focus on our true desires.

- Pay attention to what you are resisting. Let the flow take you to the places that evince changes in you.

- Nature reminds us to trust again in the positive energy of the universe.

- Connecting to your higher self can solidify your trust in the flow and help you stay in the flow.

Chapter 7

Be the Flow: Manifesting

In This Chapter

- ◆ What is manifestation?
- ◆ Manifestation's true purpose
- ◆ Living, manifestation-style
- ◆ How to flourish

Over time, creative visualization will become part of the way you live your life. It won't just be something to which you devote 10 minutes a day or do in only one or two sessions a week. We say this because creative visualization will start to bear fruit in your life in more than ways than moving you toward your goal. You'll start to see that some of the fundamental principles of creative visualization offer you, quite simply, a better way to live.

By incorporating creative visualization techniques into your life, you open yourself to the promise of manifestation in every moment of every day. What a beautiful way to live!

Manifesting Your Destiny

First, let's look at what *manifestation* is. Webster's Dictionary defines it as "to make clear or evident; show plainly; reveal; evince." This means that what we see is already in existence. We are just now seeing it. Perhaps it was there all along.

When you look back over your life, can you see the patterns that led you to where you are today and the kind of person you are? Suddenly, with the perspective of time, it all makes sense. Some of those most painful moments were the most integral in preparing you with the knowledge and strength you need to do what you're doing now. Go figure.

Author James Michener, one of the most revered and prolific writers of our time, was an orphan, raised by an aunt that he wasn't even sure was a relative. He experienced a lot of love in his life, but even so, being orphaned held an element of pain for Michener. In his memoir *The World is my Home* (Random House, 1991), he says that as he became a writer he began to realize that having no particular background could be a major asset. It was valuable to him not to know what race or ethnic group or family or population to which he belonged. He was able to fit in anywhere in the world—he could have come from anywhere. He could put himself in the skin of the people he was writing about with much more ease than someone who has to put aside an identity. Something that caused him great pain became one of his greatest strengths.

That's how manifestation works. It's a gradual revealing to ourselves of what is possible—even out of what seems impossibly painful. The word originates from the Latin *manifestus*, which means quite literally "struck by the hand, made palpable, evident." This hints that it is something not quite formed into matter, something ethereal that took physical form. Manifestation mirrors the process of a thought moving from idea to physical form. The definition goes on further to explain that when manifestation becomes clearer, it is clearer to the senses, especially to the sense of sight or to the mind.

Deeper Meaning

Manifestation is the act of making something clear or evident that was not seen before. Manifestation is breathing life into an idea until it takes form.

Michener didn't have to accept his gift, the possibility of universality of identity. But he recognized its value and he did accept it to the benefit of himself and all people who read his books.

Manifesting is a progression of the energy of the universe from what might be to what is. It is the intersection of energy changing form with our awareness of the new form. Notice that the awareness of manifestation is emphasized in the sense of sight or in the mind. These, too, are the essential components of creative visualization: Create a mental picture, and keep it in focus. Then it manifests.

The Aim That Is True: Manifestation

In his book *Manifestation* (see Appendix B), David Spangler writes, "The only successful manifestation is one which brings about a change or growth in consciousness; that is, it has manifested God, or revealed him more fully, as well as having manifested a form."

So this is the true purpose of manifestation. It is out to change us. The practice of manifesting positive results in our lives teaches us more about ourselves, what we believe about our personal power, the power of the universe, and the power of the one we call Creator. Just by raising your awareness of your manifestations, you have invited this power into your life. You become more aware of your positive and negative thoughts. You notice your habits—your daily routine, the patterns of your thoughts. You start to notice what you believe, and you may be surprised. Again, you do not have to be fiercely determined or spiritually enlightened to allow your new practice of manifesting good things in your life to take hold.

Start to notice when your positive thoughts work to bring opportunities to you. And when something doesn't go quite right, start to notice what you were giving your thought energy to at the time.

That recognition that we are not powerless, that we have an ally—our spiritual self—who can manifest in our lives what we can imagine, is the first step on a path of consciousness and personal growth. So begins a journey of getting to know this force that says, "Yes!" in such a big way.

The classic example of going from powerless to powerful with the help of a Higher Power exists in the model of Alcoholics Anonymous. Many who enter the program feel powerless to stop drinking. And at the moment they begin, that's likely true. But they learn that through use of their spiritual self, or Creator, they have all the power they need to take control of their lives. The learning curve may be high—it's not called a 12-step program for nothing—but the basis of it is the strength of turning to one's spiritual center and manifesting that energy for a positive result—in this example, achieving sobriety, health, and happiness.

The Way You Live Now: Manifestation and Intention

Weaving the practices of manifestation in your life quite naturally lends itself to an understanding of your truest intentions. It reveals your thought-habits, both negative and positive. You will start to notice how your very being—this is the ego-mind— keeps you engaged in those habits. It takes thought and effort to change them.

Take a moment to write in your Creative Visualization Journal about what you want more of in your life. What do you want less of? Take one of the "more" items and plot how you would gain this in your life. Take one of the "less" items and map how it came to be such a big part of your life. What were your decisions at the time? What did you believe? How did you get from there to here?

Now we will explore some techniques that will help you break this down:

- Control your input.

- Identify principles to live by.

- Create a belief genealogy. Clarify where your beliefs came from.

- Ritualize your intention.

- Put your virtues, principles, and beliefs into practice.

- Empower yourself as a co-creator.

What Goes In

Affirmations are the first step in beginning to shift the patterns of your mind. In addition to practicing your regular affirmations as part of a creative visualization session, start monitoring what comes into your mind.

Take note of the input into your life in several of the following areas. Make a few notes in your Creative Visualization Journal.

- Reading material

- Television, movies

- Advertising

- Your circle of friends and their attitudes

- Your co-workers

- People you admire

Take a good hard look at the quality and quantity of this input. Now take a look at your 10 Life Arenas (see Chapter 1) and be honest about some of your negative thoughts and attitudes. Do you believe that a fulfilling relationship is possible? Do you believe that hard work will pay off in your career? Do you have a positive body image? Sure, you might say yes to such a direct question—because you know you're supposed to—but commit to taking a week to be conscious of your thoughts in this arena. Do you notice any attitudes that surprise or intrigue you?

Commit now in your Creative Visualization Journal to upgrade the quality of your input.

- ◆ Collect positive stories.

- ◆ Cultivate conscious living among your circle of friends.

- ◆ Filter out negative messages from the media by being more selective in your media consumption.

- ◆ Seek out books that affirm your life principles.

Make a vow to be more intentional about what comes into your mind. Beautiful thoughts build a beautiful mind.

Imagine, See, Be

In Appendix B we provide you with a reading list to help you explore some of the topics introduced in this book and continue on your path of wisdom. We tend to want to learn things that are interesting to us—that fit our individual personalities. What is exciting to one person might be totally boring to another. Be wise about your areas of expertise. Put your learning time to good use. And always be ready to look for new sources of learning.

Principles to Live By: Activating Intention

In *The Power of Intention*, Wayne Dyer says one of the necessary requirements to activate intention is to let go of your ego identification. He outlines four key steps:

1. **Discipline.** You must train your body to perform as your thoughts desire. A good example of this principle is the way a top athlete, such as cyclist Lance Armstrong, trains. To win the Tour de France multiple times (we're leaving room here for him to win another before the completion of this book), you must have an intensity of focus—and you must put in the time training your

body. Do you think Lance's body screamed as he worked hard in training sessions? Absolutely. An athlete such as Armstrong keeps his desire to win in the forefront of his mind as he trains his body to perform, until the acts of mental and physical endurance become one in positive purpose.

2. **Wisdom.** When you create a store of wisdom, you foster your ability to focus. You know that your path is right. You are patient. You live in harmony with your thoughts. You have body, mind, and spirit in alignment and in balance.

3. **Love.** This means loving what you do and doing what you love. It's a quality you cultivate long before you reach your goal. You love what you are doing because it's bringing you what you love, even if it's waiting tables. It means loving others—and loving yourself.

4. **Surrender.** You arrive at the place of intention through the heart. Your body and mind aren't running things. It's not about drive and willpower. It's about seeing the river of intent and wading into it, letting it wash over your ankles. You step into the flow.

Your Personal Genealogy: A Family Tree

We inherit a set of beliefs from our family members so intertwined with who we are that it can be difficult to disentangle. We may have had these beliefs for so long—and they may have functioned for us—that we don't even know their origin. If you are struggling with a creative visualization, you may want to take time out and do a belief genealogy.

One of the most useful tools of self-exploration is to map out your family tree. One of Shari's clients joked that upon "shaking the family tree, bottles of alcohol came tumbling out!" While the messages you received from your family may not have been *that* strong, it's a good way to uncover your belief history.

You'll need a large sheet of poster board and some colored markers—just like grade school! First, draw a tree trunk, limbs and a few leaves—leaving room to write the names of family members.

Next, start identifying people in your tree. You are at ground level, and all of the branches contribute to your current state. Fill in three to four generations on your tree (parents, siblings, grandparents, great-grandparents, cousins, aunts, uncles). You may also want to list nonrelatives who were influences in your life. Answer these questions about the names you wrote on the tree:

- Who was a minister or person of great faith?

- Who accomplished a lot with his or her life in spite of adversity?

- Who was passionate about expressing desires, beliefs, and goals?

- Who were the alcoholics and/or substance abusers?

- Who was depressed, anxious, or constantly grappling with debilitating emotions?

- Who saw letters and words backward and was thought to be stupid even though society now recognizes dyslexia as a learning disorder?

- Did anyone commit suicide?

- Was there any abuse?

- Were there multiple births?

- Who was known for his good sense of humor?

- Who looked like you?

- Who might have seen the world the way you do?

CAUTION

Don't Panic, Focus!

Sometimes when we examine our family histories, especially if there was alcoholism, abuse, or mental illness, it can be overwhelming. If when you do this exercise it brings up troubling thoughts—or if you don't feel safe, or feel an overwhelming sadness—please seek out a therapist with whom you can talk things over.

Pretty soon, you'll see with this exercise how many of your personality attributes, habits of thought, and health conditions were handed down to you. The emotions that surface along with this knowledge constitute invaluable pieces of self-knowledge. Now you can identify which characteristics or beliefs you want to keep—and the ones to watch out for. And the nice thing about having all of this on poster board is that you have room to add information if you wish. (Or throw darts at the uncle who left you with male pattern baldness!)

We can now see that putting information down on paper is the beginning of changing what we want to change and keeping what we want to keep. We may also get a good idea of where our dreams and desires may have come from. Nighttime dreams are not infrequent when we are addressing deep material such as this. Write them down—they give you clues as to how your subconscious is dealing with your visualization work. We'll talk more about dreams in Chapter 17.

Know that the beginning of changing a pattern is being mindful of it. It takes some of the mystery out of the behavior pattern when you unveil its origin—and many patterns do originate within the context of family.

Ritualizing Your Intention

When you want to make a point of making manifestation part of your daily life, the place to which you return is intention. By ritualizing your intention, you can tap into this energy again and again. This is a good way to get back on track if you are struggling with a creative visualization.

We'll provide exercises in the following chapters of ways to ritualize your intention to change. When you create a ritual around your intention to make a change in your life, it becomes a ceremony—something concrete, something physically grounded, something memorable.

Make your ritual something that leaves a mark on you, on your life, something memorable. To be solemn is to do something according to tradition, adhering to a strict form. Of course, when we say tradition, it conjures up images of old rules and old beliefs—aren't those what we are trying to shed? In this case, let's substitute the word "timeless" for "tradition"—beliefs so brimming with vitality and truth that they hold up in any era.

To be solemn is to be serious, grave, deeply earnest. To be serious is to have great intention. To be grave is to be in awe of great power. To be deeply earnest is to be open, to believe in goodness, to act in love.

In bringing forth these qualities to your ritual of intention, you are creating something sacred. That is the sum of it. Sacred intention is serious. It is full of awe. It is good. It is love. It is timeless.

Imagine, See, Be _____

Rinse away some of your old beliefs through this aromatherapy bath ritual. First, make a list in your Creative Visualization Journal of some beliefs inherited from your family that you don't want to keep. Then fill up a tub with warm water. Add a few drops of your favorite essential oil. Soak for 15 minutes, meditating on your new beliefs. Place a few drops of oil in the palm of your hand and inhale deeply. Take your new belief into the very tissue of your being. As you rinse off, imagine the old beliefs going down the drain.

The Virtues of Intention

Author and teacher Wayne D. Dyer describes intention as a force that expresses itself in seven beneficial ways. He calls these the Seven Faces of Intention, and they are the by-products of manifestation. It's how you can tell you are doing this right—it's a confirmation. Essentially, they are virtues, and they may be the prize itself. These virtues flourish in your life when you are aligned with your true purpose and your Source. When Dyer says they have a face, he gives form to the benevolent force behind intention. These virtues are the attributes of your Source.

To allow intention to flourish in your life, cultivate these virtues:

- **Creativity**. Creativity gives birth to new ideas, new forms.

- **Kindness.** Kindness strengthens, while unkindness weakens. Kindness infinitely expands your resources.

- **Love.** Love transforms. It changes dark to light. Ralph Waldo Emerson said, "Love is our highest word and the synonym for God."

- **Beauty**. When you are heightened to an awareness of beauty all around you, you are tuned in to the intention that forms the natural world.

- **Expansion**. The practice of creative visualization opens you up to possibilities. Your world is expanded. Solutions open up to you that might not have before. Intention beckons these solutions to come your way.

- **Abundance.** This principle says that there is enough for everyone. Your prospering is not at the expense of another. The universe has unlimited abundance.

- **Receptivity.** You are willing. You are open. You stand ready to receive. Your heart is wide open.

Gradually, you raise your energy vibration to a higher level. More and more you operate from your highest self.

Beads of Virtue

Beads are used as a meditation tool in many spiritual traditions. The Christian tradition uses 33 beads, symbolizing the years Jesus Christ lived on Earth. Muslims use 99 beads, reciting all the names of God. Native American tradition uses a prayer feather, a string of precious stone beads with a feather at the end. Tibetan Buddhists use Mala beads, reciting a mantra or affirmation. Mala beads are usually 108 beads and are often made from tulsi (basil) wood, sandalwood, rudraksh seeds or crystal. Each material is believed to have a quality of energy that guides your meditation.

Some practitioners describe the meditation beads as a portable "sacred space" because you can carry them in your pocket. When you need to get centered, to be reminded of your Source, to anchor into your highest self, you can touch them, and remember.

For this exercise, choose seven beads—seven representing the seven virtues, or Faces of Intention. Choose a style of beads that represents your spiritual tradition or otherwise has meaning for you.

> **Affirmations**
>
> Today, I invite creativity, kindness, love, and beauty into my life.
> Today, I am open and receptive, and I believe in abundance.
> Today, I am seeing these virtues manifest in my life.

Before you begin your meditation, state out loud or say in your mind, "It is my intention to manifest these virtues in my life today."

As you touch the first bead, state out loud or say in your mind, "I am now an open channel for the river of creativity that flows through all life. I am giving birth to all that can be in my life on all levels—physical, mental, emotional, and spiritual."

As you touch the second bead, state out loud or say in your mind, "I am now willing to experience the kindness that is naturally part of me. I am now strengthened by my kindness."

As you touch the third bead, state out loud or say in your mind, "I am now becoming the love that transforms. I am now bringing light to the darkness."

As you touch the fourth bead, state out loud or say in your mind, "I am now receiving all the beauty that surrounds me."

As you touch the fifth bead, state out loud or say in your mind, "I have the infinite power of my Source within me, and I am allowing Divine Love to work in me here and now."

As you touch the sixth bead, state out loud or say in your mind, "I am ready now to accept all the joy and prosperity that is coming into my life."

As you touch the seventh bead, state out loud or say in your mind, "I am now being guided in perfect light to the wisdom the universe is offering to me. I embrace it."

Co-Creating with Power and Love

When you practice manifestation in your daily life, you will undoubtedly see that you are co-creating something with a Someone—again we leave the definitions up to you—an entity that is powerful and loving, an entity of positive energy.

Creating the kind of life you want can be frightening. It may seem disturbing to think that actually having all that you want could be unnerving, but the truth is, it is for most of us. Creating a life where you can express your highest good is to become aware of how powerful you can be when you work with your Source. That's an awesome power. It can shake things up.

Most of us live without the awareness of our deepest spiritual source. We feel powerless and cut off from the responsibility of the power that we do have. Tapping into the river of creativity is to tap into great power. Open the sluice gate and you flood the fields.

The creation process is continual. As we create, we empty. The Spirit/Source fills us again, and we are replenished to create again. This creative source is infinite. Meister Eckhart says it flows and flows, fills and fills and "cannot keep from flowing into every place where it finds space."

This tells us we only need to be receptive to creating more. We only need to respond to the flowing river of creativity. It is infinite.

"The task of sorcerers was to face infinity," said Carlos Castaneda, who wrote about the teachings of Toltec wisdom. No wonder only the few become sorcerers! Infinity is vast! And let us explain, in Castaneda's world of the ancient shamans of Mexico, a sorcerer is a magician of another kind. The word generally has a negative connotation, an association with the occult and the dark arts. But in his usage, the word means one who creates with the Source. A sorcerer is one who has achieved the mastery of awareness and self-knowledge—the knowledge that he creates with God/Spirit/Source.

Wisdom Well

People usually consider walking on water or in thin air a miracle. But I think the real miracle is not to walk either on water or in thin air, but to walk on earth. Every day we are engaged in a miracle which we don't even recognize: a blue sky, white clouds, green leaves, the black, curious eyes of a child—our own two eyes. All is a miracle.

—Thich Nhat Hanh, Buddhist teacher

Flow and Joy

Creativity—manifesting what we want in life—brings great joy. If you have ever been caught up in the flow of a project and lost track of time, you have known this joy. You get so engrossed in creating that you lose sense of time. You forget to stop for lunch until your stomach rumbles just as the sun is going down, reminding you. You lose all sense of physical consciousness—and at the same time, you lose a sense of self-consciousness. Temporarily, you set aside the fear of whether what you are creating will meet with receptive minds and hearts. It doesn't matter. You are in the flow.

During this coming week, take notice of moments here and there when you lose yourself in creative flow. Observe the joy you feel. Make a few notes in your Creative Visualization Journal to record what got you into the flow and how it felt.

Imagination

Wayne Dyer says your imagination is the invisible link to manifesting your destiny. That's because, as we discussed in Chapter 4, your imagination is linked with intention. Your imagination has the power to create a mental image in you so strong that you believe it will happen. Your imagination, then, is the threshold that allows the Higher Mind to enter in. Through your imagination, you are allowed to co-create with your God, your Source—to participate in the act of creation together.

When you begin to manifest in your daily life, you'll be more mindful of what is going on in your imagination. You may start to realize that when you visualize a scenario, it takes hold. It may have been a passing daydream, but if you gave a lot of energy to it, it might have happened.

Of course, this phenomenon has its opposite. Sometimes people refer to this as, "Be careful what you wish for." Be aware of when you are wishing for something so strongly that you have imagined it in great detail. This is when it has moved from wish to creative visualization. Make sure that this happens only with your permission. Notice when your imagination gives a lot of energy to a fearful idea. Commit now to only giving your imagination the tasks of formulating the life you dream of.

During the coming week, commit to noticing where your imagination goes when undirected—that is, outside of your creative visualization sessions when you are consciously directing your imagination to the goal on which you are focused. Choose an upcoming routine event—a meeting at work or getting together with a friend at a café—and notice how you visualize it beforehand.

Expansion

Expansion means that you take success with creative visualization in one arena of your life and replicate it in another. When you begin to make manifestation part of daily life, you will be able to easily migrate the techniques to other arenas of your life.

Examine arenas in your life where it's more difficult to practice creative visualization and manifestation. Many women, for instance, can be sharp and savvy about work, money, and children but play by different rules when they choose a man to share their lives. Usually the root of this is an alternate belief system in that Life Arena. Take a few minutes over the next few days to examine beliefs in your arena of success and deconstruct them. (An example: If you are good at hiring people but not necessarily good at choosing someone to date, examine how you formulated your hiring standards.) Now parallel those beliefs against the other Life Arena. What is different?

Brick by Brick

Some people define manifestation as luck, as just a coincidence when something beneficial comes your way. Some people call it "being in the right place at the right time." But manifestation is more conscious than that. It begins with a shift in focus that results in a shift in belief. The shift in belief brings about a shift in perception. Practice it, and all kinds of miracles can happen in your life—every day.

The Least You Need to Know

- Creative visualization can become part of how you live your life.
- The true purpose of manifestation is to teach us about ourselves, our personal power, the positive energy of the universe, and the power of the one we call Creator.
- The keys to daily manifestation practice are being mindful of your input, identifying principles to live by, and empowering yourself.
- Creating a belief family tree is a good way to uncover some of your underlying beliefs.
- Cultivating virtues in your life allows your truest intentions to flourish.

Part 3

Know What You Want, Set Your Intent

Intention is a powerful ally when practicing creative visualization. Intention is the force behind all of creation, from the unfolding of an apple blossom to the gentle hand of the spring breeze.

The path of attainment will lead you through many changes—among them having the courage to say what you mean and mean what you say. Your journey will require changes *within*, as change is occurring on the outside. It will train you to focus on the now, even as you contemplate the future.

In Part 3, we will further explore the mystery of this immeasurable, indescribable force called intention and teach you how to beckon it.

Chapter **8**

Finding Your Authentic Self

In This Chapter

- ◆ Real on the inside, real on the outside
- ◆ Know your values; examine your good intentions
- ◆ Is your word good?
- ◆ Agreements that work

In the children's classic tale *The Velveteen Rabbit,* a stuffed bunny yearns to be real. One of the other toys in the nursery tells the rabbit that what will make him real is the love of the boy. That part's easy enough. Soon the rabbit is the boy's favorite companion, and the rabbit knows he is real because of his great heart, which is full of love for the boy. But one day the rabbit is left out in the woods, and he notices the real bunnies can leap, using their great hind legs. "Where's your tail?" they ask.

Are you for real? Being real means being real on the inside *and* the outside. You show it to the world in what you say and do. Creative visualization provides the opportunity to integrate your heart and spirit with how you leap through the world.

The Real Deal: Being Authentic

Webster's Dictionary defines being authentic as "that that can be believed or accepted; trustworthy; reliable." Go back to the Greek root word and we find that it means "one who does things himself." In today's world, this means taking responsibility for yourself—for your thoughts, your actions, your messages to others, both verbal and nonverbal. It means that you do not play the victim, letting things happen to you and blaming the external circumstances. You choose your responses to situations. You choose when to voice your opinions and when to make decisions that sometimes set you on a different path from the crowd. This is personal responsibility.

Being authentic means you are who you are in all arenas of life, on all levels. Ultimately it means being in balance. Being authentic means that all the layers of you work in harmony. Nothing is pulling you or dragging in a different direction.

Being authentic is vital for creative visualization to work at its highest level of effectiveness. This means being conscious: Becoming aware of your underlying beliefs that may contradict what you are visualizing and wanting to manifest in your life.

Shari sees many people come into therapy with no idea of the underlying quirks that form the foundation for their presenting issues. They know that they are unhappy and have some idea of what would change that but they are not in touch with their more basic beliefs or traits. Shari tells them that being in therapy is like peeling the layers of an onion. Shari works with each person to begin with the crisis that got him or her into therapy, then to look at what comes up next. By the end of their time with Shari, clients have learned to look for subconscious motivations and beliefs and to deal with them appropriately. The interesting thing is that so many times their goals change and even move in the opposite direction when they understand their real intentions. Therapy is as much teaching people how to have a healthy psychological life as it is resolving issues. All of us occasionally have to look deeply to see why we are spinning our wheels and not getting anywhere.

> **Wisdom Well**
>
> If you cannot find the truth right where you are, where else do you expect to find it?
>
> —Dogen, thirteenth-century Zen Buddhist monk

A creative visualization in and of itself is the process of becoming authentic. You visualize what you want to bring into your life. You focus your intention on it. As you do your affirmations, at the heart of them is the belief that *this is who I really am.*

Here I Am, This Is Me

Use this next exercise to define the truth of who you are. Look back at your 10 Life Arenas that we developed in Chapter 1: love, family, work, money, health, home, personal growth, spirituality, leisure/rejuvenation, and creative self-expression.

Brainstorm "I am" statements that define who you are in these roles. Examples could be "I am a father," "I am a respected lawyer," or "I am a guitar player." Write down as many as you can think of.

Now brainstorm a list of beliefs you have about those arenas, as in "I am someone who believes it's important to stay fit" or "I am someone who believes personal growth is important." Or you can blend two, as in "I believe that working in my garden on the weekends is vital to helping me rejuvenate."

Tape these statements or have someone read them to you. With your eyes closed and with deep, even, relaxed breathing, repeat the following affirmations:

I am courageous.

I have inner fortitude.

I am self-aware.

I am wise.

I am calm.

I am creative.

I am patient.

As you say each one, notice what is happening in your thoughts and your body. Notice thoughts that arise to contradict. Notice places in your body that vibrate, twitch, or even experience pain. Notice what feels unsettled in you as you say these out loud.

Know that truth is that which never changes. The absolute constants are your authentic self, the eternal life force of the universe, and the natural rhythms of life. That is you, heaven, and Earth. Meditate on each one of these with the intention of connecting to one integrated truth. You may want to start out by saying, in your mind or out loud, "I am seeking the truth that never changes. I am bringing that truth into my body, mind, and soul right now." Visualize a golden orb of light in the middle of your forehead. Stay a few moments with it, holding the image until it becomes more vivid, keeping your breath deep and even.

Now imagine above you the infinite expanse of the firmament, filled with light. Hold this image for three breath cycles. Then bring your awareness to the place where you are seated, becoming aware of the carpet, pillow, or cushion on which you are seated. Draw your breath up from the earth, gathering its positive energy. With each inhale, raise your breath up from the earth, through the golden orb of light, up to the heavens. With each exhale, let your breath fall from the heavens, cascading over your golden orb of light, descending to Earth. Repeat the cycle until you feel your visualization and your breath have achieved a natural continuum, a good flow. When it feels complete, open your eyes. Say in your mind or out loud, "This is the truth. This is who I am."

Patience, My Friend

Let's say that you want to be more kind and patient with your children, as did Ginger, a client of Shari's. When Ginger came to Shari, she was distraught because she believed she wasn't cut out to be a mother. She had three wonderful children, but she blamed herself when she ran out of patience with them some days.

Shari saw that Ginger clearly loved her children. Her read was that Ginger needed to be better equipped to deal with her children in some situations. That was what was affecting Ginger's self-image.

So they went to work. Shari had Ginger envision a perfect hour with her children. They did it in great detail, taking about 20 minutes to develop the vision. Afterward, Ginger wrote down everything she could remember about that perfect hour she had envisioned. The setting was about bath time. The kids were all under four years of age, so they often took their baths together—a nice idea but not really workable for this mom.

Here were the steps Shari and Ginger envisioned for peaceful bath time:

◆ One child at a time

◆ Quiet, soothing games such as floating ships or playing with bathtub crayons

◆ Complete focus on that child

◆ Husband responsible for whoever was not in the tub

◆ Warm towels

◆ After bath time, only quiet play or stories with Dad

◆ Bed within 30 minutes

Quite naturally, Ginger didn't achieve perfect implementation the first time. Children are very intelligent and can short-circuit changes quite well. After a few sessions Ginger decided that a small reward after every quiet bath would be helpful—an extra story, a cookie, something she knew the child would enjoy. Ginger reported that the children were very receptive to the idea of rewards and it helped about 90 percent of the time.

As Ginger worked on implementing her vision, two things began to happen. Her image of herself as a mother shifted. She realized she was fine as a parent—that it was some of her methods that needed changing. And, most important, the success in one area—bath time—generalized to other areas. Her self-esteem and sense of efficacy improved. All of this took about six months.

Know Thyself

The key to authenticity is to know who you really are. Once Ginger saw herself as a kind, patient, loving parent—the parent Shari sensed from the first session—she was able to implement methods that revealed that to herself.

Know what you value. Know your good intentions within. Use your Creative Visualization Journal to write down five of your core values. Briefly list instances when you have had those values tested and you have held firm. List also instances when it has been difficult or impossible for you to stick to those values.

Don't be overly concerned as you list the instances where holding to your intentions proved difficult. We are much more likely to recognize growth issues and decisions that we need to make if we have the attitude that life is a process—not an end point—and that there is always something for us to learn. Here's where creative visualization can come in to help you bridge the gap—gently.

Visualize yourself as that person who holds firm to her values. Maybe, like Ginger, you visualize yourself as a kind, patient parent. Or maybe it's something else, something that you do successfully some or most of the time. Envision small steps that you can take toward closing the gap during the times when you find it impossible to maintain your values or intentions. Place your positive focus on those steps. The gap gives you an opportunity to learn about yourself and what it takes to achieve a larger goal.

Don't Panic, *Focus!*

Some goals are so big and so nebulous that we can lose sight of how simple they are to achieve. Often this is the case with interpersonal goals, such as being a better parent or spouse, because our perceived gaps—where we believe we fall short—seem so pervasive. In many cases, though, the results you seek are not so far away—they are closer than you think. But by visualizing—and then taking—simple, small steps, you may actually achieve dramatic results quickly.

The trials of life often become our best-learned lessons because we don't solve them without thoughtfulness and intention. In the hero's journey, the challenges are the lessons. They are the story. It's not the winning of the prize, but the journey. It's the stuff in the middle that's important—that makes you into a hero. In one of the *Indiana Jones* movies, the hero must step into the darkness and trust that a stone pillar will rise from the void to meet his foot. The lesson? If you do your best and understand your values and personal ethics, someone or something will always rise out of the void to help you out. (We'll talk more about the hero's journey in Chapter 9.)

How You Present Yourself to the World

Think of the mirrored balls often seen in bowling alleys, skating rinks, or discos. They look like multifaceted globes, shining light from every perspective. But each person who looks at the ball perceives it in a different way. One person may see different colors reflected; another may catch rays of light reflected off the ceiling. Our personalities are like that. In different social settings, we reflect different facets of our personalities. For instance, we react differently to a grandmother than to a life companion.

It's also comforting to know that if you are troubled about your emotional responses or your behavior in a certain situation, you can work to change your responses. Like the rotating mirrored ball, you are not fixed in time and space. You continue to grow and change.

Create this multimedia collage of yourself, as you want to present yourself to the world. Here's what you'll need:

◆ Colorful foam paper

◆ A photo of yourself (just the head)

- Magazines from which you can clip images

- Some funky scrapbooking scissors that cut in a fancy pattern—just for fun!

- Glue stick

- Paper hole puncher

- Brass brad fasteners (the kind with foldout tabs)

- A scene clipped from a magazine or printed out from a website of a favorite place (a mountain, a sunset on a beach, a formal English garden, a Vegas casino, etc.)

First, cut out the shapes of a circle, rectangle, and four limbs from your foam paper. These will be the head, torso, and arms and legs of your collage. Glue the photo of your head on the circle piece. Use clips from your magazines to adorn the rest of your body parts, adding in hair, clothes, props—anything that represents who you are. If you are known for your killer martinis or to-die-for caramel brownies, add that. If you are an avid skier or an accomplished guitarist, add that. Glue the clip of the favorite scene over your heart.

Use a paper hole puncher to make a hole in each body part where it will connect with another. Use the fastener to hinge pieces together—arms to torso, head to body, etc. Just for fun, play with your reticulated self, waving the arms and legs and wagging the head. Use this image in your creative visualizations, using affirmations that start with "I am."

> **Affirmations**
>
> Use affirmations in this style when you are seeking authenticity:
> "I am a (who you are) *patient parent*, through and through.
> I am (quality you possess) *courageous, body and soul.*"

Keeping Your Word

Up to now in this chapter, we have talked about ways to use creative visualization and take action steps to become more authentic. But at the heart of authenticity is keeping your word.

First you must start by keeping your word to yourself. Creative visualization is a vital first step in keeping your word to yourself. By committing to creative visualization sessions and keeping a regular practice, you already are keeping your word to your self that you will nurture your most heartfelt ambitions and dreams. Not someone else—you.

Keeping your word ultimately is about *integrity*, being whole, unbroken. When you are whole, all facets of you are integrated. You are not operating like a computer on a dual processor. There is one values system, one belief system. You don't have a set of values for one situation and a completely different set for another. Realistically, though, most of us allow our belief systems to evolve over time. We may have "updated" our belief system in one arena but still hold on to outdated beliefs in another. We changed, or our life circumstances changed, and we didn't go back and update the file. In the next section, we'll take a closer look at your underlying beliefs and uncover any that need to be updated.

Deeper Meaning

Integrity is the quality or state of being complete; unbroken condition; wholeness; entirety. In another meaning, it means moral uprightness. All facets of you are consciously held in your mind and are held in harmony, without friction. Integrating your conscious and subconscious beliefs and motivations allows you to function unimpaired—at optimum levels.

The second definition of integrity is "being unimpaired." When you are not living the truth in your life, it leaves you diminished. You do not function at optimum. You are quite simply not your best. This can be true even if your integrity lapses are due to good intentions, such as trying to please everyone.

Imagine yourself this week practicing letting others know where you stand, even when it might rock the boat. It doesn't have to be confrontational, and we advise you against taking on a big issue. See yourself making simple statements, such as "I disagree" or "I'm not convinced that …." Play out this scenario in your mind all the way to the end, when you have opened the door for a free exchange of opinions. Imagine the other person participating in this with you, without animosity or defensiveness. Imagine the two of you ending it agreeing to disagree.

Trying to please everyone leaves you in a situation of failing to take a stand. If people knew what *you* wanted in a situation, it might rock the boat! But if you don't know where you count in this situation, you don't know where you stand. If you don't know where you stand, others don't. Be assured that other people always want to know where you stand. It's human nature to be questioning, seeking out certainty in any personal interaction. Once others know where you stand, they can relax around you—even if they don't agree. Either that or they will run like thieves—but at least you are not fooling them!

Underlying Beliefs: Your Agreements

The third definition of integrity is the quality or state of being of sound moral principle; uprightness; honesty; sincerity. When you have an integrity lapse, it's generally because of one of your agreements. Sometimes you know exactly what these are, but sometimes you have made an agreement, and you don't even realize it. An example would be, in a family where people never have open confrontations, "I must always keep the peace." On some deep level you agree with this, and you have operated your life based on that agreement. You avoid confrontations at all costs. Therapists call these family secrets.

For this section, we'll go back to our family tree from Chapter 7. Look back over your family members. What messages were you were given about:

- Keeping the peace
- Anger
- Pleasing others
- Stating your needs
- Getting noticed
- Caring for others
- Whose opinion mattered
- What women's roles were
- What men's roles were
- What a good parent should be
- What money was for

Some of these beliefs might have been family secrets and some openly acknowledged. Of course the possible list is endless and you may have other beliefs that we did not list. Doing this exercise may help you bring into consciousness beliefs that were harmful to yourself or others. And it may make you aware of traits you are proud of that are handed down in your family.

Intention with Integrity

Intention is vital to the process of creative visualization and the role it plays in exploring your spiritual self and personal growth. For that reason, we will continue in this chapter and chapters ahead to give you ways to create a ritual around your intention. We think this one works particularly well for integrity.

First, visualize yourself in your mind's eye as a person of integrity. When that vision forms in your mind, and it feels complete, light a candle. Focus your gaze on the candle. Say, "I bring my awareness to all of me, body and soul. In this candle, I illumine all the many facets of myself. I bring light to the darkness."

Continue to keep your vision in your mind's eye as you gaze into the candle. Say, "I am light and I am dark. I am whole."

Purity of Will

Creative visualization, and the practice of positive focus that goes with it, is vital to keeping you on the path of integrity. The visualizations keep you so focused on the purity of your desire for what you are seeking that you keep your desire and your actions whole—sealed together with your intent.

If you are struggling, ask yourself what your intentions are. What do you want to get out of this? Do you have the right target? Get to the values behind your goal. What is its emotional core? "If I had a cabin by the lake, I would be able to …" "If I had the perfect relationship, I would feel …" "If I were a fashion photographer, I would have …"

Take a few of the goals from your Life Arenas. What would you be able to do if you reached this goal? How would you feel? What would you have? And why would you want that?

To purify your intention, also look at your alliances. Examine your input. What's going into your mind? Is it what you believe? Do you really agree with these messages?

You must be willing to pull back from your goal and examine your true intent. During a creative visualization, if you get the feeling of pushing or striving, pull back. Get true with yourself. Is this dream really the best thing for you? Why—or why not? What's the drawback if you achieve your goal? Are you ready for it? Examine this question on all planes—physical, mental, emotional, and spiritual.

How would attaining your goal affect your other Life Arenas? Would they change significantly? Finally, consider that the universe may have something better for you.

Sometimes it's difficult to do a creative visualization on a goal to which you are deeply emotionally attached. This is the flipside of "I will die if I don't get it." Sometimes, if you are too attached, you will tend to work against yourself. That's because the fear of not getting what you desire so much takes a tremendous amount of energy. The fear may be in your subconscious and it may be receiving more energy than the vision.

If you can identify this in yourself, you may want to stop and give some thought to your feelings about *not* reaching your goal. Take some time to write about it in your Creative Visualization Journal.

Rich Exploration

Creative visualization is not just positive thinking. It's exploring, examining and changing your deepest, most integral beliefs about yourself, others, and the world. By examining them, you are deciding which ones serve your vision for your life and which ones no longer serve. The techniques of creative visualization can help you get to the bottom of attitudes that may be holding you back—that may not match what you say you want your life to be.

The Least You Need to Know

- ◆ Knowing yourself on all levels is the key to being authentic.

- ◆ Trust that your core values and truest intentions are who you really are.

- ◆ When you practice integrity, you are whole; all facets of you work in harmony.

- ◆ Identifying subconscious beliefs that you may have formed earlier in life is a way to know the agreements you have made about how you should act and be.

- ◆ Getting down to the purest values of your goal can move you into integrity and clarity.

Chapter 9

Focus: The Inner Path

In This Chapter

◆ Working outside in and inside out

◆ Practicing inner path essentials

◆ Using negative energy constructively

◆ Intuition and the inner path

There is a Zen Buddhist saying, "Before enlightenment, chop wood and carry water. After enlightenment, chop wood and carry water." When you start using creative visualization to manifest what you want in life, you have taken on a simple yet magnificent assignment.

Trust us, these assignments are good. As they move you toward your goal, they will also bring about inner changes in your body, mind, and spirit. "Chopping wood and carrying water" means we go about moving on the path to our goal with discipline and devotion.

Two Parallel Paths

When you use creative visualization to realize a goal in your life, you are traveling on two paths. There is the outer path, as assignments come to you to move you closer to your call. These are the obvious assignments such as making a phone call to the person who can provide resources for your goal. But as you'll see in this chapter, you experience changes on the inside, too.

With the outer path, changes are unfolding right before your eyes. Let's say you visualize yourself with a grand piano in your living room. One day your vision becomes reality, and movers deliver a piano to your home. Then you practice and you start envisioning that you are good enough to sit in with a jazz ensemble. A short time later, you run into a bass player at a party. He just happens to need a pianist. Later, you learn he owns a small recording studio. One of his artists has a gig, and she needs someone to fill in with jazz piano between sets. Over time, you develop a following. That's the unfolding.

Another scenario might be visualizing living in a home with a gourmet kitchen and a view of the mountains. The outer path presents itself when just the house you envisioned pops up on the real estate listings. The house is in a good school district. It's been on the market for six months, so the buyer really wants to sell. It's meant to be.

Meanwhile, the process of creative visualization creates the experience of inner changes. In the case of the pianist, maybe you develop more discipline in other areas of your life because you develop the discipline of practicing piano. For the first time in your life, you understand how you can transfer skills from one Life Arena to another. Maybe because you feel empowered, you start taking better care of yourself. Maybe you start to experience playing piano as a meditation, and that leads to inner peace.

In the second scenario, maybe preparing for that new house gives you better discipline about your finances. Maybe preparing your house for the market gains you knowledge of your self-sufficiency as you handle the repairs yourself. These are the inner by-products of moving toward an outward goal.

You may arrive at equilibrium by approaching a situation from either the outside or the inside. Therapists sometimes prefer dealing with the inside, as in the case of insight therapy. Some deal with making outside adjustments and letting the emotional and mental systems catch up.

John: From the Outside In

John came to Shari because he wanted to be more patient with his children. He had hated it when his dad behaved lost his patience and yelled at him, and he wanted his children to have it better. Shari decided the first action was intervention—John must quit yelling at the children. So together Shari and John developed a plan: any time he started to yell, he pinched himself hard on the forearm and left the room. They worked on a visualization exercise that walked through that behavior one step at a time. Shari taped the session so that John could listen to it each day.

At first John reverted to his old habit of yelling, but after he yelled, he remembered the strategy of pinching and leaving the room. Within a week or so he was remembering the pinch-and-leave strategy *while* he was yelling and was able to quit abruptly. The children found this very amusing and began to lose their fear of him. By the third week he succeeded in pinching and leaving *before* he yelled. It took three to six months for John to internalize this habit. After that it became almost automatic.

After John learned to alter his behavior, which also altered his relationship with his children, he and Shari were able to go more deeply into his psyche and do some insight therapy. This helped him face issues with his father. But he first had to change what was happening on the outside in order to look at what was happening on the inside.

Marcy: From the Inside Out

Marcy came to Shari with low self-esteem—not just occasional feelings of low self-esteem, but a chronic sense that she was inferior to everyone else in the world. In the first session with Shari she wouldn't lift her eyes and make eye contact. She talked about wasting her money and the therapist's time.

Because Marcy functioned well at her job as a librarian, lived on her own, and was not talking about ending her life, Shari decided to start with insight therapy rather than intervention. A few sessions in, Shari led Marcy through a visualization of what it would look like for her to go through a day feeling good about herself. Marcy had to "borrow" behaviors from people she admired and pretend she had them in order to complete this visualization.

Next Shari asked Marcy to make a list of how she was keeping herself from being that person she envisioned. Then they spent several months discussing each item on the list, deleting some, adding others, as Marcy began to understand her personality more objectively. It took about a year to deal with all of the issues that Marcy needed to put to rest. Marcy kept a vision of herself as a person with healthy self-esteem and moved steadily through that year toward living out her vision. In Marcy's case, she had to work from the inside out.

> **CAUTION**
>
> **Don't Panic, _Focus!_**
>
> What if you don't know which path to focus on first—the outer or the inner? Generally, it's best to start on the outer path if your concern is about a behavior or response in specific situation. If you are encountering the challenge every day—if an outward change is needed urgently—then take the outer path first. The inner path may be the place to start if the changes you want to make are not focused or if they arise from feelings more than behaviors.

The Hero's Journey

In every hero's (and heroine's) tale, the hero is tested along the journey. The story is as much about the journey as it is the destination. From King Arthur to Harry Potter, from Dagny Taggart in Ayn Rand's _Atlas Shrugged_ to Buffy the Vampire Slayer, we are just as fascinated with the way the hero changes as we are with the goal.

Many visionaries and spiritual mystics of the ages have described their journeys as visualizations. St. Teresa de Avila compared her spiritual journey to that of walking through the many rooms of a mansion. St. John of the Cross compared it to ascending a mountain. In the accounts of Abraham and Moses in the Old Testament, both ascend a mountain—Abraham to be tested, Moses to receive the commandments of God.

In literature, Alice in _Through the Looking Glass_ moves across a chessboard. Harry Potter and his two pals must cross a chessboard to reach the inner chamber in _The Sorcerer's Stone_. In both cases, it's not about becoming a queen, as Alice does when she reaches the other side, or the clever "checkmate" victory for Harry Potter. For Harry, it's about teamwork and sacrifice and friendship. He is learning the traits that are the true attributes of a wizard. Alice, on the other hand, learns how to get along with difficult people and become more confident of herself.

So, as you see, both paths come into play when you use creative visualization. Think of them as two parallel paths. The outer path is the conscious, goal-directed you. The outer path is the movie screen of you living out your goal and people around you responding to the new role you are playing. The inner path is integral to remaining calm in the face of a storm of changes.

If you typically have been goal-focused and results-oriented, you may not feel you need to recognize the inner changes that take place. However, if you discover, examine, and understand some of those changes, it will add power to the external changes you have made.

Inner Path Essentials

The key to the inner path journey is knowing that it's not the external circumstances that influence your happiness, but rather how you respond to them. In *Man's Search for Meaning* (Beacon Press, 2000), Victor Frankl, neurologist, psychiatrist and Holocaust survivor, wrote that the last of human freedoms is the ability of an individual to choose his attitude toward any set of circumstances.

Training yourself to maintain a positive focus during a creative visualization is one example of practicing finding your happiness in the way you choose to respond to a situation. Your happiness is no longer at the mercy of the whims of fate. Through the affirmations of creative visualization, you are training your mind to keep the positive thoughts and shed itself of the negative thoughts. You are creating a reservoir of positive thoughts and beliefs from which to draw when you get into reactive mode.

Reactive mode can be defined as thinking with the mind of the lower self—the petulant child, the wounded child. You are in reactive mode when you are quick to anger, quick to take offense, quick to project on others, quick to find malice in other people's actions, words, and motivations. This is where John was going when he lost his patience with his children—only he wasn't ready to explore the feelings he had about his father's yelling until he got a handle on his own outward behavior.

You must be gentle with your less-than-loving thoughts when they sneak into your mind. Don't banish them. Instead, let them bemuse you. Therein lies the distinction between positive thinking and aligning yourself with the positive energy of the universe. In positive thinking, you are imposing your will on your less-than-positive thoughts. You want to punish them and send them into oblivion. But that's not where they go—these negative thought loops can be quite persistent. When you recognize that you are merely the observer of your negative thoughts—that the real you, or wiser self, is aligned with the positive energy of the universe—you can simply watch those negative thoughts go by. You can choose how you will—or will not—react to them.

You get there only through practice. Practicing the positive focus of creative visualization creates a reservoir of positive beliefs so that you *can* quickly get back to that place where you "know better."

Imagine, See, Be

You can use affirmations to stop reactive mode dead in its tracks and snap you back into your higher self. Another technique is to clap. That's right, just a loud clap. The sudden noise breaks the buildup of reactions to a fearful thought. One man Carolyn knows just says, "Next ..." when the crazy "monkey mind" thoughts rise up. We like that approach because it sort of suggests a detached bemusement. He doesn't give the thought much energy, just sends it on its merry way.

We can't just pretend negative thoughts don't exist and have no power. What we can do is use the power of negative thoughts against themselves. This maneuver is a little like martial arts, in which you use the weight of your opponent against him. In her book *Wishcraft*, Barbara Sher gives an example of how to use this. She says that bitching, moaning, *kvetching*, griping, or just all-out complaining can be constructive—even cathartic. Negative feelings have powerful energy. You just have to know how to use this energy.

There are times you can't force yourself to have a positive attitude. You feel what you feel, right? Denying it, bottling it up, banishing it—these things only give your negative feelings more energy. And what you want is to release that energy so that it gets smaller, not bigger.

Sometimes negative feelings can be so powerful that they feel like they can only be expressed physically. You just need an outlet. So find a healthy outlet: a hard workout at the gym, a vigorous jog along a nature trail, punching a pillow. It's sort of like the line in the Bruce Cockburn song, "Kick the darkness 'til it bleeds daylight." Just don't kick any*one* or any*thing* that *lives*.

Another way to take away the energy buildup of negative feelings is to just let 'em rip—either in your Creative Visualization Journal or in a "big spill" with a kind, supportive friend. If you do it with a friend, make the ground rules that your friend doesn't respond, protest, or argue you out of your position. (And make sure the negative feelings aren't about *him or her*.) When you unleash the flood, your goal is to really go for it. Try to uncork some really good lines. And reward yourself for the most clever ones.

Finally, when you need to have a negative energy release, train your supporters (more about that coming up in Chapter 12) in how to respond and translate it. Generally, a complaint is a plea for encouragement. In New Mexico's Hispanic culture, it's common to say *pobrecito*, which means "poor little one" in Spanish. In surfer culture, the term is *bummer*. Either way, the communication is sympathetic. And sometimes that's all we need: sympathy and a pat on the back.

We tend to complain when we are driving ourselves too hard and we hit a snag. That's when it occurs to us that our efforts may not be acknowledged. Maybe no one knows how hard you're trying. So train those around you that when you say, "I did all this work. I swept the floor and did all the laundry and scrubbed the tub and made an apple pie from scratch, then I organized all the spices," they don't feel guilty they didn't work as hard as you or feel accused of some wrong or shortcoming. Instead, they just say, with all sincerity, "You're absolutely amazing. How do you pull it all off? And you're rich and beautiful, too!" That's what you need to hear!

What's Necessary: Packing Your Suitcase

On any journey, you would pack a suitcase of the essentials. The following are qualities that you can cultivate during your creative visualizations and will help you enhance your experience of the inner path.

Solitude

You must spend time alone, meditating with positive focus, on your vision. Solitude creates the open, empty space that allows the "what might be" to come into your life. Solitude is the way to fill your spiritual self.

Psychologically, solitude is a wonderful antidote if you are struggling with personal boundaries. By spending time in solitude, you become clearer on who you are and what you believe in. By spending time in solitude with your creative vision in your mind, you become friends with it. (So you're not alone!) You create a nearly inseverable bond. When you are tested by others around you, your boundaries hold firm.

> **Wisdom Well**
>
> In solitude, we give passionate attention to our lives, to our memories, to the details around us.
> —Virginia Woolf, British author

Courage

To have the willingness to explore your deepest self is to have tremendous power. When you allow yourself to be vulnerable, you open yourself, yes, potentially, to agony, but also to exquisite joy.

Imagine, See, Be _____

Symbols of courage abound in the history of time: the mighty lion, the Purple Heart, the sword, Saint George and the Dragon. What other symbols of courage come to mind? Write in your Creative Visualization Journal about a moment when you showed great courage. It could be when you were in the throes of childbirth or when all you did was rub chamomile salve on your mother's back after cancer surgery. Acts of courage are great and small. Choose a symbol that reminds you of that act of courage. Meditate on it in your creative visualization sessions.

Trust

Growth hurts. Okay, we admitted it. We weren't exactly trying to hide that, but we didn't want to scare you off. So it's true. The reason growth hurts, in a nutshell, is because we must let go of ego identification in certain Life Arenas. When we move into uncharted territory, our natural tendency is to cling to what we know. Even old emotional pain is more comfortable than new joy. New joy is uncertain. "Is it real?" we may ask ourselves. This other stuff, this old pain—we know it's real because we've been living with it for a long time.

Once, when Carolyn was facing the decision of moving to Arizona from her hometown of Lexington, Kentucky, her sister asked, "But aren't you afraid of the unknown?" Carolyn replied, "It's *all* the unknown." She recognized that staying in her hometown also was the unknown—many things could change.

Carolyn did move to Arizona—the unknown—but what created a strong reservoir of certainty for Carolyn was the *vision* she had of moving to Arizona. Her vision was so vivid it was indelible in her imagination, even as she and her then-husband agonized over the decision. Every time she closed her eyes, she saw herself in her little Dodge Colt, piled up with suitcases, boxes, and two cats, listening to Nanci Griffith all the way along the open roads of Texas. She could feel the sway of the car and the rumble of the road. She knew she was going.

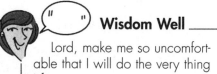

Wisdom Well _____

Lord, make me so uncomfortable that I will do the very thing I fear.

—Ruby Dee, film actress

When your vision is that strong and that vivid, you *can* trust it. You can let go of what you think is the "known."

Receptivity

What if you *don't* know? What if all you know is you love photography but you hate your job? What if all you know is you think you'd be a great chef, but you have two children to support so you can't imagine having enough money for culinary school?

You can use creative visualization to create the receptivity in you so you will receive the answer—and sooner than you think. Remember, solitude is one of the first items to pack in your suitcase. Solitude and receptivity work hand in hand. Solitude allows you to tune your heart to your deepest desires. Solitude is a way of finding your true north, your compass. Solitude is a practice of receptivity, of learning to be open, to allow spaces in yourself that can be filled.

Receptivity also has an element of trust. Receptivity is saying, "I don't know how I will get to culinary school. But what I do know is I would be good at this. I would enjoy being a chef. So I am open to hearing the answer. I am open to the wonderful opportunities that are coming to me now. I am open to listening to the guidance and encouragement from others that will help me know the next steps I should take." Then you keep visualizing yourself as a chef, working in your favorite restaurant.

Bird's Nest Visualization

Use this visualization when you need to fortify your courage and trust. Envision a bird's nest, with all of its branches and mud. Envision the swallows scouting out the place for their nest and choosing a spot. Envision the swallows returning with bits of branches in their beaks. Envision the branches, how they are intertwined—how when assembled they become strong enough to bear the weight of tiny baby bird eggs and hold them safe until they can hatch.

A bird's nest is an example of the instinct for the principle of intention. A nest is a sign of optimism. A nest is an act of trust.

In your visualization, see the nest as a place you can safely stow the tiny baby bird eggs of your dream. Each time you return to your visualization, you are bringing bits of branches that fortify your dream. Your affirmation for this can be, "I know that just like the bird's nest, there is a place being prepared for me and my dream. In this nest lie all the trust, creativity, and imagination I need to reach my goal."

A real-life example of optimism in action is the hawk's nest story in New York City in late 2004. For 12 years, a hawk family had a nest at a Fifth Avenue apartment over-looking Central Park, but the building co-op had the nest destroyed. Actress Mary Tyler Moore, a tenant in the building, led the cries of protest, which ranged from the

Audubon Society to nature lovers across the nation. The building co-op agreed to restore the nest, negotiating even as the most famous of the Fifth Avenue hawks, Pale Male, hovered overhead. If this story of a community joining to intervene to do the right thing works for you, by all means, use it in a visualization for what you want to restore in your life.

Up Ahead: The Intersection of Preparation and Opportunity

Some define luck as when preparation meets opportunity. Preparation entails many aspects—envisioning, trusting, listening, believing. Preparation is driven by your willingness to do what's necessary and your belief that it will pay off—the Zen Buddhist chopping wood and carrying water.

If luck is when preparation meets opportunity, then *intuition* provides the introduction. Inevitably, when you commit to using creative visualization, you will encounter intuition. Intuition can be a tremendous tool to use on your inner path. It also can make great things happen on the outside!

Deeper Meaning

Intuition is a way of knowing something without conscious reasoning. Intuition draws upon information and knowledge we may already have stored within but have not yet brought to consciousness.

Intuition is a way of knowing something based on understanding information that you already have. You may not be aware of having this store of information within, because the information may not have come to you cognitively. We live in the age of rationalism, where everything must be explained through thought—through conscious reasoning. But we are taking in much more information than words and thoughts.

Nonverbal communication is an example of a way of collecting information intuitively. We may walk away from an encounter with someone in which that person was saying with his words that he agreed to what we were asking. Yet we know that it didn't feel right. We know he wasn't on board with the idea. How did we know that? We just felt it.

Because intuition is often based on information we have collected through our other senses—that is, not cognitively—we may or may not immediately trust it. The more aware you are of your subconscious motivations, the more likely you are to trust your intuition. If your learning style is highly verbal, you may not readily trust the information you receive that is not verbal. Highly verbal learners access information through words, but visual learners see pictures, not words. Tactile or kinesthetic learners want to get their hands on something to learn about it. If your learning style is aural or visual or kinesthetic—most people are a blend—you may already have practiced receiving information on many levels—and trusting it.

People we label as naturally intuitive are people who recognize at an early age that the information they are hearing is coming from within. They may or may not be able to explain it. Again, because intuition is knowledge that bypasses conscious reasoning, its source cannot immediately be explained, though people who practice using their intuition often come to recognize the source of their intuitions.

Wherever you are with understanding your intuition, know that it doesn't have to be explained or analyzed. You just have to get to the point of trusting your intuition.

The value of cultivating your intuition is that it will lead you to those moments when you recognize an opportunity—and you are prepared for it. Cultivating intuition will help you get more in touch with *all* of you—with your complete capacity to take in knowledge and use it toward meeting your inner and outer goals.

Looking Back

Take some time to reflect on ways your vision has come to you through the years. Think back to any promptings you have had to pursue something you were interested in bringing into your life. Recall coincidences that struck you that at the time you might have filed away. Let's say you have always dreamed of being a singer. Now that you look back on it, you can remember a time when someone told you that you had a fine voice. Then there was that time three months ago when you ran into someone who remembered you had taken singing lessons 12 years ago and asked whether you still did that. Now that thought is in your psyche. Perhaps the coincidence is enough to bring it to your awareness. Are you ready to make it your vision?

These promptings and coincidences can come to us in the rational world. But more often than not, they come in sideways, through intuition. Listening to our intuitions is what brings them to consciousness and prompts us to act.

Dream a Little Dream

Paying attention to your dreams is another way of cultivating your intuition. Again, you can use creative visualization to do this. Each night before you go to sleep, envision yourself having a vivid dream—and remembering it. State your intention to have memorable dreams. Buy a notebook that you can keep on your nightstand to record your dreams. Just by stating your intention and creating a receptive thought-space and physical space (your notebook) for your dreams, you'll bring them forth. You'll be surprised!

Why do dreams matter? They bring up those strong desires, motivations, and yes, fears that we have stored inside, the emotions that form the matrix of intuitive thought. They are the subconscious feelings trying to break to the surface. We'll talk more about dreams in Chapter 17.

The Inner Work

So you see, the internal changes can power the changes you are bringing about on the outside. Not only can they help you reach your goal, they can migrate to other arenas of your life. But most importantly, they can bring you the true happiness within that makes your vision-making seem effortless.

The Least You Need to Know

- ♦ When you use creative visualization, you are traveling on two parallel paths: the inner path and the outer path.

- ♦ Your ultimate freedom lies in your ability to choose how you will interpret and respond to your circumstances.

- ♦ You can use the power of negative energy constructively.

- ♦ It requires trust, courage, and receptivity to cultivate the inner path. Solitude is a vital component in enhancing those qualities in yourself.

- ♦ Opening yourself to your natural intuitive powers goes hand in hand with the way creative visualization works to prepare you for the changes you are manifesting on the outer path.

Chapter 10

Focus: The Outer Path

In This Chapter

- ◆ Breaking down the steps toward your goal
- ◆ Holding on to your vision
- ◆ Criticism and countermoves
- ◆ When you're faced with obstacles
- ◆ Testing your devotion to your dream

"Gonna be some changes 'round here," proclaims pop singer Bruce Hornsby in the title of an invigorating, catchy tune. In this song, Hornsby sings about getting to the point where he is no longer willing to keep things as they have been. He wants something new, and it's going to happen right now. Folk singer Shawn Colvin sings with a similar sentiment in *"Sunny Came Home,"* when she sings about a woman who returned home with a list of "a few small repairs" for her life. Sunny came home intent on fresh start. Sunny was a woman with a mission.

It's time to rearrange the furniture. It's time for new carpet and fresh paint. It's time to open the windows and let in the fresh air. It's time for some changes.

Change Is in the Air

The changes on the outer path can be invigorating. When you start to change, everything changes around you—people, places, things, situations. You may find you encounter some unexpected reactions—in others around you and in yourself.

In this chapter, we will help you enhance the external benefits of the changes that are coming about because of your creative visualizations. And we'll help you navigate the rough spots. But for starters, let's get practical.

The Picture of You

Many people instinctively use photos to motivate themselves to reach a goal. A teenager who is saving up for a car may hang a poster of a Ferrari on her wall. An overweight man might place photos of himself as a thin person on the refrigerator to motivate himself to stay on that low-carb diet.

Placing a photo or physical symbol in a place where you see it every day is an excellent way to keep your vision in the forefront of your mind. Many people find it useful to place a photo that represents their dream on the bathroom mirror so they are thinking about it as they are shaving or putting on makeup in the morning. Other ideas might be your desk, your computer, your nightstand, your front door, your kitchen sink. Or you may want to hang a symbol from the rear view window of your car.

Some people like to make their picture a shrine, bringing little emblems of their devotion to it over time. This can be especially useful if you have a long-range goal that unfolds over time.

Using a Flow Chart

It can be helpful to set up a flow chart, particularly if you have a long-range goal such as changing careers. Flow charts also can come in handy when you have a more nebulous goal, such as manifesting a meaningful relationship. A flow chart helps you move your vision from your mind to a concrete form. It can help you identify steps you can take now to create the opportunity for your dream to flourish.

> **Affirmations**
>
> Every day in every way I am seeing the steps for my vision unfold.

Let's take a big goal such as the bed and breakfast in the mountains and break it down into manageable steps. Let's say it will require you to leave your 70-hour-a-week job that requires bicoastal travel but pays well. This kind of goal falls into several Life Arenas. It's a career goal because that's how you will make your living. It's a financial goal because it means you'll have to pull together your assets. It's a lifestyle/leisure goal because it means relocating in a vacation spot with more recreational opportunities and possibly more leisure time. It's definitely a home goal, and it could also be a love and family goal because it will mean changes for your spouse and children. It may have undertones of spiritual goals (maybe you dream you will take more hikes in the forest) and creative self-expression (maybe owning the B&B will allow you more time to do your watercolors or grow herbs that you make into handmade soaps). So you see, it transcends many areas, and it's going to mean big changes.

Let's enter the end-goal on the chart:

Buy and operate a B&B.

Brainstorm a list of things you would need to do this. Be as specific as possible:

Identify a location.

Have enough money for a down payment.

Have enough money to leave my job.

Take the first step on the list—identifying a location. Ask yourself what you would have to do. You might come up with:

Research mountain areas and find one I like.

Research business real estate prices in those areas.

Research financial viability of B&Bs in those areas.

Research tourist interest in those areas.

Now let's say you have come up with a dollar figure of how much money you need to make the transition, but there are obstacles. Here are a few we can think of, right off the top of our heads:

You need $100,000, and right now you have only $45,000.

Your company's stock options are down at the moment.

Your children like their school.

You need health benefits.

You need to replace your monthly income.

Your spouse doesn't want to leave his/her job.

Now let's figure out what steps get you from here to there. This is called building a bridge. Let's brainstorm a few ideas:

Buy company stock while it's low.

Research financial statements for B&Bs, in general and yours specifically so you know approximately how much you'll have to live on.

Brainstorm supplemental forms of income for once you have relocated into the community.

Brainstorm passive forms of income (investments, real estate) that can help you make the transition.

Plan to sell your current house, in which you have $40,000 in equity, when the kids go off to college in five years.

So you see the way it works. You just keep breaking down the steps until you hit upon a step you can take tomorrow. Maybe tomorrow's task is that you call a friend who knows a good CPA who can help you read financial statements and come up with a budget. Then you build a creative visualization around that step. Use creative visualization every step of the way, and you will not falter.

When You Hit a Snag

Sometimes, in spite of your best efforts—with strong visualizations and flawless planning—you hit a roadblock. Let's look at how you might go around, through, over, or under those unexpected obstacles.

Get Encouragement

When Shari was in analytical/pastoral counseling training, she and four friends formed a support group. The group allowed people to share their stories of facing discrimination and helped people heal from past wounds. For about three years, the group met one night a week in a cozy room where one member worked. Peanut

M&Ms were their goddess food. Each time they met, they set up a little altar with a candle and random items of symbolic significance.

Much pain circled about the flame of the candle in that room. They cried, they laughed, they raged. Sometimes discussing the changes in their beliefs felt like sawing off a limb of a tree that they were sitting on. But they *had* to have that exchange in order to honor their emerging sense of equality and the changes that were happening to them. It was exciting and terrifying at the same time. Because of the group's support, each was able to go out into places that were unfriendly toward women.

As each member's birthday came around, one member started a tradition of giving a marble apple. Shari still has hers. Shari describes being a part of such a group as a gift of grace. She wouldn't have had the knowledge or courage to go forward with her life and career had she not had the group.

Your friends can be your best allies in creative visualization. They can be your vision keepers when you temporarily hit a snag and lose sight of your goal. They can help you remember.

Get a Taste of It

One of the best ways to make your vision stronger is to move it out of fantasy realm directly into the realm of experience. Allow yourself to get a taste of what it would be like to experience your dream. Start taking trips to bed and breakfasts and interviewing owners. Maybe spend a weekend with a gallery owner setting up a show so you can get a sense for what it's like to own an art gallery. Maybe sit in with your friends who play in a jazz band the next time they play at a party. Afterward, you may use your experience to develop your creative visualization in more detail. Or you may use your experience to sharpen the focus of your affirmations.

Imagine, See, Be

Try your dream on for size. Set up a situation in which you can live in the life you want for a while. Spend a day with an artist in her studio. Ask if you can shadow the set designer at the opera. Borrow your friend's toddler for the day. (Believe us, she'll hand him over—diaper bag and all!)

Criticism: An Obstacle of Choice

When you make changes in your life, it undoubtedly will affect those close to you. Your life has been in a delicate balance with theirs. Imagine your life and theirs like the scales of Lady Justice. If you put more stones on one side, the other side rises.

When you alter the balance of your relationship, it's rare indeed not to experience pressure from others to return to the way things were. God bless them, this isn't because they don't want you to realize your dream. In many cases, it is a subconscious need bubbling to the surface. They are mostly afraid they will lose you. Somehow if your identity changes, you won't be the person they know as friend, spouse, or parent.

Imagine a 5-year-old girl with a new baby brother. Even though she's been encouraged to help with the baby and been given praise for playing the big sister—all that goes out the window when she realizes she's no longer the center of attention. At that point, she is likely to ask Mommy and Daddy to send baby brother back to where he came from!

So how to deal with other people's reactions? That depends on who the person is to you and how much you care about what they think or feel. Maybe your best friend has been unrelentingly critical about the man you are going to marry. She won't go out on double dates with you, and when you are together, she is barely civil to him.

> **CAUTION**
>
> ### Don't Panic, *Focus!*
>
> Sometimes even people who have known you a long time don't understand your deepest motivations. You yourself may just now be discovering them. You may find that taking the time to explain why you are pursuing your goal and how much it means to you will pay off. You may find it's worth it to expose your vulnerability and share your heart.

Consider that your best friend may have lost sight of how important she is to you. Consider that her survival needs have kicked in, and she is terrified at the thought of losing you to someone else. She feels displaced by your husband-to-be. As tempting as it might be to tell her she's overreacting, the best thing to do is to sit down and listen to her feelings. These may not be feelings you want to hear because they may be laced with criticism of your mate-to-be and you—but listen to her. Talk it out and seek the common ground. Reassurance is the best gift you can give—to others and yourself. Listening may be the greatest gift of all.

Barking Up the Right Tree

While friends and lovers can often do with reassurance, family can sometimes require reassurance and more. That's because the belief systems can go back quite a way. So you have to do a little reprogramming. Let's return to the family tree exercise you did in Chapter 7. Brainstorm for a few minutes on each family member's core beliefs, the ones that were communicated to you strongly. Don't edit or evaluate. Just write as many beliefs as you can think of.

Here are some statement starts to get you going:

I could never _____

_____

I must always _____

_____

The way to be loved is _____

_____

Don't ever talk about _____

_____

It was never questioned when _____

_____

To be together, we must _____

_____

Think about what the risk was if you didn't adhere to the same beliefs. In a family, it's dire. If your beliefs fall outside the family's, you no longer conform. You are no longer within the circle. Ultimately, it's about pure survival. Families band together to survive. Families form to protect everyone from the cold, cruel wind. We keep each other safe and warm, physically, psychologically and emotionally. If you venture outside the circle, you may not be safe or warm. Ultimately, says Erich Fromm in *The Art of Loving*, we learn to conform in order to receive love.

Devil on My Shoulder

It's vital for the success of your creative visualizations that you approve of yourself now, as you are. When you disapprove of the way you are now, you create a struggle.

CAUTION

Don't Panic, *Focus!*

Don't be too surprised or dismayed if your loved ones sometimes don't "get it." It may mean they feel threatened by the changes they are seeing. It's inevitable that when people encounter uncertain situations, there will be some countermoves. Stay centered and keep your vision in focus. Through your creative visualization sessions, you will gain the insight for how to meet this new challenge.

Your goal may be to improve your decision-making or to be more patient, but you must live with your flaws and foibles or you will engage in a struggle to hide them from yourself. The affirmations you create for your visualizations will be a struggle because underneath you will sense the negative voice, ever at the ready to point out that you are not *all that*. Shari believes—because she's seen it unfold too many times—that self-criticism and lack of confidence in one's ability to achieve goals often prevent perfectly capable people from fulfilling their dreams.

Shari asks her clients to identify the negative voice. Surprisingly, almost always it is usually only one person—someone close to the client when she was growing up. Once the client identifies the negative voice as a person outside of him or herself, Shari works with the client to eradicate that negative voice. The first step is to identify when you are listening to the negative person's words. Next, Shari asks him or her to picture that person on their shoulder rather than inside of them. Finally, the client envisions the person as far away, perhaps in another room, perhaps miles away.

The challenge is that the negative voice is often someone they love. But once a client begins to listen to her own voice, she starts to discover her positive traits. She starts making her own decisions and believing in herself. When she is no longer listening to the negative voice, the voice takes care of itself. It goes away.

When You Change

After you have been on the outer path for a while, you may look back and realize that behind you is a great divide between you and the people who made up your inner circle. At first, becoming aware of the differences between the emerging new you and your spouse, your family, or your culture can be unnerving. At the same time, you may discover that once you are on the other side, your relationships deepen. When you realize that you can agree to disagree, yet reiterate your commitment to share your life with that person *even though you are different*, you start to see a stronger bond emerge. *This* bond is based on choice. You may not have the same common ground you once had, yet you choose to love this person anyway.

With this kind of bond, you experience the gift of freedom. You allow the other person to be as he is *and still be loved.* And in return, you receive the same gift. To experience this gift is to experience the rewards of what intuitive healer and author Caroline Myss calls *soul clarity*—the weaving together of your inner and outer paths to achieve higher wisdom of your purpose in life.

> **Deeper Meaning**
>
> Intuitive healer Caroline Myss defines **soul clarity** as "the capacity to recognize that the material contents and relationships of our physical world are here only as props or parts of our service to our Contract." Soul clarity is the convergence of the outer and inner paths. When we recognize that the external results we are experiencing are intertwined with changes within, we have achieved soul clarity.

The Assignments

Your assignments are simple. Remember, creative visualization is, at its essence, quite simple: See, believe, affirm. Just keep your focus on the vision—and keep listening to the directions that come in.

There are two sides to the power of creative visualization, then—the quieter side where you meditate and you focus within, and the other side, which is active. There is something powerful in directing your energy into activities. It bolsters your intention. It keeps your focus on the vision. The activity alone can help block out the doubts.

Staying Busy

In the year before writing this book, Carolyn had visualized herself moving into a beautiful home in a good school district for her children. She saw it clearly in her mind, and she devoted prayer, meditation, and effort to that goal. She knew that when the right house in the right neighborhood appeared for the right price, it would be time to act. On the day she made an offer on her house, she returned home terrified, wondering, "What have I done?"

But in her mailbox was a letter from a prospective buyer for her townhome. It was just too good to be true, but yes, there indeed was the Divine saying, "Go ahead, buy the house. Trust, and I'll sell your townhome for you." It was hard to remain calm in the face of such a powerful answer to Carolyn's intention. There was nothing more for her to do, other than get her townhome ready to show the prospective buyer. That's when Carolyn relaxed into trusting the Divine to guide the process, and it came to her that all she had to do was vacuum the carpet so her townhome would present well to the prospective buyer. "What a relief!" she thought. "You take care of the big stuff," she said in her prayer. "I'll just run the Kirby (vacuum cleaner)." She performed her personal Zen Buddhist act of chopping wood and carrying water.

There will be times when you near the culmination of your vision when you may want to get into the action. You may be energized by the realization that your intention has brought this good thing into your life, and it may feel too powerful to remain receptive. This is the time to direct your energies to an activity that plays a supportive role in letting the forces of the Universe do the work.

Staying Devoted

When paired with creative visualization, the practice of self-devotion takes your burning desire one notch higher. Self-devotion is living from day to day with your desires held clearly in focus. Think of self-devotion as an enhanced, proactive version of self-discipline. That means you are not coming back to your meditative focus and your Creative Visualization Journal out of duty or discipline, but out of love for your ambition. You pour your heart out for it. You wake up in the morning, and you greet your dream with a smile.

> **Wisdom Well**
>
> Power is the ability not to have to please.
>
> —Elizabeth Janeway, American novelist

Self-devotion comes when you are willing to do something that will move you toward your goal, even when you don't feel like it. It's a form of service to yourself. It's a form of self-love. You play mother to your dream, looking out for its best interest, even when you yourself may flag after a disappointment or a bout of doubt.

Self-devotion requires you to have a strong heart and strong will, but more than that, it requires you to have faith in yourself. When you follow the path of self-devotion, it means you have the willingness to continue beyond the point at which you really want to stop. You are tired. You think it's taking too much out of you. But what overrides your fatigue and doubt is how much you really, really want this. It's when you say, "I knew I was going to die if I didn't do this."

This kind of commitment to your dream and this kind of faith in yourself is *not* about pushing yourself to the point of burnout. Remember the natural law of the universe, the power of intention. Remember the workings of the universe are toward the fulfillment of your highest potential. The difference, then, in how you push yourself, in ~~with the flow of the universe~~, not *against* the grain.

Soon it will feel right. It's the natural rhythm of the process of creative visualization. After you practice, again and again, it will become as natural as breathing.

Testing Your Vision

By this point, your dream is getting clearer and clearer. So when you reach the point of encountering obstacles from circumstances of other people, test it! This is a little bit like saying, "Go ahead. Make my day." You'll see …

Use the following cost-benefit analysis exercise to assess your self-devotion to your dream. By gaining a clearer picture of the risks and the rewards—both of continuing to follow the path and of halting your dream in mid-journey—you can become get clearer and more at ease with your choice.

Worst-Case Scenario

We'll start with this one, because no doubt this one is more prominent in your mind, if you are feeling tested. What is the worst thing that could happen if you continue on your path? Create a scene and describe it in your Creative Visualization Journal.

What is the most terrible fate you could imagine? Might you lose your marriage? Might you have to relocate? Might you have to skimp and sacrifice for a few months? If that happened, would you live on tuna and saltines? Would your 401(k) be wiped out? Okay, so then what would you do to recover?

By picturing yourself in the scene, you make your response to it more real. You can see yourself as empowered. You may realize that you would summon the fortitude to save your marriage, if heading toward your dream would put it on the line, and you may see yourself doing whatever is necessary to rescue it. Then again, you may feel that any soul mate who would not support this dream is no soul mate at all. While that may be a terrible thing to realize, what you can glean from it is the realization of how vital to your essence this dream might be. It may renew your courage in speaking about it to your mate so that he or she *does* start to buy into it.

The other thing that might result from a visualization about the worst-case scenario is that you may realize that you can handle it. This happens to many people. Once they know that they can handle even *that*, they are freed. They feel a sense of release. They can now pursue their goal with fierceness and without fear.

Imagine, See, Be

Cynics say "I'll believe it when I see it." With creative visualization, it works the other way around. "You'll see it when you believe it." That is, it will begin to unfold in your life when you believe it. You'll see what you wish for unfold right before your eyes.

Best-Case Scenario

Now, flip it and create a mental picture of the best possible outcome. Maybe you have not even let yourself imagine it yet. Now, you have our full permission. Create the most vivid scene you can imagine. What is the setting? Where will you receive the recognition for a dream well-realized? What will you wear? Who is standing by your side? Who will congratulate you and wish you well, and what will they say? What kind of hors d'oeuvres are they serving? Is there champagne?

One Year Later

Now imagine your life one year from now if you abandon your goal. If your dream is still on the shelf, what will you be doing instead? Who will your friends be? Where will you live? How will you feel?

When Carolyn got to the point in her life that she knew she was ready to have children, she had many tests of her courage and commitment. At that point, she created a vision for having a child and summoned her intent. She asked herself if when she was 45 she did not have children, would she be happy? The answer was such a resounding no that she knew she would do infertility treatments or adopt in order to reach that goal. A few years later, when she was experiencing a miscarriage, she was presented a choice: Lose the baby, or drive all the way across town and pick up a prescription for progesterone that was not covered by insurance (and therefore quite costly) at the only pharmacy still open in the city. It was a no-brainer. She had already envisioned how her life would look if she *didn't* try to realize her dream. "I WANT THIS BABY!" she chanted all the way to the drugstore. (Carolyn did lose that pregnancy, but we're happy to report that on the next try, she conceived twins, who are now six years old!)

Keep the End in Mind

Now imagine yourself at the end of your life, when you have realized your goal and you have lived it. Imagine yourself reflecting on a life lived well, looking back at the choices you made and the joys you shared. How will you feel when you look back on that time in your life when your goal came to fruition? How will you remember the struggle? How will the rewards of reaching your goal bear fruit in your life? Imagine sitting back in your favorite chair—in the living room or on the front porch or on your favorite beach—talking with your soul mate about your dream.

Trusting

Some of the struggle within and without arises from not knowing if you will get there—yes, even with those affirmations. If your goal is to become a chef or a fine art photographer, you may have some years of hard work ahead. Use this visualization of a bus stop when you have mapped out a long-range plan for yourself and you need to trust.

When you are waiting for a bus (presuming you are on time), you are not anxious about whether you will get to your destination. You know the route the bus will take. You checked it on the placard by the bus stop. You know the approximate distance between your location and your destination, so you know how long it will take to get there. You have studied the bus schedule so you know what time the bus will arrive at your stop, and you know when it's supposed to arrive at your destination.

Now visualize your long-range goal. You know where it is, and you know the route because you did your flow chart. You know how long it will take to get there. Visualize yourself waiting at the bus stop. Visualize the bus sliding up to the curb. Visualize yourself stepping up the two steps to the bus and finding a seat by the window. Now visualize yourself feeling so relaxed that you just lean against the window and take in the sights and sounds of the city as the bus rolls past. Take in the sycamore trees that line the boulevard. Catch a headline on the newsstand, the movie title on the theater marquee, the woolly sweaters on display at Banana Republic. Now imagine yourself stepping out at your destination. You have arrived. Did you enjoy the journey?

The Least You Need to Know

- ◆ Mapping out a flow chart can help you break down the steps toward your goal. Break it down until you get to a step you can take tomorrow.

- ◆ You may face criticism of your pursuit of your goal—even from loved ones. Stay centered, keep your vision in your mind, and reassure them.

- ◆ By identifying the negative voice in your head, you take the first step to banishing it.

◆ Staying busy and staying devoted are two key techniques you can use when you are facing external obstacles.

◆ Test your vision by imagining a worst-case scenario. Visualize yourself not just surviving it but thriving.

Chapter 11

Living in the Now

In This Chapter

- ◆ Connecting to mindfulness
- ◆ Disconnecting from the past and future
- ◆ Techniques for staying in the now
- ◆ Solving the spiritual paradox
- ◆ Techniques for getting back to the now

The present moment is the best friend you have. It is a pure, unadulterated taste of life. Every moment offers us the chance to fully experience life at its most authentic—on all levels—the physical, mental, emotional, mental, and spiritual.

When you practice mindfulness with creative visualization, you enhance its benefits. Mindfulness—a focus on the present moment—instills in you a clarity of purpose and a calm assurance.

It may seem paradoxical that a focus on the present would be vital to attaining a future goal, but it's true. The answer lies in the authenticity the present offers in every moment, and in this chapter, we'll show you how it works.

"A Slow Sort of Country:" Practicing Mindfulness

We live at high speed. It's like when Alice, hoping to make it across the chessboard and become a White Queen, encountered the Red Queen in *Through the Looking Glass.* The Red Queen grabs her hand, and they run and run and run. Alice's heart is bursting from her chest, and she is gasping for air. "Now! Now! Faster! Faster!" the Red Queen exclaims. They stop, and Alice realizes she is still under the same tree. "Why I do believe we've been under this tree the whole time!" Alice says. Alice explains to the Red Queen that "in *our* country, you'd generally get to somewhere else—if you ran very fast for a long time as we've been doing." The Red Queen pronounces Alice's country "a slow sort of country." Then she says, "Now, *here*, you see, it takes all the running *you* can do, to keep in the same place. If you want to get somewhere else, you must run at least twice as fast as that!"

When we live at high speed, we lose sight of all the gifts the present moment has to offer us. Whether you have practiced creative visualization for years or just started with some of the meditations in this book, you no doubt have experienced how simply and easily meditation can bring you back to the present moment—and the calm within. Though we live at high speed, that mindfulness and inner peace is only one moment away, one breath away.

Shari's sister-in-law is a Protestant minister. In one of her churches she developed a ritual called a breath prayer. It's just what the name implies: one prayer, one breath and always the same prayer, specific to each church member—or each application. You can use a breath prayer in a moment of trouble. Silently say your breath prayer and bring yourself back to your spiritual center. Develop a breath prayer of a sentence or two that taps into your spiritual center and brings you instantly back to a state of mindfulness, conscious of your wholeness.

Deeper Meaning

Mindfulness is keeping your mind on what you are experiencing in the present moment. Mindfulness is experiencing a moment of life with full awareness, engaging all the senses.

Prayers, affirmations, or meditations are all ways to return to *mindfulness*—to be in a high state of consciousness in the present moment. Mindfulness is not the same thing as *thinking*; indeed, it is quite the opposite, and we'll explain why.

Meditation and mindfulness work hand in hand. Meditation creates the gaps in our active thoughts that allow us to recognize the stillness within. When you find the stillness within, you have found something bigger than the stream of thoughts that rushes through your mind. You have found your spiritual self. This wiser self can draw you away from the activity of the mind. This wiser self reminds you that you are not just a thinker—your mind. You are a body, you are emotions, you are a spiritual being. We repeat: You are not your mind.

But, you might say, "I like my mind. It helps me solve problems. It helps me make decisions. It's a pretty smart mind. I use it all the time."

So we'll say it this way: You are *more* than your mind. In a state of mindfulness, you are highly alert but not thinking. You are experiencing life in its fullest expression—in its truest expression. Your wiser self is in control.

Mindfulness is key to maintaining the positive focus that is vital to creative visualization. Practicing mindfulness means being aware of your negative thoughts as they come up. But again, you don't engage those thoughts. You watch them. When you become the person watching them, you take their power away. Just by observing your negative thoughts, you have noted that these negative thoughts are not who you are. They are *not* you. You are the one who will choose whether you have these thoughts or not.

Right here is where the present moment fits into creative visualization. The present moment brings you back to your wiser self—your whole self. What exists in the present moment is calmness and completion. You feel calm because you are connected with the life that exists in the moment. You feel calm because for a moment, you drop out of all the energy you are devoting to the past and the future. You feel complete because you are connected with the wisest part of you—and because you just remembered how complete you already are. To visualize from the place of this wise, complete self is to have great power indeed.

Wisdom Well

To be free of time is to be free of the psychological need of the past for your identity and the future for your fulfillment.

—Eckhart Tolle, author of *The Power of Now*

Past Tense: Why "Then" Has a Hold on Us

We spend a lot of mind-energy apologizing for, regretting, or revising the past. We spend a huge amount of mind-energy formulating ways to avoid re-experiencing the pain of the past. In *The Lion King*, Simba experiences a lesson in facing his past from Rafiki, the baboon/seer. Simba resists returning to rescue his father's kingdom because he will have to face his past. Rafiki bonks him on the head with a coconut. "What did you do that for?" Simba says, rubbing his head. Rafiki replies, "What does it matter? It's in the past." "Yeah," Simba replies, "but it still hurts." When Rafiki moves to swing at him again, Simba blocks him. Of the past, Rafiki says, "The way I see it, you can either run from it or learn from it."

Ultimately the lock that the past has on us is about a feeling of incompleteness—and an energy-robbing feeling of not being in control of our lives. In Simba's case, he was letting his past control him and hold him hostage to an erroneous belief.

Take a moment to do this next meditation. Get comfortable in the place you have set up as your sanctuary or meditation spot. Take in a deep breath, filling up your lungs, letting your chest expand. With the exhale, let your breath lift to the sky. On the next inhale, draw your breath into your belly, letting it expand. As you exhale, send out all the stale, empty breath. Send out all the waste, all the clutter, all the sediment, all the thoughts that do not nourish you. Take in a third breath. Draw it deep into the deepest, most secret, intimate part of you. (If you are familiar with the chakras, send it to your root chakra. More about that coming up in Chapter 13.) As you exhale, release all that is not your wisest self.

Now, turning your gaze inward, continue to breathe, taking in nourishing energy, imagining it falling like glittering sand to the deepest part of you and rising back up and out with the exhale. Imagine this glittering sand falling and rising, circulating freely. Stay in this for six or seven breaths.

Say in your mind or out loud, "I draw nourishment from the heavens to the highest wisdom that dwells within me. I am now remembering this is my authentic self. I now let this wisdom flood my body and my soul." Now say out loud, "I am complete." Say your name: "I am _____, and I am complete." Repeat it, letting your voice grow stronger each time. Continue until this feels complete. Close out the meditation, remaining silent through three breath cycles. Open your eyes.

Future Perfect: Why "What Might Be" Dazzles Us

In our "buy it now" world, we spend a lot of time planning the future, imagining some material thing will enhance our lives. In the face of the barrage of cultural messages enticing you to spend money, many of us steal our own future. When we go into debt, we trade future life energy for a thing that may or may not give us lasting pleasure.

It would be hard to find anyone who is completely immune to the glitter and glam that entice us to spend our hard earned dollars on brand-new stuff. We're (only somewhat) amused at the plethora of television shows that focus on clearing out clutter and remaking your home (or yourself!) so you can get new stuff. And don't forget the countless stories about shopaholics who turned their addictions into eBay entrepreneurship with great success, thus validating their "gotta have it" material mentality.

> **Wisdom Well**
>
> Happiness is a butterfly, which, when pursued, is always just beyond your grasp, but which, if you will sit down quietly, may alight upon you.
>
> —Nathaniel Hawthorne, nineteenth-century American author

Learning to live in a state of mindfulness gives us the ability to pull back the veil of "must have" so that we have a much healthier perspective on how to use our available resources. Each of us is but one soul in a vast sea of creation. Centering ourselves into mindfulness helps us see clearly how we need to, and can, contribute to all life that exists.

Back to the Now

Remember with creative visualization that you act as though your goal has already manifested in your life. It has already happened. This is where the *now* comes in and starts to do its work. The moment you want to experience in the future is something you experience *now*, in the present moment, in your visualization. The *now* that you visualize is complete, and it brings you assurance—at first, an assurance that what you hope to achieve is possible. And then, an assurance that what you hope to achieve is good for you (and not hurtful to anyone else).

This is the paradox. The certainty we can experience during creative visualization, when we devote a positive focus to experiencing our ambition in the *now*, is what allows us to push back all of the negative thoughts about what we have not yet become. Focusing on what *is* in the present moment brings our focus to the gifts the present moment has to offer. The first of these gifts is simply life itself.

> **Imagine, See, Be**
>
> Creative visualization isn't daydreaming, mind you, though daydreaming *can* be a component of creative visualization. Daydreaming can activate the imagination, though, and you can use those vivid scenes for creative visualization techniques. So think of daydreaming as a window to creative visualization.

The present moment restores us. Being mindful of the now reminds us that the mistakes or shortcomings of the past do not exist—they are in the past. Being mindful of the now reminds us how perfect the present moment actually is. We no longer need some future imagined event to fill us. We are full now.

This precisely is why creative visualization works so beautifully. Yes, you are visualizing some future event that you desire. Yet the techniques you use with creative visualization—mindfulness, compassion toward yourself, purity of intention, and affirmations—bring to you the awareness that you are complete *now*.

Your Now, *Now*

To understand how you can use the present moment to make your creative visualizations the most effective, let's start by analyzing your beliefs about the past, present, and future.

Most of our thoughts in the average day are connected to either the past or the future. Very seldom are we connected to the present moment. More often we are replaying a past event or unconsciously acting in a certain way because of a past event. Or we are concentrating on an immediate goal, such as shopping for groceries, preparing a meeting agenda, or just trying to make a work deadline. These kinds of thoughts clutter our minds and block our awareness of the beauty of life in the moment.

Carolyn had "the Now" knock loud and hard on her door when she was in the store one night during the holiday season and looked up from an intense price analysis of Christmas lights to notice her daughter dancing to the Scooby Doo Santa singing "We Wish You a Merry Wish-mas." "Be here now." Just be here. Just dance.

Affirmations
I embrace my past and everything I perceived it was. I see it clearly and I am at peace with it. Seeing that, I am now free of my past to experience the present, just as it is.

To get to the crux of this, commit to being aware of the very instant your thoughts escape to the past or the future. Start becoming aware of how much your thoughts about the past influence your moods and actions of the present.

It's also vital to notice the times when your mind leaves the present and takes a whirlwind trip to the future. It's human nature to do this. Life's present circumstances throw too many challenges our way, and suddenly everything's on fire, and we say, "I need a vacation!" So we imagine a trip to Italy or the beach—or, Carolyn's current favorite fantasy coping mechanism after a week grappling with ever-changing twenty-first century technology: the lavender farm, à la the French Provence.

Why is it human nature to let our minds run off to the past or the future? Escaping to the past or the future is resistance to the truth of the moment that is. It's too painful—or sometimes too magnificent—so we flee to the places we know. The more you can accept the present moment, as it is, the less you will resist.

Imagine, See, Be

It can be just as difficult to stay in a magnificent moment as it can to stay in a painful moment. But it's much more fun to practice staying in the magnificent! The next time someone pays you a compliment—or the next time you catch your lover admiring you—just stay in the moment. Take in a deep breath. Receive the compliment. Hold the gaze of your lover. Note where you feel it in your body, and let that feeling expand with your breath.

Ultimately, both escapes—to the past or future—are about resistance. Look at what you are resisting in the present moment. What do you believe is lacking? What struggle are you identifying with in your mind? Another way of saying it is: what were you expecting this moment to be? Was there a picture in your head of what you/your spouse/your house/your job should look like? The more you are able to honor the present moment, accepting it as it is, the more you will be free of the struggle. You are creating pain for yourself when you do this. You are failing to see the gifts of the moment.

We find it's pervasive in our media-saturated culture to have expectations of what a moment should be. The holidays are a prime example, when the media barrage us with images of the perfect family, complete with the trimmings of perfect turkey dinners, abundant merriment, warm familial ties, and unlimited gift giving. Romance is another area that gets the glamour treatment. We are exposed to so many of these messages, we may not even know we hold these expectations, or believe them to be true. We may not even stop to ask whether the ideal family holiday gathering or perfect relationship ever existed—or question whether it's possible to attain, or worthwhile. Or we may not stop to question whether someone else's ideal is *our* ideal experience.

The Five Senses and the Now

This simple meditation offers a good technique for anchoring yourself in the now. In your meditation spot, dressed comfortably, free from distractions and eyes closed, begin to calm your breathing. Keep your mind in stillness for about two minutes. Then on your next exhale, look up around the room.

Notice one thing you *see*.

Notice one thing you *hear*.

Notice one thing you *taste*.

Notice one thing you *smell*.

Notice one thing you *touch*.

Repeat the rotation. Notice each time how your awareness deepens. You see more detail in things. You listen more deeply for the sounds beneath the sounds—for the stillness. Suddenly, stillness has a sound! The current moment begins to take on an unexpected sweetness. You are creating your experience of it, and it belongs only to you.

Rough Waters: Now and Challenges

It can be quite a challenge to stay in the present moment if your life is particularly difficult right now. If you are struggling with your career, if you are going through a breakup, if you have a severe illness, your thoughts about a better future may be the very things that keep you going.

But we're here to tell you that the present moment offers more solace than you can imagine—even in rough times. Author Eckhart Tolle says it's impossible to be unhappy *and* feel fully present in the moment. That's quite a statement, but that's how powerful the now is. It's pure happiness.

Wisdom Well

Every moment lived fully is a moment of transcendent alchemy of fire transforming dull metals into dazzling gold.

—Anonymous

The key distinction Tolle makes is between your present situation and your life. Make a list of the problems you have in your life right now. Ask yourself if you really have this problem *right now*. If three weeks from now you will be laid off unless your company picks up a new contract, you do not have this problem *right now*. If Thursday morning you are meeting your estranged spouse at the marriage counselor's office, you do not have this problem *right now*.

If you're experiencing a highly stressful situation in your life, you'll be tempted to argue with us. Don't worry too much if you are. If it were our situation, we would argue, too. The argument would go something like this: my problem *right now* is that I must look for a job. My problem *right now* is that I must be prepared for what my spouse might say in the counseling session.

But life is underneath every situation. It is the heartbeat. Take a deep breath. Experience your senses to the fullest. Touch, taste, smell. See the light, shapes, colors and textures around you. Listen for the sounds and the sounds beneath the sounds. Feel the rhythm of life around you.

When you feel this much alive, you remember that you have this wiser, stronger self that will walk with you through even the most difficult of circumstances. Let this life energy infuse your creative visualization sessions, in which you imagine yourself meeting your challenges as a wise, strong person.

Now, the Spiritual Paradox

It may seem paradoxical to talk about the importance of staying in the present moment when we are talking about realizing a goal in the *future*. Isn't creative visualization about imagining the future? Isn't "staying in the now" a process of letting go of attachment to a certain outcome?

It seems like a paradox to devote yourself to visualizing an outcome that you desire while at the same time you focus on contentment and completeness in the present moment—when in fact you do not have the thing that you so desire. It seems contradictory to talk about devoting such an effort to visualizing and realizing a goal at the same time we talk about not being attached to the outcome. It's much more natural to be very attached to anything to which we expend great effort.

So let's go deeper to break down this apparent paradox. No doubt you have heard the saying that goes something like, "No problem can be solved on the level of the thinking that created it." The answer lies within that statement.

In our culture, most people live most moments of their days cut off from their spiritual selves—from wholeness. The window through which they view the world is cloudy and smudged, hiding the real truths. This leads to a sense of incompleteness—of "less than, or not enough." And so we try to become enough, to become "more than." We become very goal-oriented, very attached to things going a certain way. We are focused on what is missing in our lives, not on the abundance we already have. But at this level of consciousness—focused on what we lack—we create our own barriers. Maybe we subconsciously set up obstacles that thwart our goal. Instead of cleaning the window of spirituality we simply move the smudges around and further obscure our view of the truth. In the meantime, our higher, spiritual self stands just on the other side of the window waiting for us to clean it and to ask for help in doing so. It's just that simple.

The first obstacle is this belief that you are cut off from your spiritual self, and it's the first thing that needs to go. Just toss that idea right in the circular file. When you reconnect with your spiritual self and start cultivating this side of you, you are restored to a feeling of completeness. So perhaps your goals shift. Perhaps some of them fall away; others transmute into something that touches your deepest desires. You may still hold your vision in your mind's eye—you may still set goals. But you are not pursuing them from a standpoint of incompleteness. You are pursuing them with more wisdom.

Wisdom Well

We are tasting the taste this minute of eternity.

—Rumi, thirteenth-century Persian mystic and poet

When you reconnect with your spiritual self, you can trust that good is coming to you. Miraculously, you let up on the struggling. Another way of saying this is "high participation, low attachment." Letting go is the beginning of the end of the struggle of the now vs. past and future. When you see the good you already have, you truly cease the struggling. So the highest level of functioning that creative visualization can attain is when you stop resisting what *is*. That's powerful stuff.

Back to the Now

Quick! Right now! Lace your fingers together. Did you automatically place one thumb on top of the other? Probably it was your dominant hand. Now break your hands apart and lace your fingers back together again, this time with the other thumb on top. It doesn't feel natural, does it?

That's a little bit what practicing the discipline of "now" in your visualizations is like. It's easier said than done. It doesn't feel natural at first. It takes time, discipline, commitment, and practice. But here are three simple techniques for getting there.

Home Sweet Home: Arriving Back at Now

Practice this meditation and the following affirmations as a close to any creative visualization session. Move your focus away from your future goal to what you want now. You may live in a big city but imagine that you want to run a horseback riding stable in the Rocky Mountains. Still, that goal is still a year or two out there. So ask yourself, "What do I want now?" Is it financial stability? Financial independence? Time on the weekends to go horseback riding?

Or maybe you have put in some time with your visualization to the point of feeling frustrated that it's not happening as soon as you would like, or maybe new barriers have presented themselves. Today you may want to strengthen your intent or bolster your faith.

- **Peace.** "Today I am surrounded by peace. I have peace in my life right now."

- **Focus.** "Today I am one with my ambition and my vision. It is all I see."

- **Strengthened intent.** "Today I am certain this vision is right for me. Knowing that, I have peace."

- **Consciousness.** "Today I am directing my consciousness to all that is right now. All around me I see gifts."

- **Compassion.** "Today I am receiving love and kindness from my spiritual self and Creator. I feel enveloped in loving arms."

- **Clarity of purpose.** "Today I am seeing the meaning of my life. I know my purpose is this."

Breath and Now

We can't emphasize enough the power of the breath to bring you back to the now. Buddhist monk Thich Nhat Hanh offers this breathing meditation to help you remember the beauty that exists right here, right now, in this moment.

As you breathe in, say: "Breathing in, I calm my body." Bring your focus to directing your breath to the parts of you body that need calming.

As you breathe out, say: "Breathing out, I smile." Bring your focus to releasing your breath in joy. You exalt in being alive. You exalt in what this moment offers to you now.

Say: "Dwelling in the present moment I know this is a wonderful moment."

Repeat, and as you breathe in, take in the energy of this beautiful moment. With each cycle, increase your awareness of the calm, the joy, and the beauty of the present. Do this for at least six cycles, until it feels complete.

Nature and Now

Nature is an anchor, bringing us back into mindfulness. It's difficult to be out in nature and not be reminded of the life force energy of the universe. It's difficult to miss how peaceful it is—how creativity, rejuvenation and serenity are built in.

Remember the walking meditation we did in your outdoor sanctuary in Chapter 6? We have found that one of very best ways to engage in a fulfilling meditation is to walk and go into a light trance state. You are noticing, seeing. Quieting the mind lets your subconscious and your higher spiritual self flow up into your conscious mind.

Embracing the Present

So embrace the handsome ogre that is the present moment. It's here on your doorstep, bearing a bouquet of flowers and a crooked-toothed smile. Accept its lovable imperfections. Make it a habit each day of blessing the day—*as is*. Say yes to the thoughts, feelings, perceptions, and sensations in every day. Open yourself to its sights and sounds. As the Indian playwright Kalidasa said, "Dreams of today whisper to me; visions of tomorrow beckon. Yet it is today where I must live …" This kind of letting go leads to the most valuable type of information and growing enlightenment. There is something to be learned or understood in every now.

The Least You Need to Know

- ◆ Practicing mindfulness is a way to befriend the serenity we experience in the present moment.

- ◆ Finding the completeness in the now is the way to break the strong links our minds have to the past and the future.

- ◆ Fully engage your five senses, use meditation, and practice affirmations to stay in the now and enhance your experience of creative visualization.

- ◆ Embracing the now seems like a paradox when visualizing what we want in the future, but it connects us with our spiritual selves, which empowers our creative visualizations.

Part 4

You've Got to See It to Be It

Creative visualization taps into powerful stuff.

In Part 4, we'll look at the source of this energy. Understanding that everything you see is energy is the first step. It's all energy, from your belief and your intent, to the flow of time and the power of the present moment. Your thoughts *are* energy, and they have the power to attract changes in your life and initiate changes in the energy fields around you.

We'll explore the way energy moves through your body, mind, and soul. We'll explore how it moves out through the world. Then we'll show you how creative visualization can become more powerful when working with a partner or a group.

12

Are You the Conductor?

In This Chapter

- ◆ Your physical capacities
- ◆ Taming all of your personalities
- ◆ Visualize plenty, visualize harmony
- ◆ Training your support system
- ◆ Harnessing your spiritual power

Creative visualization connects you—through your belief and your intent—with some powerful, positive energy. At first that connection with the natural energy that creative visualization brings forth can be a little bit like grabbing a live wire. You get a jolt.

But once you are aware of the role *you* play as the conductor of that energy, you will begin to see how you decide how much you access and absorb at any given time. *You* are in charge of the change and growth in your life. In this chapter, we will help you see how you can truly be the conductor of that positive energy.

You: The Super Conductor

When you practice creative visualization, you connect with the power of the present moment and the serenity and happiness it offers. It connects you with the flow of time and energy. It connects you with the life force energy of creation. It connects you, most of all, with the conductor of that energy: you.

What does it mean to be a conductor? To delve into all the possibilities that exist in that word, we will look at three definitions of conductor that can further define your personal growth:

- Someone who makes sure the trains run on time.

- Someone who leads an orchestra made of musicians playing their instruments in harmony.

- A way to move an electrical current from a source to an outlet.

A train conductor is concerned with timing. It's the conductor's job to make sure the trains arrive at their destination on time. Up ahead, we will show you how you can identify ways to conduct the many "trains" in your life—the "engines" by which you "transport" yourself to your goal.

In the metaphor of the conductor of an orchestra, we will explore ways to create your support team so that the members work in harmony together. And we will explore how you can work in harmony with yourself by attaining a greater self-knowledge.

> **Wisdom Well**
>
> Recognize what is before your eyes, and what is hidden will be revealed to you.
> —The Gospel of Thomas

Electricity is light and power. In this metaphor, we will explore the source of this positive energy. We will explore how to connect with it. We will delve into how to allow it to flow in your life. At first, it may seem unnecessary to have to learn how to let something good and powerful occur in your life, but sometimes it is a lesson you truly need.

All Aboard: The Train Conductor

A train conductor makes sure, first of all, that the trains—and all the passengers—are heading to the right destination. When you get on board, the conductor checks your ticket. Ask yourself—really ask yourself—if you have the right ticket. Maybe you are lucky, and you have more than one possible destination. Maybe you must decide which goal takes you on the path of the heart.

Can You See Your Destination?

Have your goals changed since starting this book? Have they become broader, maybe a little bigger, affecting more than one Life Arena? Or have they become more focused, more concrete? Great, if they have become a little bit of both. When Shari worked at the counseling center of a major university, she counseled many students pursuing degrees in fields that they knew they no longer wanted to pursue. Flexibility is key in setting goals and amending them. Change doesn't mean you were wrong the first time or made a wrong decision, it means you have more information or have grown in your perception of life. Statistics show the average person changes occupations (not just jobs) seven times during a lifetime.

Ask yourself if this is the right time in your life for this goal. What is right about it? What's not right? Can you clearly see the destination? If not, visualize the next stop. What do you like about your goal? What don't you like? Test yourself to see if you are still "on board" with this goal.

Modes of Transportation

Taking the train is about getting somewhere. It's about transportation. What will transport you to your goal? Give some thought to your physical capacities as you write about this in your Creative Visualization Journal. For instance, while writing this book, Carolyn gained the insight in the deepest, most lasting way possible of just how vital exercise was in allowing her to write. She strengthened her commitment to cycling and yoga because she knew both were vital in supporting her goal of meeting manuscript deadlines. She held this time as sacred. It would take a child emergency or an act of God to make her compromise her goal.

What are your physical needs? Take an assessment now of where you stand, giving each a number, with 10 representing that you are at optimum and 1 representing … well, that you need to get to work on an area, to say the least.

Nutrition _____. You eat a variety of healthy foods. There are a lot of ways to eat right and a lot of ways to think about it. It may mean you have a diet of lean proteins, low fats, and high in fresh vegetables and fruit. Or it can mean a low-carb diet.

Healthy attitude/relationship with food _____. You do not eat to indulge your moods, mask depression, or compensate for low self-esteem. You eat to have a healthy body. You enjoy the tastes and textures of the foods you eat.

Body image _____. You have a healthy, realistic view of your body, its beauty, and its capabilities.

Exercise _____. You exercise regularly doing something you enjoy. You have found your exercise style.

Energy _____. You have plenty of energy. You are enthusiastic about life.

Stamina _____. You have a healthy heart. Your vital statistics point to a thriving system. Your cholesterol is low; your blood pressure is within normal range. Because you exercise, you have good muscle tone and your body mass index is good.

Clear mind _____. You take care of your mind by controlling your input and cultivating mindfulness. When you need to think about a problem, you have clarity and purpose. You are good at making decisions.

Shelter, physical _____. Your home meets your needs and you easily make your mortgage payment (or rent payment) without straining your budget.

Shelter, emotional _____. You love to be in your home. It's a sanctuary for you—a place where you can be yourself.

Security _____. You can feel reasonably certain that you are safe. You aren't overly concerned about crime, death, divorce, job loss, or any other event that could cause a great upheaval in your life.

Roots _____. You are connected to your childhood. Even if you don't live in the place where you were raised, you know how it shaped you and you value that. Even if you do not live near your birth family, you are emotionally connected. You know quite a bit about your family history and where you fit in. You feel you understand your family, for all of its strengths and weaknesses.

Plenty _____. You believe you have all you need for survival and happiness. You believe the universe has plenty for everyone. You do not believe the good in this world is scarce and that you are only getting the scraps.

Trust _____. You trust people easily. You have good judgment about who to trust. You have good skills in discerning people and knowing when to trust them. You win others' trust easily.

Add up your total score: _____.

If you scored well on this list, how powerful art thou!

- An excellent score is 111 to 130.

- A score of 91 to 110 puts you at above average.

- A score of 65 to 90 indicates you have some definite areas to work on.

- A score below 65 is cause for alarm.

If going through this list revealed some weak areas to you, then you have just uncovered some vital information. Use it to make your creative visualization sessions more powerful. And what's the strategy for working on that, you might wonder? Right. Visualize it. Make a point in your next creative visualization to build a positive image around that area.

Affirmations
I am strong. I am powerful. My mind is healthy, and today I am free of worry.

For instance, if you feel somewhat disconnected to your roots, try using a photo from your childhood in your visualization. Send positive energy to it, saying, "I am experiencing a deep connection with my roots. I am feeling the serenity of that connection now."

If you find that your belief in scarcity overrules your desire to believe in plenty, then meditate on a large buffet table overflowing with luscious foods. Imagine that as the guests circle around the buffet loading up their plates, the platters are instantly replenished. Your affirmation for this visualization could be, "I believe that my supply of love is infinite. I believe that abundance is here in my life now. I am recognizing the abundance that is my life."

I Hear a Symphony

Italian psychologist Robert Assagioli used the metaphor of an orchestra to define the makeup of the human personality. He saw our personalities as though they were made up of many sub-personalities—each a different musical instrument—playing in harmony. Each sub-personality contributes a rich range of tones. Some provide the melody; others provide harmony, while others provide percussion.

An orchestra conductor brings order to a cacophony of sound. He keeps all the musicians playing their instruments in time. He may signal when to play louder by raising his arms and expanding them out. He may signal to play softer with a gentle caress of his palm in the air, as though he is soothing a powerful beast. He brings a perfection to the music that would not be possible without his presence.

As the conductor of your life, you decide when to play louder, when to play softer. You command the orchestra of your sub-personalities so that they play in harmony. You command the energy you summon—the positive energy, the power of the present moment, the natural flow of the universe—to play together, in time, in one key.

A Harmonious Whole

To be in harmony with yourself, you must know yourself. A cellist knows his instrument. He knows just the amount of resin the bow needs. He knows the way to glide the bow over the strings because he has rehearsed it and rehearsed it. It's second nature. The trombonist knows that sweet spot that yields just the right pitch, neither too sharp nor too flat.

In your Creative Visualization Journal, describe the various parts of your personality. Write each down as you think of it and then describe an episode when that personality or trait was dominant in what you were doing. Remember it takes all of the sides of your personality to complete the perfection of the whole.

Let's throw out some ideas:

Adventurous, risk-taking

Nurturing

Driven

Childish

Passionate

Mellow

Discerning

Could all of these attributes exist in just one person? Absolutely. Notice the dichotomies that exist in you. One children's book by actress Jamie Lee Curtis, *Today I Feel Silly, and Other Moods That Make My Day* (Joanna Cotler, 1998), helps children identify their moods and feelings. Another one that Carolyn's twins were fond of in their toddler years has the creature/character turning different colors on different days. Some days he is blue, some days he is orange, some days he's purple. How many colors are you?

You must not only know yourself, you must like yourself. Healthy self-esteem is simply having a positive regard for oneself. It means having a positive, fairly accurate vision of yourself. You consider yourself to have mostly positive attributes. While you have flaws, you know you are likeable. Many people like you, and you count yourself among them. It would be difficult to find an area of our lives that *isn't* affected by our self-esteem.

Healthy self-esteem gives us a sense of hopefulness when we take on a new task or perform an old one. We have a reasonable expectation of success as opposed to someone with low-self esteem, who likely expects to fail. If someone has low self-esteem, one of the best ways to help him or her is to point out the Life Arenas that are succeeding. If successful in one area, he or she can use that reminder and feeling of success to build other areas.

> **Don't Panic, *Focus!***
>
> Global low self-esteem is the psychologist's term for people who have low self-esteem in all areas of life. Generally, they are clinically depressed. If you don't feel like you can attempt the exercises in this book or feel like you can't be successful at attaining your goals, perhaps it is time to be screened for depression. It may be more than low self-esteem that is affecting you.

Have Baton, Will Travel

Now, with a deeper understanding and a growing respect of self, you may approach others in their role in reaching your goal. Remember, you are conducting an orchestra, and that means teamwork. How do you work in harmony with others? How do you create a support system that doesn't deplete people around you? After all, you don't want to drain your family and friends. If it's hard for you to reach out for help, how do you learn to do that?

If you are used to being self-sufficient, you may not even realize how much other people can help you—and with only a small contribution. If you are accustomed to being self-reliant, you may take so much pride in being responsible for yourself that it doesn't occur to you that you can get there faster with a little help from a friend.

But remember that *you* are the conductor. *You* have put in the time visualizing your goal. *You* have put in the time developing your vision and sending positive energy to it through affirmations. You have journeyed this far because your belief and intent strengthened with each step. So know that reaching out and relying on others is not a weakness. It's a sign of the strength of your vision; you believe in it so much that the people around you believe in it, too. They are starting to see it with you.

Let's think of the ways a support system can help you reach your goal:

◆ **Encouragement.** Of course, you need people around you who believe in you. These are the people who say, "You can do it" or "I believe in you."

◆ **Resources.** Your friends and family have a wealth of resources to offer, and they want to help.

◆ **Skills.** Do you have a friend who has a Master's degree in finance and you need to develop a business plan? Offer to make him dinner one night a week for a few weeks if he'll lend his expertise. Do you want badly to remodel your house? Maybe you are good at marketing. Propose to your architect friend that you can write copy for her website in exchange for her sketching out some ideas for your house.

◆ **Sounding boards.** Use your supporters to sound out ideas. Talking about it out loud is a terrific way to get to the heart of any concern you have. Often just the talking it out—just explaining it to another person—yields the insight that you need to move to the next step.

◆ **Connections.** There are only six degrees of separation between you and every other person on the planet. A degree of separation is you to your father. Two degrees is you to your father to your father's business associate. Say your father's business associate knows an art therapist and that's what you want to do. That's three degrees. And so on. It's very likely you are already connected to someone who knows someone who will help you meet your goal.

◆ **Heavy lifting.** Sometimes you need your supporters to roll up their sleeves and just help. Maybe it's to take care of the kids so you can meet a deadline, or maybe it's to build a brick patio. Make sure you reward your support team well.

◆ **Vision keeping.** Supporters can hold your vision as sacred as you do. They can be your reminders when you lose sight of your goal. This can be extremely valuable with broad-ranging goals, such as wanting to build a community or wanting to break into an artistic career. Tell your friends about the community you want to create, and share your vision. When the going gets rough, they will remind you. Tell your friends that you feel contentment in your soul when you paint and you want to sell your paintings to galleries. That day when you waver and you think about taking a corporate job with benefits, they will remind you that it's not the true path of your heart.

◆ **Out-of-the-box solutions.** Sometimes you put yourself in a box. You believe you can't pursue a career as a filmmaker because you have a family to support. You believe you can't relocate because you have to keep your children in a certain school district. You believe you have to do the work yourself because there's no one to delegate it to, and you end up spending endless hours on the weekend to catch up—when it's really true that someone else in your company eagerly wants to learn some skills and would gladly take it on. Supporters can encourage you to get out of the box. They can help you see when you are putting yourself in a box.

Getting Out of the Box

For the following exercise, you will want to assemble a brainstorming group of about 7 to 12 people (more about that coming up). You sit in a chair, surrounded by your supporters in a circle of chairs. Tell them your dream, and tell them why you can't do it. Let them interview you about what's stopping you. Every time you say something like, "That's a fine idea, but I could never do that because …" your supporters scoot their chairs closer to you. Eventually you are cheek to jowl with them, if you throw out enough "can'ts."

When you are knee-to-knee with your supporters, have them say, "What if you did (fill-in the blank)?" Let's say you want to start your own business and the question is, "What if you asked your friend who has a Master's in finance to dinner?" You might say, "He would say no." Your supporters would say, "What if he didn't? How would you feel then?" You might say, "I would feel good. I would feel encouraged." Each time your mind starts to open up, your supporters scoot their chairs away from you. Keep going until you have a specific set of action steps.

Let's Get This Party Started!

So how do you begin? Start with a brainstorming group—call it your Master Mind group. You may find you want to develop different groups for different Life Arenas. You can have a Master Mind group as small as two (yourself and your spouse, yourself and your best friend), but it's more effective to have several people in your group. Some Life Arena goals (such as getting back into shape after pregnancy) can best be achieved one-on-one, say, with an exercise buddy. But many, particularly in work, creativity, and relationships, benefit best from a group of creative minds.

Kick off your Master Mind group with a brainstorming session. For that, the more great minds, the better, but we recommend keeping it under 12 people. Four to six is the ideal number for maximum effectiveness. Go through your address books, cell phone directories, e-mail lists. Put together your Master Mind group with an eye for a diversity of backgrounds, skills, and personal styles. When you recruit a person for your Master Mind group, you can even ask that person to bring someone along whom they think might contribute. It can be someone you are loosely acquainted with—or someone you have never met. Having a few new people in the group creates maximum energy and excitement.

Training Great Minds

When you cultivate a support system, the most important thing is that you know what you need. You have to train your supporters to support you in the way that works for you. You have to be as specific as possible. Being specific will lead you—and your supporters—to the best possibilities for you.

Remember, as the conductor, you give your supporters the signals. Sometimes you want proactive solutions. You just want to take action steps. But other times, all you need is for someone to listen. It's your job to say sometimes, "Just listen. That's all I need right now."

There are several reasons good listening is so important. First, all of us derive great encouragement from knowing that our ideas are valued. This sense of encouragement is reinforced with eye contact and affirming acknowledgment ("yes," "I see," or just "uh-huh."). Second, good listening prompts the speaker to keep on talking, and the longer you talk the deeper you go.

It's vital that your listener avoid being shocked or judgmental about what you are saying. You must feel safe and know that nothing you say can be turned against you or taken outside of this conversation.

Listening—or receiving good listening—is a form of affirmation itself. Sometimes just a little goes a long way, even if it's only praise for being able to talk so deeply or for being able to take on change in the first place.

Finally, the best way to get a terrific support system is to give the kind of support you envision to your friends. It's the old adage, "To have a friend, be a friend."

Imagine, See, Be _____

Empathetic listening techniques take reflective listening one step beyond. With reflective listening, you replay to the other person what you thought she said, almost verbatim. With empathetic listening, you are trying to get into the skin of the person you are listening to. As you watch her compose her thoughts and you watch her face, listen for the emotion behind the words. Empathetic listening injects the emotional back into the equation: "I bet you felt pretty mad about that." Or "I bet that really hurt you."

Rules to Live By

Here are some specific strategies for creating a support system. Follow these, and you'll have a support system with bench strength!

◆ **Be generous in your heart.** Don't hold grudges. Forgive people of their shortcomings. Remind yourself that we are all just doing the best we can with what we know now.

◆ **Get the giving spirit.** Tune your heart to giving, making it a habit. Know that the positive energy that you give out amply renews itself. We'll delve into this more in Chapter 14.

◆ **Accept yourself now.** Don't tell yourself you will be okay once you reach your goal. You are okay now. Treating yourself this way opens the door for others to come nearer to you. Even if you believe you are harder on yourself and more accepting of others, when others sense negative beliefs you direct toward yourself, they feel the tension. They wonder if you have accepted them if you cannot accept yourself.

◆ **Surround yourself.** Cultivate warm, generous, accepting people who are proactive. Surround yourself with their energy, enthusiasm, and grace.

◆ **Appreciate.** Be vocal and be specific in your appreciation for others.

Power and Light

The third definition of *conductor* is a conduit for power. A wire conducts a current of electricity. It brings us power and light. Electricity illumines our worlds.

Think of electricity as the source. Think of yourself as the conduit. What are you allowing to happen? Are you allowing power to work in your life?

As we mentioned at the outset of this chapter, sometimes when you grab on to a live wire, it's hair-raising. You want to let go. It's just so powerful. Every instinct in your body is telling you to let go, while at the same time every instinct in your soul knows you just got to something good—that is, if it's just a metaphorical wire! The test is whether you will let it juice you.

This is often the reaction people have when they first access their spiritual self. But people who have had a spiritual practice for years also know that the further along the spiritual path you progress, the more powerful the lessons and experiences, and the deeper and more profound they become.

Conduct Your Spiritual Power

When you encounter the fear that comes with realizing you are the conductor in *this* area—your spiritual self and your personal spiritual curriculum—here's what to do:

◆ **Practice acknowledgment.** Acknowledge that the power comes from outside of you. Acknowledge that you are the conduit. Visualize yourself opening up to it. Visualize yourself doing this and *not getting burned*. Many spiritual traditions believe that spiritual power exists inside of each of us. In that regard, spiritual power is seen as something that can be recognized within and expressed, rather than accessed from without.

◆ **Practice gratitude.** When you see the positive energy of creative visualization working in your life, send it gratitude. Make it a habit to express gratitude whenever an opportunity comes your way.

◆ **Practice compassion.** Make a commitment to soften your heart, to see others as spiritual beings just like yourself. Make a point of seeing their inner heart.

◆ **Practice sending positive energy to others.** You can send positive energy to others—through prayer; by visualizing a world free of conflict; by supporting your leaders; by sending it to your influences, your mentors, and your role models. Make a point each day also to send this positive energy to your Master Mind group.

Super Connectors

Super connectors are people who are connected to infinitely more people than the average person. They are generally people who have an unlimited interest in everyone they meet. They are connected to many circles. They are the kind of people who can make things happen "in a flash" because they know just the person to call—or if they don't know the name, they know someone who can find out.

Who are you connected with? Let's find out. Make a list of your various communities. Everything counts, even the people who did gymnastics with your kids when they had six weeks of lessons. You can go back in time, too. Of what university are you an alumnus? Communities can be defined by institutions and organizations, such as your alma mater or your work team. They can meet regularly or just every once in a while. Think of every group, past or present, that comes to mind.

Finals Week

Now let's check in about how you're doing. For each Life Arena, rate your support system in that area on a scale of 1 to 10, with 10 being the highest.

	Ideas	Encouragement	Listening	Task Master	Out of the Box
Love					
Family					
Work					
Money					
Health					
Home					
Personal growth					
Spirituality					
Leisure/ rejuvenation					
Creative self-expression					

Allies and Supporters

So you see, you are your own best ally, and you have the ability to cultivate other allies and supporters. When you do begin to channel this new energy, you'll find you can power the engine to your dreams. In the chapters ahead, we'll show you more techniques for harnessing this power inherent in creative visualization.

The Least You Need to Know

- As the conductor of your vision-making, you have control over your destination and your timing.

- There are many facets to your personality. To make your visions, you must be a harmonious whole.

- Taking care of your physical capabilities is the underpinning of reaching your goals.

- Train the members of your support system in how they might give you support.

- To nurture your support system, remember to give what you want to receive.

- Use contacts with the super-connected people in your life to meet your goals.

Chapter 13

Seeing All the Layers

In This Chapter

- ◆ The four layers of energy
- ◆ Ch'i: Life's give and take
- ◆ Chakras: The color of power
- ◆ Epiphany: The ultimate energy shift

In creative visualization, you are turning an idea you have about where you want to go into form. You are quite literally turning mind into matter. You receive an inspiration, and you make it a reality. This is the manipulation of energy.

In this chapter, we will look at what is happening in creative visualization on an energetic level. We will also explore several energetic body theories to see how they might be useful in moving your vision from inspiration to reality. And understanding that, you will gain an understanding of the myriad of ways you can tie in the energy of your idea with the natural laws of energy in the universe. Just as Neo in the movie *The Matrix* can see energy, *you* can see and manipulate it, too.

The Energy of an Idea

It's helpful to understand that ideas and thoughts are energy. With the dawn of the atomic age came the scientific shift that matter is energy, too. At the atomic and subatomic level, all particles are made of energy. So everything is energy. Matter is vibrating at a slower level, and therefore becomes solid. It takes a form that we can see and we can manipulate. But thoughts and ideas are merely a lighter form of energy, and they are quick to change and take other forms.

Let's start with this parallel. An idea, let's say, is moisture in the air, something you can't see but might be able to feel in a humid climate. The moisture changes form through condensation. It becomes sweat dripping down the back of your neck, or dew on the blades of grass at daybreak. Similarly, water becomes solid (snowflake or a cube of ice) if the temperature reaches freezing. So our idea has gone from something we couldn't see to something we can hold in the palm of our hands.

What We Do—and Don't—Know

The movie *What the (Bleep) Do We Know?* explored through the blending of a story line, special effects, and documentary interviews the way idea, thoughts, and emotions work to create our reality. Starring actress Marlee Matlin, the story line showed how the energy of ideas and thoughts move out from the mental plane to work on the physical plane. In turn, Matlin's thoughts and emotions form the way she perceives her world—and therefore, the energy that she takes in and sends out.

The movie splices in scientists who try to explain this phenomenon—the power of our thoughts. Where do our memories reside, and where does the energy go? How is the energy of a memory expressed when activated by one of our senses, such as the smell of baking bread that reminds of us of childhood? What is the power of prayer, and how can the power of collective prayer change the crime rate in Washington, D.C.?

Somehow we are beginning to know that energy has a magnetic quality. Positive energy attracts positive energy, and negative energy attracts negative energy. Ideas and thoughts that are infused with intention gain power and become form. An idea that we empower with intention during creative visualization creates an image of form. This gives the idea more energy, and it vibrates on a stronger level. The idea draws physical energy to flow into the form we create in our visions, and eventually it manifests on the physical plane becoming our reality or something we call the truth.

Four Planes of Energy

Creative visualization works with energy on all layers of experience—the spiritual, emotional, mental, and physical. It may seem that it starts out in the mental—because that's the place ideas come from. But a vision can start out as energy on any other plane before it becomes an idea.

The most effective way to use creative visualization is to be aware of the energy moving through all the layers. It may not be natural to us in the Western world to understand how integrated these layers are. In the ayurvedic tradition of East Indian medicine and in traditional Chinese medicine, the body is not seen as operating separately from the mind, emotions, and spirit. They work together as a whole.

Each tradition rests on the belief that there is a life force that infuses the universe with energy. In India, it is called *prana*, or breath of life. In Chinese philosophy, it is called *ch'i*. Prana and ch'i form the basic understanding of how energy moves through the four planes of spiritual, mental, emotional, and physical being. Let's take a closer look at ch'i, prana, and energy forms of other belief systems and how they work with creative visualization.

Through the viewpoint of Eastern medicine, then, we can see that using creative visualization to manifest our dreams is an energy shift. So we'll also work with some techniques to create energy shifts that can lead to manifesting your vision. Body work such as massage therapy or disciplines such as yoga or tai chi are excellent ways to create energy shifts—but for that matter, so is vigorous exercise. What is happening on the physical plane can shift the energy dramatically on the mental, emotional, and spiritual planes. Moving energy in the body frees up space for our minds to imagine and implement new possibilities. Breath work in particular accesses the life force energy that links us to our higher selves.

Imagine, See, Be

Body therapy work such as massage, acupuncture, reiki, or breath work can provide significant shifts in your creative visualization work. Shifting the energy in the body can often get you unstuck as you are moving toward a goal. So schedule a session now!

Energy Pathways: The Ch'i of the Moment

In traditional Chinese medicine, optimum health depends on the optimum flow of ch'i. If there is pain in the body, practitioners believe, it's because the energy pathway is blocked. Acupuncture is just one way that traditional Chinese medicine removes the blocks along the energy pathways, called meridians.

Feng shui (pronounced *fung schway*), which literally translates as "wind/water," is the Chinese art of arranging your home for good ch'i. If you have good feng shui, you manifest prosperity, health, creativity, and rewarding relationships in your life. A well-placed potted plant or mirror can make a difference in bringing a relationship or career into your life—and many people swear by this, Carolyn being one of them. When she read that it was good to place images of pairs and the color pink in the relationship area of your home (each of the nine areas is called a *gua*), she moved a pink scarf and a sculpture of two figures dancing together, embracing one another, into that area. Within a few short weeks, she started a good relationship—ironically, with a sculptor who liked to dance! (We can't attest that feng shui is always this direct and clear!)

In Tai Chi or Qigong, you use movement to draw good ch'i through your body, enhancing your physical health, inner peace, and sense of personal power.

Look back to Chapter 3 at the yin/yang symbol pictured there. The yin/yang symbol illustrates how this energy of ch'i flows through the universe. Yin and yang are two complementary yet opposing forces. One continually is flowing into the other, becoming the other. In each one is the seed of the other. Yin needs yang to balance it, and vice versa. We commonly see yin and yang as the feminine and masculine energies, respectively, though there is more dimension to yin and yang than that. But it's a useful comparison, because men can't exist without women and vice versa. We balance each other out.

Traditional Chinese medicine defines diseases or pain in the body in terms of yin and yang. Every organ has either yin or yang energy. When an organ is out of balance, it needs to be balanced with the opposite energy.

A Time to Yin, A Time to Yang

The energies of yin and yang define the seasons and the forces of nature. Many believe the symbol itself arose from the observing of day turning to night and night turning to day. The ancient Chinese measured out the days on a circle and marked the length of the shadow of the sun. Connecting the dots resulted in the yin/yang curve. The "seeds" or "eyes" of the yin/yang symbol mark the winter and summer solstices. Winter solstice is the beginning of yang energy, when the earth turns forward, heading toward the light (at least in the Northern hemisphere). Summer solstice is the point at which the earth moves away from the sun, retreating.

Let's experiment with this idea that yin and yang mark the timing of the natural energy of the universe. We'll use yin and yang energy for a creative visualization, and you'll see what we mean. Let's say you have pushed for months with your creative visualization sessions but you are at the point where you feel you have done all that you can do. Say it's a career or relationship you want to manifest, and you have "put it all out there." You have a resume out to the companies you'd like to work for, or you have your profile up on an online dating service and you have been meeting people. Whatever it is, you feel you have left no stone unturned. Yet it just isn't clear to you what the next step is. Maybe it's time not for yang energy (direct action) but for yin energy (receiving, waiting).

Start by choosing a pair from this list, or think of one of your own:

◆ Light/dark

◆ Rain/ocean

◆ Heaven/Earth

◆ Sun/moon

◆ Movement/stillness

◆ Summer/winter

Begin your meditation by focusing on the yin/yang symbol. Keeping your breathing even and deep, focus on the dynamic energy of the two forces in constant movement, ever changing, one becoming the other then becoming the other again. Let your in and out breaths follow this pattern. Think about the pair of words you have chosen. See them not as distinct opposite but as two interdependent forces continually flowing into each other. Your breath is parallel to this: With each inhale, your lungs fill with oxygen. Your blood receives the oxygen and sends nourishment through your body. With each exhale, you release carbon dioxide, which nourishes the plants and trees that surround you. The plants and trees receive nourishment from the carbon dioxide and produce oxygen, and the cycle begins anew.

As you hold this image in your mind, feel the energy flowing. Move your focus back to the word pairs you chose from the list. Feel the movement from light to dark to light, from rain to ocean to rain. Hold yourself there in the

> **Affirmations**
>
> I am heaven. I am earth. I am cloud. I am rain. I am action. I am stillness. The energy of the universe flows in me. I allow myself to receive this energy, to let it flow through me.

harmony that exists within this dynamic. Say, "In this constant flow, I find peace. I see that all is as it was meant to be."

Now invite this energy to reside in you. Create in your mind's eye a vessel in your body to receive this flow. Imagine the light descending to dark, the rain being received by the ocean, or the stillness holding the movement. You have put it out there—all of your energy. Now it is time to wait, to receive. It was time to yang; now it's time to yin.

Feng Shui: Wood and Water

Remember the Zen Buddhist "chop wood, carry water" metaphor from Chapter 9? No matter how dedicated you are to visualizing and meditating on your goal, sometimes you just need to take action. Sometimes you need to chop wood and carry water.

Feng shui can be an excellent way to move the physical energy around and create big changes on the other planes of your life, the emotional, mental, and spiritual. The principle of feng shui is based on the five Chinese elements of wood, water, fire, metal, and earth, and each of these elements attracts energy at a certain vibration.

Use feng shui to empower your creative visualizations.

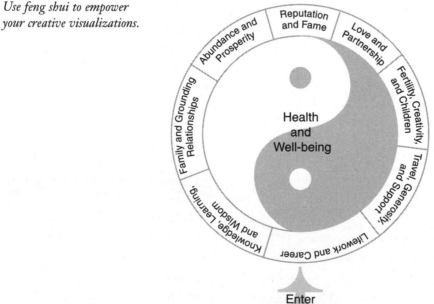

Feng shui divides your living space into nine areas called guas (or really, any personal space: your desk, your car). The center gua is health. The entrance of your home is career, and the others move around a circle clockwise: skills and knowledge, family, prosperity, fame, relationships, creativity and children, travel and helpful people, arriving back to career. Each area is enhanced by certain elements—for instance, career is enhanced by water, so it's good to put a fountain in your foyer or anything that evokes the image of water, such as a painting of a waterfall, seashells, or mirrors.

Entire books exist on the topic, including *The Complete Idiot's Guide to Feng Shui, Third Edition* (Alpha Books, 2005). You can hire a feng shui expert to come and do a makeover on your home. But for purposes of this book and creative visualization, let's experiment with the energy of feng shui in connection with your vision.

Say your vision relates to career. Other areas that might be associated with career are skills and knowledge and prosperity. So we'll give you some Feng Shui 101 tips for those areas. We already know that a fountain in your foyer is good for career. We'll add that it's important to make sure your front door doesn't stick, and you should never have a potted plant on your front porch. That keeps the vital ch'i from entering your house. It's also good to have the color black somewhere in your career area. For prosperity, it's good to have the color purple. The elements that enhance prosperity are wood and water.

Commit now to spending a weekend clearing out the clutter from your skills and knowledge area. Take a trip to the home decorating store for a fountain or mirror for your career area. Take a trip to the home improvement store for some paint. Put on your work clothes, roll up your sleeves and get to work on moving the energy around your home. As you work, visualize this energy starting to flow. Visualize your career dream manifesting in your life.

Chakras: Your Power Source

Ancient Indian seers were the first to identify a system of energy centers known as the chakras. Through these energy centers, seven of which are located in the body, prana, or life force energy, flows. Chakras are like energy intake centers. They are seen as whirling pools of light, each vibrating on a different level, and each with a color. In Sanskrit, chakra means "wheel" or "circle."

The chakras are aligned with your spine, starting with the base of the spine and rising up to the crown of your head. The lower the chakra, the denser the energy and the lower the frequency at which it spins. The chakras follow the colors of the rainbow, with the first chakra being red and the seventh being violet.

The seven chakras have many associations you can work with to enhance a practice of creative visualization.

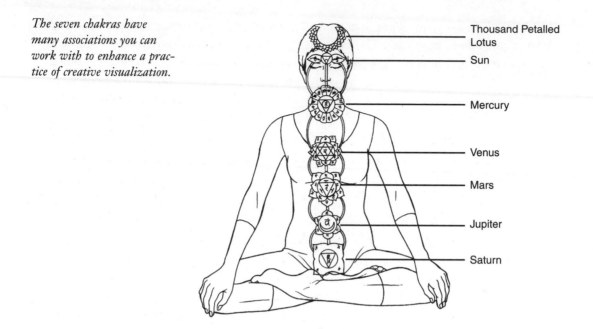

Thousand Petalled Lotus

Sun

Mercury

Venus

Mars

Jupiter

Saturn

Here's a quick rundown of where the chakras play into creative visualization:

◆ **First—survival chakra.** This chakra governs your basic survival needs: your family, your roots, the way you identify yourself, your will and self, your shelter. When this chakra's energy is good, you feel secure and grounded. You feel provided for and taken care of. In the spiritual sense, you know that we are all one. This chakra is centered on your tailbone, at the base of the spine or your rectum. Color: Red.

◆ **Second—allegiance chakra.** This chakra governs sex, money, and creativity. We call it the allegiance chakra because it's where you form your allegiances with power and love. This is where you form many of your basic agreements about what you will allow in your life—your beliefs about creating and taking risks and who you will be with. When this chakra is healthy, you are resilient and courageous and you treat others with honor. This chakra is centered just above your pubic bone. Color: Orange.

◆ **Third—integrity chakra.** This chakra is sometimes called the self-esteem or personal power chakra. It's where you get your gut instinct, your sense of what's right for you. It governs your interactions with other people, so it also influences your sense of what's the right thing to do with others. This is where you define your code of ethics, and it's also where you define your personal boundaries. It's located in the solar plexus. Color: Yellow.

◆ **Fourth—love chakra.** This chakra is your heart center. It's where compassion resides, and because of that, it rules the process of transformation. Compassion softens everything. This is the center of forgiveness and release. Your heart is the keeper of wisdom. When your heart chakra is open, your life is infused with a love that animates your existence, giving your life flavor and texture. Because the fourth chakra is the center, is it the link between the lower and upper chakras and the center of power. You need your heart chakra in order to manifest in your life. Quite naturally, it's centered on the heart. Color: Green.

◆ **Fifth—voice chakra.** In this chakra, you express your choices—your love, your allegiance, your power, your needs. This is where you are who you want to be and know you really are. This is the chakra where you make the vows to bring into your life what you want. This is the chakra of affirmation. It's centered on the throat. Color: Blue.

◆ **Sixth—imagination chakra.** This is the chakra of wisdom. Because it's the center of the imagination, thinking and visioning, it's quite essential to creative visualization. Its energy affects your ability to see, articulate, and trust your vision. It is here that you gain the energy to focus your mind on your inspiration. It is the instrument through which you gain the skills to focus your attention and turn the energy of ideas into form. Here, the seed of inspiration (which, as you'll see, comes from the seventh chakra) is transformed into a workable plan. It is centered in the "third eye," the center of the forehead. Color: Indigo.

◆ **Seventh—inspiration chakra.** This chakra is imbued with spiritual and creativity energy. It is the place where inspirations are born. Its energy is light. It's here that we are able to see things afresh, with the innocent eyes of a child, with no preconceived notions or limitations. This chakra vibrates most closely with the spiritual forces of the universe, so it has the energy of limitless power. Suddenly, it all seems possible. This is the place where we can make dreams comes true. It is centered on the crown of the head. Color: Violet.

The chakras often work in pairs, with the first working with the seventh, the second working with the sixth and the third working with the fifth. So it's useful to know that when you are working with the imagining and planning of the sixth chakra during creative visualization, you are also working with the second chakra. That only makes sense, doesn't it? How many of your ambitions and dreams are about sex, money, and power? But seriously, it is true that when your imagination is paired with the place where you store your deepest desires, only great things can happen.

Each chakra represents a power source that you may draw upon for moving toward your vision. Each chakra also represents a life lesson. Once you have mastered the life lessons of each chakra, you will find you are living your life at optimum energy.

Take a few moments to study these descriptions of the chakras. Which are strengths for you? Which might represent lessons you need to learn? Evaluate yourself on the following:

Wisdom Well

Wisdom is finding the balance between head and heart, upper chakras and lower chakras, earth and sky, masculine and feminine, joy and sorrow, yin and yang, energy and rest, human and divine, cosmos and psyche.

—Matthew Fox, author and Episcopalian priest

- ◆ Living in the present moment
- ◆ Seeking only the truth
- ◆ Surrendering your will to Divine Will
- ◆ Speaking your truth
- ◆ Loving with compassion
- ◆ Honoring yourself
- ◆ Honoring others
- ◆ Seeing yourself as part of a whole
- ◆ Being who you say you are
- ◆ Seeing yourself as whole

Energy Shift #1: Imagination Meets Your Deepest Desires

This exercise will help you make your second and sixth chakras work in synch. Your sixth chakra is largely the one we have been working with as we envision a goal, send positive thought-energy to it and give form to our plans. To enhance the power of creative visualization, draw upon the power of the second chakra, the power of creativity, the source of your most cherished desires.

Here you explore where you limit your creativity. Where are you afraid to take risks? Remember that creative visualization is not changing something that exists. It is creating something new and fresh—something that did not exist before. You are giving birth to something new.

To create is to share. To create is to realize all of your gifts. Creating is about giving and receiving. Where are you afraid to give? This is where you look at your allegiances. To whom are you willing to give, and how much? Look at your most intimate relationships. Where there is pain you'll find some of the ways you have failed to give—or give wisely, in alignment with your truest desires. Where are you afraid to receive? Receiving, as wonderful as it is, may be the hardest of all, because it means being vulnerable.

For the following exercise, you will need a partner with whom you feel safe. This is someone you know well and trust, someone you know would not harm you and would cherish your deepest desires. Lie down, and allow your partner to place both hands on your lower abdomen, just above the pubic bone and above the belly button, with light to medium pressure. Allow his hands to merge into your abdomen. Hold in your mind the picture of his hands melting into you, fusing with the inside of you. He in turn visualizes the same. Notice when both of you feel the true merge. Now, switch roles.

CAUTION

Don't Panic, Focus!

What if the energy shift exercises here unleash a tumult of emotions? It's entirely common that when we first examine the emotions linked to the survival and sexual chakras, strong emotions present themselves. If any of these exercises brings up information that is too disturbing, don't face it alone. Find a good therapist with whom you feel comfortable.

Energy Shift #2: Fit for Survival

In Chapter 12 we had you assess your physical needs. Take a look at how you rated yourself in those areas. Write in your Creative Visualization Journal about your beliefs in these areas. Select some of these that you'd like to change.

Return to the family tree you drew in Chapter 7. We were somewhat focused on the negative traits of family members before, in an effort to understand that we did not come into the world unburdened. This time we want to also look at the positive. So take a moment and look at each name. For all of those that you remember, add a positive trait or two. List traits that you have, would like to have, or think are especially important.

Get three containers. You may use plastic jugs, grocery sacks, shoe boxes—whatever is handy. Label one container TRASH. This is for traits that are absolutely unhelpful. You don't want them. Your relatives who had them didn't want them. Out they go!

The second container is for NEUTRAL. These are nice traits. You have no special feeling for them one way or another. An example would be having red hair or being the middle child.

The last container is the stuff you really want. Label it GREAT. Maybe you already have some of these traits or maybe a parent or a distant relative has them. At any rate, you want these to be a part of you.

Look at your family tree. What traits do you see that can go right into the TRASH? So put them there. They get no more attention. Identify the neutral traits in your family tree, too, dropping them in the NEUTRAL container.

Now for the best part—the keepers. Write down traits in your ancestors that you admire and put them in the GREAT folder. Dwell on each one as you drop it in. Take a minute to appreciate the good traits that you inherited—lustrous hair, a nice shape, being tall. Thank the ancestor who gave you those traits or thank your higher self that they belong to you.

Energy Shift #3: Integrating the Eighth Chakra

Sometimes our survival needs seem so vital that they might overrule our good intentions. We can think of our lower chakras as being the more instinctive areas. When something is out of balance in these areas, we tend to be more reactive. That is, we fail to react from our wisest self.

From our description of the chakras, you'll remember that the heart chakra is the link between the lower chakras and the higher chakras that rule the mind and spirit. Another link is the eighth chakra, an energy center that is outside the body, generally centered above the crown of the head. Because it is outside the body, it transcends the individual. The eighth chakra is the link between the individual consciousness and the collective consciousness. This is where some of the natural laws of the spirit link up with the body. This is where you can access your higher wisdom. Think of the eighth chakra as the collective body of Divine Wisdom.

> **Affirmations**
>
> I hold within me the clarity of my purpose. I am watching it as it unfolds.

Use this meditation to link the higher consciousness of the eighth chakra with your higher consciousness of the upper chakras and your lower chakras of survival. When used in conjunction with breath work and massage, it can be very powerful. Do this lying down in a comfortable spot.

With each breath, imagine drawing a nourishing breath down into your body, pulling it to your feet and beyond. With each exhale, let it rise up the length of your body, going past the crown of your head. Continue breathing in this way, envisioning over your body a beautiful petal of emerald green and sea blue. The petal floats above your body as your breath flows, following the energy path of your breath from the eighth chakra, pulling it down beyond your feet. Feel the gentleness of this petal, unifying all of your chakras.

Stay in this meditation for about seven minutes, allowing yourself to let your mind gently touch the visions you have been working on. Don't let them take over. Keep your primary focus on your breath and the beautiful petal. But let your visions meld into the energy flow of this beautiful petal.

When the flow is good, collapse your beautiful petal into a blue butterfly. Imagine her wings caressing you. Now let this beautiful blue butterfly grow smaller, to the size of a real butterfly. Place it on your abdomen. Let her merge into your abdomen, your allegiance chakra. Imagine tucking this beautiful butterfly within you. She is the vehicle for all of your dreams to fly. She will be there when you need her.

Epiphany: The Light of Dawn

The ultimate energy shift is an *epiphany*. This is when a realization touches us so deeply that the shift is permanent. We see the world with new eyes. It's the shift of perception that births a miracle. What we believed to be impossible now is entirely within our grasp. What we were unable to comprehend before is now clearly under-

stood. Now that we understand it in a whole new way, we can create a whole new way of being. When we trace the root word of epiphany back to the Greek, we find it means "to manifest."

Deeper Meaning

An **epiphany** is a profound realization that provides lasting insight. It often results in dramatic new understanding and significant changes on the inner and outer paths.

We can experience an epiphany through a profound experience, through the energy shift of body work, through a spiritual awakening—in just about any way, as long as we are open to it.

If it comes through an experience, it may be called a "quantum experience." This happens when your whole paradigm shifts and you experience new lasting, life-changing behaviors, based on new understandings that have become a part of your very soul. You leap to a whole new plane of experience, and you are not going back. This is the mountaintop experience. This need not be brought on by a life crisis or a catharsis, as we have commonly thought. Something must make the "lights go on." For some it comes after a long period of study; for others there must be a strong motivating factor—your intent.

For some it is an out-of-the-blue mind-altering experience. That person may not know anytime soon why that experience was her gift, but it becomes clearer as time goes by. Sometimes this sort of experience comes when we are in deep grief, or in a state of profound joy. The point is that we cannot know when or why this might happen to us and we may not understand why we have been given this gift but it is the most profoundly mysterious experience that a person can have.

Author Caroline Myss defines epiphany as "a sudden illumination of our intimate union with the Divine." All of a sudden, we realize we have a greater power source. We see beyond our limitations. We see that we are united with the Divine, not separate. Many people who have this kind of experience define it as a comprehension of union with God and all living creatures.

The Energy Way

So you see it is a matter of channeling the energy within and around you in the direction of your goal. We have primarily worked with the mind and the imagination, but there are more tools available to use in creative visualization, if we understand that energy works on several planes. When you harness the power of that positive energy on all levels, you optimize the power of creative visualization.

The Least You Need to Know

- ◆ Ideas and thoughts are energy. They become form and create our perception of reality.

- ◆ Optimize your creative visualization sessions by optimizing your flow of ch'i, the life force energy of the universe.

- ◆ Body therapy work such as Tai Chi, Qigong, acupuncture, or massage can create shifts in your energy and often get you unstuck if you are meeting obstacles on your journey toward your goal.

- ◆ Attending to the arrangement of certain objects in your home, such as mirrors or plants, can improve the positive energy flow in your environment, and ultimately bring positive energy toward meeting your goal.

- ◆ The chakras are whirling centers of energy in the body. By working with these energy centers, you can enhance each as a power source for creative visualization.

- ◆ An epiphany is a dramatic shift in energy in which a profound realization takes place.

Chapter 14

Life-Affirming Visualization

In This Chapter

- ◆ Identifying nonintentionality
- ◆ Making compassionate agreements
- ◆ Eradicating grudges and resentments
- ◆ Letting generosity flow

Discovering creative visualization is a little bit like looking down and seeing that you are wearing ruby slippers. Like Dorothy in *The Wizard of Oz*, you have had the power to go where you want to go all along. Close your eyes, visualize Kansas, and click your heels together.

But with this magic power comes an obligation. You must remember it's not all about you. Your creative visualizations must always support the higher good. In your relationships with others, with your community, and the world, you have an obligation to create visions that affirm the best life for all of us.

In this chapter, we will explore how to use creative visualization with compassionate intentionality. We will show you where you can take it to its highest good—to create unity in your heart and in your community.

Intentionality vs. Nonintentionality

Speed kills. When you are going high-speed toward your goal, you not only miss out on the mindfulness we discussed in Chapter 11, but you also lose sight of compassion. Here's a scene: you are running 15 minutes late for a theater production. You know that they won't seat you if you don't get there before the curtain rises, and that would mean you miss the first act. But even though it's Sunday, you run into a snarl of mall traffic. Then just as you get clear of that, you encounter a parade of earth-moving equipment going 15 miles per hour in a 45 mph zone. If you are tempted to think of the mall shoppers and backhoe drivers as "stupid," then you're only human.

But remember that when you rush at a breakneck speed, living life like it's an extreme sport, the people around you can only fail you. They can't go as fast as you—or as fast as you think they should go. Stunningly, they think differently from you. They are going somewhere else. What gets lost in this is compassion.

Deeper Meaning

Nonintentionality is at work when you get results other than what you desired. Despite your best intentions, you hurt someone or you got yourself "in a pickle." If you got results that seem to be the opposite of what you intended, examine whether you are giving energy to the underlying intentions of your subconscious.

To move into life-affirming creative visualization is to really take a hard look at where all your intentions lie. Closely examine the arenas of your life where you are not conscious—where you are allowing *nonintentionality* to influence your practice.

Nonintentionality is showing up in your life when you say, "I didn't mean for it to turn out this way." It happens when we inadvertently hurt another person, or when we intend to help someone but fail to do so, or do so clumsily. Nonintentionality shows up in your life when you have not taken into account how your actions—or omissions—might be perceived by another person.

We realize that's a terribly high standard, and no one can avoid occasionally obfuscating the truth. We're all human. Nor can we live our lives concerned about how others perceive us. But we should be conscious that our intention—and lack of intention—ultimately does matter.

On a deeper level, nonintentionality happens when you aren't absolutely certain you desire your goal, and you sabotage it. It happens when you let the concerns of others constrain you, perhaps without realizing it, and you hold yourself back from your truest desire. Call it fear of failure or fear of success. Call it fear of abandonment or fear of exclusion. These fears can be strong forces that undermine our intentions.

Doing Your Best

In Don Miguel Ruiz' best-selling book, *The Four Agreements* (see Appendix B), one of his rules to live by is "Always do your best." When you adapt this axiom, you commit to being conscious and intentional in your actions. That's not to say you commit to being a perfect life-affirming being, destined for accelerated sainthood. It doesn't mean that you always do the best that any human being can do; it means you do the best that *you* can do. You may, several years later, realize what you could have done differently. But that doesn't mean you didn't do your best. You did the best that you knew how at the time.

And that is where you can bring compassion back into play. Be compassionate with yourself. And remember: we are all doing the best we can with who we are now.

A friend of Carolyn's (we'll call her Tamara) once invoked the Four Agreements (which we'll discuss in a few pages) when she said she hadn't been able to keep in touch with a mutual friend who had just had a baby. The baby was born with only one kidney and had to be hospitalized. At the time, Tamara was helping her elderly mother after her father's death, going back and forth between New Mexico and Texas. But Tamara expressed regret—and more than a little guilt—that she hadn't contacted their friend. Tamara said, "I wasn't doing my best." But it was her best at the time, given the demands of her own family.

Being compassionate with yourself means accepting your best when it's less than your ideal. It means accepting your limitations and finding your best within those circumstances. The key word here is "can." Do the best that you *can* do. At that time, Tamara couldn't do more for their mutual friend other than send her good wishes via Carolyn. When you are this compassionate with yourself, it opens the door in your heart to be this compassionate with everyone else.

Metta: The Buddhist Practice of Compassion

You can combine the Buddhist meditation practice of metta with a creative visualization to bring more compassion into your life. Metta is a world from the Pali language that means "lovingkindness." It is based on the principle that you must make friends with yourself first, embracing yourself in love and affection. Having done that, you are ready to let that love and affection ripple out to others and the world.

Start by visualizing yourself held in the white wings of an angel. Repeat the following phrases:

May I be free from danger.

May I be happy.

May I be healthy.

May I live with ease.

Next, imagine another person, someone who inspires you and supports you. You may want to make it specifically someone who is supporting you through the creative visualizations you have used in this book, but it is not necessary. Visualize this person in the arms of the angel. Say:

May you be free from danger.

May you be happy.

May you be healthy.

May you live with ease.

Now move to a friend, someone with whom you have exchanged kindnesses over the years. As you visualize that friend in the arms of the angel, repeat the four phrases.

After that, visualize someone to whom you feel neutral—your barista at Starbucks, the crossing guard at your children's school, or the man you saw walking his dog in the park. You neither like nor dislike this person, and you probably don't know her or his name. Visualize that person in the arms of the angel, and direct the four phrases to him or her.

Now you are ready to extend the lovingkindness to someone who has hurt you. Think of someone with whom you have experienced conflict. This person has been difficult to extend compassion to because she may have threatened you. You may feel pain, anger, or fear when you think of this person. Know that visualizing sending compassion to this person is not condoning her behavior, nor is it agreeing to allow the hurt to happen again.

 Wisdom Well

When you begin to touch your heart or let your heart be touched, you begin to discover that it's bottomless, that it doesn't have any resolution, that this heart is huge, vast, and limitless. You begin to discover how much warmth and gentleness is there, as well as how much space.

—Pema Chodron, Tibetan Buddhist monk and author

You may or may not be ready to forgive her. Your goal is to access your capacity for unconditional love. Now visualize her in the arms of the angel. Say:

May you be free from danger.

May you be happy.

May you be healthy.

May you live with ease.

Finally, visualize all of us—all six billion of us—in the arms of the angel, without conditions, distinctions, or exceptions. There is no fine print. It is all-inclusive. Say:

May all beings be free from danger.

May all beings be happy.

May all beings be healthy.

May all beings live with ease.

You may not be able to do all progressions in one session. You may want to build up slowly. By spending more time focusing on each one, you magnify the power of your compassion. By the time you get to the person with whom you have experienced conflict, you may find it easier to extend compassion—because you have already experienced it for yourself.

Your Underlying Motivations

Take a good hard look at the goals you have set in your 10 Life Arenas. What are the motivations behind them? Would achieving these goals hurt anyone in any way? Would it call on a loved one to make a change that he hasn't bought into? Would it ask her to make a sacrifice? What unintended results are possible?

Here's an example: let's say that your goal in your work Life Arena is to change careers. That might mean that, for a few years, you are going back to school. Your spouse might have to be the primary breadwinner for a while, and he might see a little less of you as you manage the coursework. How does this affect him? Is he on board with this idea?

Your concern for his feelings should not limit you from pursuing a life-affirming goal. But it's important to be aware of those feelings. You may use creative visualization to manifest in all of your arenas the skills to navigate the changes in your life.

Your Agreements

Let's get back to your agreements. Agreements are beliefs that you have adapted and incorporated in how you make choices for your life. What are your agreements? They are actually fairly easy to find. They are in what you are resisting. What are you struggling with, and why? On some level, you believe that you must struggle to manifest your best life.

In the Ruiz book *The Four Agreements*, the agreements are:

1. Be impeccable with your word.

2. Don't take anything personally.

3. Don't make assumptions.

4. Always do your best.

It might be useful to think of your agreements as poison management. Ruiz talks about not taking the poison when other people seek to diminish us or limit us from reaching our goals and manifesting our best selves. "Don't take anything personally" means remembering that when people criticize you, restrict you, or challenge you, it's not about you. It's about them. It's about their pain. It's about their recognition of their limitations. (The irony is that the more focused you are on your creative visualization practice, the more others may see their own limitations. The more you stay true to your practice, the more criticism you may invite. Again, this is not about you and whether you have to cast aside your dreams because others do not always wish you well.)

"Not taking the poison" means recognizing when criticism is not productive. If you agree with the nonconstructive criticism, you will take it in, and then you have taken the poison. The best way to immunize yourself against the poison? Stay true to your vision.

 **Imagine, See, Be** _____

One key to staying centered is perspective-shifting. Breath work and body work such as massage or yoga can create these perspective shifts because they change the energy within your body. The key to staying centered is to shift back to that place where all your selves—physical, emotional, mental, and spiritual—are integrated. See your life through the long view. View it through other lenses: cultural, historical, symbolic, or archetypal.

Grudges

Staying true to your vision means staying pure in your heart. You can immunize yourself from emotional poison by not letting grudges take hold. Think of someone that you hold a grudge against. You may think you have forgiven that person and have agreed to let bygones be bygones, but if every time you think of that person, you remember what she or he did, then you haven't.

Create a visualization that portrays that person in a whole new light. Imagine the whole of her life. She is not just this one deed that is your focus. Imagine her in all of her Life Arenas, sometimes being impeccable with her word, sometimes not. Imagine her giving and receiving love. Imagine her as her soul mate, her mother, or her children must see her. Do not see this as hypocrisy, that these individuals who love her have failed to see the deceitful person that she is. Resist the temptation to go there. Imagine that the way they see her is the core of her, and this one slight against you is the exception. This is a moment when she was not doing her best.

What if someone is holding a grudge against you? Remember to not take it personally. It's about that person's inability to work through it, not about you. Not taking it personally means not absorbing another person's weakness. Yes, by all means, do what you can to clear the air with this person. But know that each of us processes in our own time. If you let this grudge become an agreement, then you have let this person's weakness become your weakness.

These affirmations can help you on your way to letting go of a grudge. Practice writing some of your own:

I surrender my need to protect myself now. I surrender my thoughts about how _____ has failed me, and I commit these thoughts to healing.

I am releasing _____ now.

I am feeling this grudge lifting from my heart. My heart grows lighter and lighter every day.

Anyway, you get the idea!

Janna: Courageous Visualizations

Janna, who was in her mid-20s, came to Shari for therapy because her uncle had sexually abused her. She was having nightmares about him and was afraid he would be at family functions. It was the first time she had told anyone about the abuse. It had begun when she was about 8 and ended when she was about 12. At that time he moved on to her younger sister, who had never spoken to anyone but Janna about the abuse.

After assuring herself that this man did not have any access to children, which would have required intervention, Shari set about to use creative visualization to equip Janna to meet the emotional challenges of this wound. Janna's story is an excellent example of someone who took steps to visualize and realize an emotional goal.

Shari asked Janna to describe her uncle now. Janna replied he was now disabled, in a wheelchair, hardly able to speak or move after several strokes. He had to be fed and wore "diapers." Shari and Janna developed a strategy of envisioning the uncle not as he was when she was a child but as the sick and helpless old man he was now. Every time Janna had a nightmare or memory, she switched to visualizing him as a disabled man. That took a lot of the power out of her fears. Gradually Janna began to see him as this frail man, no longer acting as an abuser. Janna even talked about who she thought must have abused him.

The next step was to equip Janna to attend family functions. Janna told her mother and father what had happened to her and her sister. After the initial shock and grief, they supported her wholeheartedly. They decided that uncle would simply not be invited to most family functions. On the occasions where an invitation couldn't be avoided, they made sure that Janna knew she was empowered. Here's how:

- She didn't have to attend.

- Her mother always told her if the uncle was expected to be there.

- She had a safety word or phrase. When she said that word to a trusted someone, that person would help her make a graceful exit.

- She told her family that when he died she would not be attending the funeral, nor would she visit him should he be in the hospital.

Staying in the Light

The pop-folk duo The Indigo Girls sings about the immense power of darkness, saying it has a hunger that's insatiable. They go on to say of lightness that its call is hard to hear. There are times when the conflicts in our lives cause so much pain that it can seem that darkness is more powerful than light. But it only takes the light of one candle to change that. That is, it only takes a little willingness to hear the call to lightness.

For your next creative visualization session, you will need a mirror and a candle. Light a candle and sit before the mirror in its glow. Envision yourself in the light. Meditate on this image for a few moments.

Write affirmations for this exercise. They might go something like this:

I know this light is more powerful than the dark.

I invite this light to shed wisdom and insight on my path.

I invite this light to overtake any darkness I may encounter.

I dwell in this light.

Wisdom Well

Human virtues, like glistening jewels, or beauty itself, ask for nothing in return for what they give.

—Marcus Aurelius, Roman emperor and philosopher (121–180 A.D.)

Whenever you are having trouble believing in the light and you are dwelling in the darkness, return to this visualization.

Change Yourself, Change the World

Margaret Mead once said, "Never doubt that a small group of thoughtful, committed citizens can change the world. Indeed, it is the only thing that ever has." When our thoughts turn to global matters, the tasks can seem arduous. Can creative visualization bring about world peace? Render a world in which there is a reverence for nature? Create better schools? Reduce crime? Heal others?

The answer is yes, and we devote all of Chapter 23 to global visualizations. But here we will lay the groundwork for global changes by working on change within, focusing on these practices: acceptance, gratitude, humility, generosity, being, and giving.

Being, Doing, and Having

Shakti Gawain identifies three arenas of life activity: being, doing, and having. Most of us spend most of our energy on doing and having. Doing is the outer path of creative visualization—making things happen. Having is what we want—that's the ultimate goal of creative visualization, to reach our dream. Being is just living, being conscious, being mindful, being aware that we are alive in this present moment. Being is contentment with what exists now.

How does cultivating this state of being and bringing it in balance with doing and having affect the world around us? It is said that the path to global peace begins with peace within, and we believe it is true. When you are content with what is, you bring that contentment to others around you. You practice gratitude, and others see the fruits of gratitude in your life. You practice acceptance, and others feel your centeredness. You practice a generosity of spirit because you feel complete. Your completeness completes others around you.

Another way to think about it is: your need to "take" from others is diminishing. You have everything you need. Through your creative visualizations, you are bringing into your life what you want to manifest—and with it comes peace and contentment. Take a few moments now to build some affirmations around these concepts:

- Finding peace within

- Practicing gratitude daily

- Feeling alive

- Being present

- Feeling complete

Outflowing

One of the side benefits of creative visualization is a completeness that enables us to give more generously. You are "well fed" because you are pursuing your highest ambitions. You believe there is enough for everyone. You are no longer starved, focused on doing and having. You enjoy just being, because you inhabit a life that you have chosen. You have visualized it and manifested it in your life.

Many people believe they are receiving so little—and that what's out there is finite—that they keep a stranglehold on the small amount of love and affection they have in their lives. Outflowing is a conscious decision to reverse the flow. Make notes in your Creative Visualization Journal about what you have manifested in your life so far. You see! You are so well taken care of. There is an infinite supply of love, fulfillment, and contentment. You have found your inner source of happiness.

Channel this flow outward, and you'll find you only make room for more to flow in. What are ways you can give? Find ways to share your appreciation of others throughout your day. Give away possessions you no longer need. In Samoa, people think of possessions as simply tools. If you are not using it, you give it to someone who can use it. Notice what happens after you start giving like this. Notice what it manifests in your life. It will come back to you multiplied.

To write affirmations about outflowing, build from these key phrases:

♦ Infinite supply of love

♦ Finding your inner source of happiness

♦ Feeling "fed"

♦ Knowing that you are well taken care of

♦ Experiencing love and affection

♦ Multiplying this feeling

What kind of affirmations did you come up with? Remember that generosity is self-renewing. You will find powerful energy in that. Find that joy simply in being generous without expecting reciprocation or acknowledgment.

> **Wisdom Well**
>
> An open and loving heart, seeking a higher good without selfish motive, without any shadow of negativity or harm, can invoke a powerful manifesting energy in order to accomplish its goal.
>
> —Brian Weiss, psychiatrist and author of *Same Soul, Many Bodies*

Unification

Finally, one key step to creating this outflowing is to see yourself as part of a whole with all of humanity. There is a bumper sticker that says U&IR1, meaning "you and I are one." We only think we are separate beings—that is the illusion. We are part of a greater whole, all parts working together. When you see yourself this way, you drop out of all sense of selfishness. You don't need to protect yourself from others.

By the same token, you recognize that any harm you do to another is doing harm to yourself. When viewed that way, it starts to seem like your misguided efforts to right a perceived wrong are backfiring, doesn't it?

Too often, as we go through this world, we see ourselves as separate. We are separated from one another by separate bodies. We drive around in our separate cars, thinking that we are driving defensively and responsibly and all the other drivers are "crazy." We live in separate houses, each with our own little sofa, television, and phone. Sometimes we lose sight of the fact that everybody has to deal with the same set of challenges, whether they are rich or poor: waking up in the morning, showering, feeding oneself, dressing one pant leg at a time. When we're hungry, we all get rumbly in the tummy, as Winnie the Pooh would say.

The Buddhist meditation of tonglen is about the practice of "sending" and "taking." It moves the focus from ourselves as separate beings to ourselves as vessels that receive the life force energy of the universe. By moving the focus away from ourselves as separate—which by turn creates self-absorption—we remove the obstacles that block our natural sense of kindness. We start to put others first.

Tonglen works in four steps. The first step is, quite simply, stillness. You create a gap in your thoughts, an empty space. Take a deep breath. Allow there to be a crack in your life that lets in fresh air. In this step, give permission to see something beyond yourself, something bigger and higher.

In the second step, shift your meditation to your emotions. As you hold that awareness, breathe in, focusing on the taking in. (In previous meditations, we have used the inhale as the breath that takes in nourishment; in this meditation, though, the mental shift is that as you breathe in, you are taking energy from the universe to tend to your emotions. This is needy energy. It has a taint of selfishness to it. You are grabbing what you can get.) Now, as you breathe out, send out cool, clear, refreshed energy. Imagine this energy flowing out of you, invigorating the world around you. This is the sending energy.

On the third step, begin with a specific issue in your mind's eye, an emotional challenge that is manifesting in your life at this moment. Maybe someone is directing aggression toward you. In the "taking" and "sending," you transform that energy they send to you, and you imagine it being redirected. As you breathe in, take in that person's aggression. Remember, you are not going to take the poison. You are not going to let this aggression form a belief in you that you will keep and use in your operating system. You merely take it in because it *is*. It does not change the core of you. As you breathe out, send out a wish to that person, a compassionate intention that the person be free from anger, fear, and doubt. Visualize that person now.

This is the essential concept. First, you breathe in what you do not like, then you breathe out the energy of what you do like. Breathe in the attack on you; breathe out your soothing of the attack. Next, if you feel angry about the attack, breathe in the anger you feel; breathe out your affirmation that you will not take the attack personally. Choose not to send it out in the world. With each breath cycle, go deeper into the layers of your emotions.

Affirmations

I am breathing in only what I need to nourish myself. I am sending out purity, kindness, and compassion.

The fourth step is to broaden the reach of your tonglen practice. As you breathe in the aggression of the person who attacked you, imagine that expanding to all aggression, everywhere on the planet. As you breathe out, include in your visualization everyone who has suffered. Visualize all those souls being soothed.

A Whole New World

Tonglen and other life-affirming visualizations we have used in this chapter have the effect of lifting creative visualization out of the self. No longer does it feel like you are just one person wielding a magic wand, trying to get the blessings of the universe to fall your way. You begin to see yourself, and the blessings that can come into your life through using creative visualization, as part of a whole. The positive energy you receive is part of a continuum. As you take it in, you let it flow outward. As you receive, you send it out again, expanding it to others, freeing them to receive the blessings, too.

The Least You Need to Know

- ◆ Creative visualization should never be used for harm. Examine and purify your intentions. Notice where you are being nonintentional.

- ◆ Always do your best, and be compassionate to yourself, even when your best is less than the ideal.

- ◆ Use creative visualization to release yourself from grudges and resentments.

- ◆ Contentment and centeredness have ripple effects. When your need to "take" is less, more positive energy flows in.

- ◆ Generosity is self-renewing. The outflowing brings in more positive energy.

- ◆ See yourself as part of a unified whole.

Chapter **15**

Power Groups: Partner Visualizations

In This Chapter

- Creating a shared vision with a partner
- Setting life goals
- Visualization—in the family way
- Ways to encourage collaboration

"Love does not consist in gazing at each other but in looking outward together in the same direction."

—Antoine de Saint-Exupery, French pilot and poet, 1900–1944

If two heads are better than one, it certainly follows that two visualizations are better than one. There are many ways to create a shared vision, and infinite ways to apply them in your life for dramatic results. In this chapter, we'll explore the power of two—and more.

A Shared Vision

When two or more people share the same vision and intent, the results can be profound. A shared vision, given twice the intention, twice the positive energy and twice the affirmations can only be stronger for the effort. Here we'll explore the types of visions that work best with a partner or with a group.

You can recruit a partner for two-on-one goal making or start a group. What kind of group and for what purpose? The sky's the limit! You can build power visualization groups. You can use visualization to enhance emotional support groups, to bolster family unity, or to build community awareness.

The benefits of partner or group goal making can be:

◆ **A broader vision.** Together you accomplish more.

◆ **Out-of-the-box thinking.** The ideas and problem-solving style of another person can add originality and vitality to your visioning.

◆ **Emotional support.** You are not alone. You have someone to support and encourage you.

◆ **Partner buy-in.** If you have a life partner, involving him (or her) in your vision making, even if it's for personal goals, is a great way to get buy-in. To quote Saint-Exupery again, "If you want to build a ship, don't drum up the men to gather wood, divide the work and give orders. Instead, teach them to yearn for the vast and endless sea." What is joy for you is joy for your partner.

◆ **More resources.** Together, you have more energy and more ideas. You automatically double your network of allies and supporters.

◆ **Test lab.** A partner will challenge your thinking. One oft-quoted axiom comes to mind: "If two partners agree, one of them isn't necessary." You don't want someone who is a clone of your thinking. You want someone who will test your assumptions.

◆ **Vision keeping.** Your partner will help you keep your vision intact. Together, you commit to hold this vision sacred. If you lost sight of it, he or she will remind you.

◆ **Discipline.** Pure and simple, your partner can be a taskmaster, keeping you on track when you'd rather just surf the Net or watch TV.

♦ **Focus.** When you work on a goal together, you work to keep the vision high on your radar. A partner can be a buffer against life's distractions, filtering out everything but emergencies.

Partner and group visualizations can be applied to home life, the workplace, creative endeavors, or fitness goals. They can be done as a couple, as a family, or as a professional group of collaborators. Although our first example has two partners, bear in mind that many of the principles apply whether you are vision making with your spouse, your corporate team, or your community.

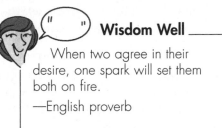

Wisdom Well

When two agree in their desire, one spark will set them both on fire.
—English proverb

Life Partner Visualizations: A Marriage Made in Heaven

Marriage is probably the most common two-on-one vision making experience many of us have. The wedding ceremony itself is a commitment to a shared vision of a life together. That shared vision often is what keeps a couple *motivated* to practice the skills and gain the knowledge that make the marriage work. Together, two people see their lives as enhanced by sharing them with the other. Two individuals see themselves as being better people because they are with the other person.

Take a few minutes to write in your Creative Visualization Journal about the person with whom you are sharing your life. If there is no one in your life right now, write about who that person might be and how the two of you would live out your lives. What is possible for you because you are with this person? Write anything that comes to mind, from the sublime to the mundane, from traveling to Machu Picchu to weeding the garden.

If you *do* have a partner, have him or her do the same and then share your lists with each other. This exercise will help you lay the groundwork for effective creative visualization sessions with your life partner. Again, this exercise can be useful for launching any group creative visualization: what do you envision you will be able to accomplish by collaborating with this person or this group?

Affirmations

I see us together, thriving, as we enjoy the fruits of our efforts. As we look outward at the life we share, we are filled with contentment.

Setting Goals

In Chapter 20, we'll develop some loving visualizations that you can use to enhance your relationship with your life partner. Right now, though, let's brainstorm some life goals you'd like to pursue with your partner. If topics come up about improving your relationship, jot them down and save them for Chapter 20.

We returned to the Life Arenas list from Chapter 1 to come up with some possibilities, but feel free to come up with ones unique to you and your partner.

Love

Be a better listener

Become better about communicating needs

_____

_____

Family

Find more balance in division of labor

Help kids do better in school

Help teenager select a college (and make sure she is prepared)

Help aging parent get home health care

_____

_____

Work

Find a more rewarding job

Buy a business together

Move to a farm/the ocean/the city

_____

_____

Money

Develop and implement a plan to save money for children's college tuition

Save for retirement

Save for vacation

Buy a big-ticket item (car/refrigerator/computer)

_____

_____

Health

Make positive changes in diet

Make positive changes in exercise

Reach health goals (lose weight, lower cholesterol, improve blood pressure)

_____

_____

Home

Remodel home

Get home ready for market and sell for a good price

Build garden shed/greenhouse

_____

_____

Personal growth

Develop more confidence

Become more compassionate

_____

_____

Spirituality

Find a spiritual community where we can practice together

Become more charitable (volunteering, donating)

Be less judgmental

_____

_____

Leisure/rejuvenation

Go bike riding together

Go to a Caribbean beach together

_____

_____

Creative self-expression

Sell screenplay

Show watercolors in art gallery

Act in theater festival

_____

_____

We're hoping this list really sparked your imagination and you came up with a whole list of topics. Did your partner's topics surprise you? How many topics appear on both of your lists? Which topics are high priorities for you? Which are high priorities for your partner?

Undoubtedly you noticed that some goals are truly shared (helping your daughter choose a college or remodeling the home you share) while others are individual (get a more rewarding job, sell screenplay, lower blood pressure). It's important at the outset to identify what type of goal you have, because it determines which techniques you will use. Here's a guide:

- **Two-on-one** vision making is when both people have a stake in the outcome _and play an active role in making it happen_. If the goal is to remodel the house, then both of you have ideas about what you want, and both of you will work to make it happen. You may have different roles, but you are both working toward the same goal.

♦ **One-with-one** vision making is when both people have a stake in the outcome but *only one person can make it happen*. An example is if one person wants to find a more rewarding job. In this kind of vision making, the secondary partner plays a supplemental role. In other words: "Behind every great man is a great woman" (or "behind every great woman is a great man").

♦ **One-plus** vision making is when one person primarily has a stake in the outcome but the other's life would be enhanced when the goal is reached. An example of one-plus vision making is when one partner wants to lose weight.

♦ **One-to-one** vision making is when *each* partner desires a parallel individual goal. An example is to train for a triathlon.

Supplemental Vision Making

When the goal is equally shared, such as buying a cabin in the mountains, both people develop the vision. But when the goal is primarily one person's goal with the other supplementing, as in one-with-one or one-plus vision making, the primary person takes the lead in developing the visualization.

It's important to recognize the subtle difference because there is the danger that the primary vision maker will feel undue expectations from the supplemental person. This can be the case when the goal is to lose weight, for example. On a bad day, "How much did you weigh in at Weight Watchers?" can sound too much like, "I just think you're so fat." Or, in the case of looking for more rewarding work, checking in can seem like checking up. When you are the supplemental partner, you are a sounding board. Your job is to explore, not *expect*. Ask the person who is looking for a job questions like, "What's become clearer to you this week about your goal?" Or, "Among those options, which one can you see yourself doing and enjoying?" Remember, the only thing that matters here, even if you have a stake in the outcome, is that your partner can visualize it, want it, and affirm it.

Ask your partner what parts of the vision he sees most clearly. What parts are fuzzy? Where could he go to get more information that would

Don't Panic, Focus!

As a primary vision maker, you have an obligation to ask for what you do and don't need from your supplemental vision maker. Feel free to say, "I need encouragement today" or "I need to know you love me just as I am now."

fill in the picture? Who could he talk to? Your role is to get your partner to externalize his or her inner dialogue.

Once your partner can articulate the vision (even if the visualization is "I want to see myself getting clearer about this goal this week"), then you spring into action. You have an assignment. Your assignment is, having clarified with your partner and gotten confirmation that this is his or her vision, to send affirmations to it.

Two-on-One Vision Making: An Example

Here's how a couple might work together on two-on-one vision making. Let's use the example of remodeling a home:

1. Make a list of the ways it would enhance your lives. Discuss these in detail. Together, paint a mental picture of what your lives would look like. This will be the seed of your visualizations.

2. Discuss the challenges you would face. This is acknowledging the negative visualizations. Later on, you'll visualize triumphing over these obstacles.

3. Discuss in detail how you envision the project moving ahead. What's important? That it be peaceful and not disruptive? Get specific: not disruptive *how?* Not affecting the children's school routine? Not interfering with one partner's work? Not losing sight that the relationship is more important than a house?

4. Develop an action plan for the rough times. You might want to agree that you order out for pizza on tough nights. Or go out for a martini. You might want to develop a code word to remind each other to chill out.

5. Now, make the vision. Gather clippings. Visit the Parade of Homes in your city. Interview builders. Get blueprints drawn up.

6. When you have blueprints, make your visualization. Go back to step 1. Now that you can see the details of your remodeled home, see your lives together in it. Send positive energy to this vision. Agree to voice affirmations about it. You may want to exchange affirmations and visualizations by sending each other e-mails each day or posting notes on the refrigerator. Agree on a method to keep the visualization active.

7. Map out the steps. Set up a schedule.

8. Divide the labor. Decide which roles you'll play. Who is more suited to handle the money? Who is more suited to manage the subcontractors?

9. As you break ground, tend to your visualization for the process. Send affirmations to it, asking for a graceful, smooth process.

10. Keep repeating steps 6 and 9 until the project is complete. Then enjoy your new home!

One-to-One Visualizations

While one-to-one visualizations can be done with a life partner, they are just as often done with a friend or someone who has expertise in the area of your goal. Expert visualization partners can be personal fitness trainers, nutrition/weight loss specialists, sports coaches, career coaches, or life coaches. We have even heard of people who serve as dating coaches. (It's about time we acknowledged that you should not be out there alone in the dating jungle!) But one-to-one visualizations can be done with anyone. The main criterion is someone who has a parallel goal. Training for a triathlon this summer? Want to save money? Want to look good in a bikini by the time you vacation in Belize? One-to-one visualizations work very well for specific, short-term goals like these.

Here are some ways to get set up for one-to-one visualizations:

1. Agree on how often to meet. Agree on how you'll communicate in between.

2. Agree on individual, specific goals.

3. Share why you want this goal—why it matters.

4. Visualize, for each of you, what it would look like when you reach your goal.

5. Agree on what would feel like a reward to you.

6. Develop a strategy. Be specific.

7. Brainstorm affirmations. Create an affirmation data bank.

Now keep following the steps, and you are sure to reach your goal.

Family Visualizations

Family visualizations are a natural outgrowth of partner visualizations. Before you start with the whole family, we urge you to practice with your life partner. It's good to sort out your different values and techniques with your partner, using some visualizations that involve your children, before you take your techniques out on the road.

When you feel ready to try it in a family setting, take the time to sit down and discuss with your partner what you appreciate about the other's approach to creative visualization. Acknowledge each other's strengths. Observe what is different about your techniques. How do these different approaches complement each other's techniques? Be honest and discuss anything you might resist or not understand about your partner's technique. It doesn't have to be good or bad. Your approaches are just different. For example, by admitting that you sometimes bristle at your partner's unbridled optimism, you're opening up the lines of communication. Ultimately, this can help you steer clear of getting into locked-down, polarized positions. For instance, maybe you become more pessimistic when you perceive your visualization partner as having rose-colored glasses, and you tend to want to confront her with challenges that you perceive she doesn't recognize. By having this discussion, you can present yourselves to one another not as black-and-white optimist-pessimist, but two people who more than likely come in shades of gray.

By taking the time to reveal your motivations and perceptions, you reveal your inner complexity, and it provides both of you with a wider range in which to operate emotionally. Through this discussion, you invite your optimistic partner to take more responsibility for examining the challenges and you give yourself permission to ring out the affirmations.

A good place to start with family visualizations is with elemental problem-solving. By getting an immediate payoff—such as getting a handle on laundry—everyone shares in the success. Everyone buys in. Small successes build trust in a process that won't seem natural at first. They lay the groundwork for the family to address larger issues such as respect and tolerance. Creative visualization also gives your children valuable life skills.

Sacred Circle Family Time

Brainstorm activities that you enjoy doing together as a family. Put a suggestion box on the dining room table and let everyone add their ideas on a slip of paper. Commit to spending time together doing one of these activities each week. Make it a block of time, a whole morning or a whole afternoon. Afterward, let each person write down a brief sentence or two about why the time shared together meant a lot to him or her. With small children, let them draw a picture.

The suggestion box is an excellent technique for any group bonding or group problem solving because no idea can be judged or revised. All ideas are valid and considered. It can really get the creative process flowing.

Collaborative Visions

Group visualizations can be very effective ways to accomplish larger goals. A power group of professional peers can help you gain the skills to move ahead in your profession. Visualization can be very effective with volunteer groups, where volunteers often have diverse skills. Visualization can work well to improve the effectiveness of corporate teams. Working together to formulate a mission statement is group visualization at work. It's a way of encoding the individual visions into one.

With your group, write a mission statement using these steps:

1. Define your group, using an adjective and a noun. Let the adjective describe your group's personality, such as "authentic."

2. List three or four values. What matters to your group? What counts? How would someone who benefits from your work be transformed or touched?

3. Think about where your group carries out this mission. In your community? In everyday life? Carolyn likes this mission statement from her church: "An authentic biblical community where others matter, community counts, truth transforms and authentic worship is lived out in everyday life."

Deeper Meaning

Collaboration is when two or more people work together to encourage creative ideas, achieve shared goals, and solve challenging problems. In a collaborative group, the whole is greater, stronger, and more effective than any individual working alone would be. It goes beyond coordinating your efforts and sharing knowledge to refining collective ideas and visions for superior solutions.

Start with some ground rules. Group dynamics can be interesting, to say the least, and the important thing is to head off any potential for the group to affect you negatively. (Refer to our discussion of nonintentionality in Chapter 14.) Having these conversations up front heads off the possibility of outcomes that you never intended. We won't say feelings won't get hurt, that people won't feel their egos stepped on, or get discouraged. Working together and getting along is part of the human experience.

But you can minimize some of the potential for destructive blow-ups if you set some ground rules right from the get-go.

Here's a start, but we encourage you to develop ideas with your group:

♦ Everyone must feel heard.

♦ Everyone must be able to speak.

♦ Everyone must feel empowered.

♦ Everyone must be challenged to be his or her best self.

♦ Everyone must be honest.

♦ Everyone must be honored. This means that each person must be able to trust that what he or she says in the group will be heard, held, and considered.

♦ Everything stays in the circle. The group holds what is said confidential.

Confidentiality is vital to the success of any group visualization. If you are truly to get the most out of creative visualization with a group, you must feel that you can reveal—and envision together—your most heartfelt desires. If you are not sharing your most heartfelt desires out of fear of censure, then what are you doing with this group? You are wasting your time, giving a big effort to a small priority.

It's important to give plenty of time for the process. More than anything else, this will ensure the success of your group. Specifically:

♦ Allow time for incompletely formed, nascent ideas to be voiced, honored, and discussed.

♦ Recognize that consensus-building takes time. Even if there is a clear majority, take the time to hear the minority viewpoints thoroughly.

♦ Allow all participants to disagree, even strongly, and engage in lively and respectful dialogue. Even if in the end, the decision is made to go with the majority, everyone will feel heard.

♦ Be willing to tolerate ambiguity and uncertainty. Acknowledge that you don't have a sharp vision yet. Persist in spite of it, asking for the vision to take shape.

When visualizing with a group, it's essential that the group give voice to what succeeds. By recognizing successes collectively, you form a group visualization of the ideal. Now everyone in the group has the same picture. Everyone can point to the picture and say, "See, this is what we're striving for. This is who we are." Without taking this step, you risk at some point having competing visions to take root in individuals' minds. Even if a success is mixed—because success doesn't happen overnight, but incrementally—it's good to discuss what worked and what didn't.

Test *your* satisfaction with the group with these statements:

- ◆ I feel accepted as I am.

- ◆ I feel my ideas are heard.

- ◆ I feel a part of this vision.

- ◆ I am proud of the way we collaborate.

- ◆ I am willing to take the extra time to uphold the tenets of this group.

- ◆ I am willing to take responsibility for my role in the group.

- ◆ I feel I am a better person because I am part of this group.

- ◆ I feel I am growing and learning new skills.

- ◆ I feel comfortable giving voice to any and all concerns.

- ◆ I feel there is a balance between what I am giving and what I am receiving.

- ◆ I trust the group and feel I can be honest and open with them.

- ◆ I feel we have a forum for addressing imbalances.

> **Wisdom Well**
>
> In a truly creative collaboration, work is pleasure, and the only rules and procedures are those that advance the common cause.
>
> —Warren Bennis, American lecturer and author on organizational management

With all levels of group visualization, whether it's in the corporate, community, or family environment, create a collaborative space with these elements:

- ◆ **Encourages interaction**. Have a round table or comfortable sofas.

- ◆ **Is visually stimulating**. Put art, origami, or flowers in your meeting space.

- ◆ **Is fun**. Have mind-bender toys such as squish balls, Rubik's cubes, or geometric puzzles on hand.

- **Suggests abundance.** Have bowls of fruit or platters of finger foods to munch on.

- **Is beautiful.** An aesthetically pleasing setting opens up the imagination.

A Big Payoff

Over time, we're pretty sure you'll get sold on partner and group visualizations. You'll find that the power of two—or three, or more—is pretty powerful, indeed. Beyond that, we think you'll find it emotionally rewarding. Your relationships will deepen, and your bonds with your community will strengthen. You'll find that your communication improves. A shared vision brings the purpose of the relationship into a clear focus. It keeps you on common ground, and it gives you techniques for resolving conflict. The shared sense of accomplishment you'll derive is bound to create contentment.

The Least You Need to Know

- Shared vision making gains you out-of-the-box thinking, emotional support, more buy-in, and more resources.

- Goals for partner visualizations can be two sharing in one goal or two supporting each other in individual goals.

- Family visualizations can first be applied to solving day-to-day challenges, then used to enhance more bonding and character building.

- In collaborative group vision making, it's essential to allow enough time for the process of generating ideas, discussing and developing them, and building consensus.

- Partner and group visualizations can deepen relationships and build stronger bonds.

Part 5

Manifest Creative Ways to Visualize

Using visuals is just one way to create a picture for yourself of the life you want to manifest. We all learn differently. Some ways of learning may resonate for some, but not others.

Some people respond to tactile experiences; others are kinesthetic and explore their world through physical action. Still others respond through aural experiences. So whether it's a dream journal, a spiritual epiphany, a sports competition, a blueprint, or sheet music, there are many ways to fix your vision in your body, mind and spirit.

In the chapters ahead, we'll explore other ways to create and use mental pictures and physical symbols of the life you want to create.

Chapter 16

Use Your Hands

In This Chapter

◆ Active hands, fertile imagination

◆ Connecting to the natural rhythm of life

◆ Rhythm and no more blues

◆ Elements of the earth, the nature of ideas

Just imagine a fulfilling life. But how do you unlock the imagination? We admit it might come readily to us, a psychologist and a writer. It's part and parcel of our trades, something we do every day.

But there are many styles to creative visualization. One sure-fire way to unlock the imagination is by working with your hands. Hand work frees up your mind to visualize new possibilities. In this chapter, we'll explore how to do hands-on visualization.

Hand-to-Mind's Eye Coordination

Hand activities bring out what is already within us. By freeing our minds, they work much like hand-eye coordination in reverse. Hand-eye coordination comes from outside. There is a stimulus. Your eye captures the information and sends a message along the optic nerve to the brain. The brain decodes the message and interprets it. It then sends an electrical impulse to the hands to take action. This all happens in a nanosecond.

In reverse, when your hands are active, you are sending impulses to your brain to see. Your brain tries to decode the information flooding in from the activity of the hands. Think of the bits and pieces of information flowing in as pixels assembling pictures in your mind.

So hand-eye coordination is taking in, responding to the outside world. There is no room for creation. But hand-to-mind's eye coordination is sending out, responding to your inner world. Hand-to-mind's eye coordination is giving form to that inner world—in the form of mental pictures that take shape as our hands are at work. (Remember in Chapter 15 we suggested adding geometric puzzles and mind-bender toys to your collaboration room? There was a reason for that!)

Getting Started

Many activities fit the bill for this kind of imagining. Here are some we brainstormed. Take a few minutes to brainstorm your own:

- Knitting
- Quilting
- Needlework
- Cooking
- Washing windows
- Vacuuming
- Folding laundry
- Carpentry
- Painting a wall
- Tiling a floor
- Drumming
- Repairing a car engine
- Washing a car
- Bathing and grooming a dog

- ◆ Gardening

- ◆ Scrapbooking

- ◆ Watercoloring

- ◆ Sculpting

- ◆ Playing piano

- ◆ Working a jigsaw puzzle

- ◆ Designing and coloring a mandala

- ◆ Refinishing furniture

- ◆ Dancing

What activities did you think of? What hobbies or pursuits do you have that fit the bill? Have you noticed how they affect your imagination? Of course, other activities such as exercise can have the same effect, and we'll talk about those in Chapter 18.

Don't Panic, *Focus!*

It might be tempting to pick up a new hobby as a hand activity, but for creative visualization, it's best to stay with something you know well and enjoy. According to Mihaly Csikszentmihalyi, author of *Flow: The Psychology of Optimal Experience* (see Appendix B), the first step to achieving the flow that we believe activates the imagination is a sense of playfulness. Choose something that you enjoy for its own sake. Choose something in which the challenge matches your skills.

Why It Works

Whether it's knitting or cooking or drumming or playing piano, when you work with your hands you are clearing out a vast space in your mind. Educator Maria Montessori called it "making silence." In this inner stillness, you allow your imagination to flourish. This is why hand work is so effective for creative visualization. It sparks the imagination, and it creates a fertile mind.

Again, it's the reverse of hand-eye coordination. Hand-eye coordination, in which your hands spring into action upon seeing a stimulus, is the brain filling up with external stimuli. Hand-to-mind's eye coordination can be described more like an emptying out. The repetitiveness of the hand activity calms and soothes the neural pathways that so very often transmit information that needs to be acted on at high speed. The hand activity is sending information back: no need to act now. All systems at rest. Gradually, the mind empties. You become engrossed in your activity, and you sink into mindfulness, the simple awareness of the moment. At that point, you can start taking in information *from within*, from your highest self. This is the self that is often not allowed to speak. Our minds tend to send a stream of constant survival messages, which creates a great amount of static along those neural pathways.

Working with your hands can help you achieve the mindfulness we discussed in Chapter 11. Activities like this keep you in the now—and keep you *safely* in the now—and allow you to go deeper within. They allow you to become vulnerable, which means getting to your truest desires—and those are the basis for your most effective creative visualizations.

When you are engrossed in an activity with your hands, you are doing something that brings you into your full aliveness. Most of us spend our working lives doing something mental, something that involves thinking, planning, or typing on a computer. We are no longer an agriculturally based society. In those days, people spent their time in the fields, shucking corn or picking apples. For women tending to home and family, they spent time cooking and sewing—and we mean cooking the *real* way, with fresh ingredients straight from the garden, not the lettuce-in-a-bag you grab at the supermarket! Of course, some of us build bridges or dig ditches, but most of us are using our minds and rarely our hands for most of the working day.

Wisdom Well

If our dreams weren't already real within us, we could not even dream them.

—Gloria Steinem, American author and feminist

Natural Visualizations

Working with your hands is a way to connect to the natural rhythm of life. When you get engrossed in activity with your hands, you turn off your mind to the external distractions, opening up to the vast landscape within. Yet the activity of your hands is stimulating. You are physically connected with the flow of life, which leads to being emotionally, mentally, and spiritually connected as well.

Hands-on visualization is like standing with your feet in the mud and casting your eyes to the stars. When you are grounded in a simple physical task that brings you joy, it leaves your imagination free to roam. There's something a little frightening about letting your imagination loose with no tether, no tie to the world you inhabit. But when you maintain that connection to Earth, you allow it to flutter in the breeze, like a kite. This is particularly true when you engage in activities that connect you with the rhythm of the earth: kneading bread, with your hands immersed in the dough; knitting, with your hands weaving in and out of a cloud of wool; gardening, with your fingers sifting through the dirt; dancing, with your feet gliding across the floor.

Shari often recommends physical exercise, in an outdoor setting, for people who are struggling through therapeutic issues. The very rhythm of walking—step after step after step until one no longer counts the steps—allows the mind-body connection to flourish. From this walking, running, skating, horseback riding, or biking, subconscious material surfaces much more easily. Sometimes Shari recommends working with the hands outside—gardening or bringing the sewing or knitting outside. Remember, we are born with a passionate drive to be whole and healthy in both body and mind—and to be connected with the earth. All we need to do is create the opportunity.

> **Wisdom Well**
>
> And forget not that the earth delights to feel your bare feet and the winds long to play with your hair.
>
> —Kahlil Gibran, Lebanese novelist and poet

Earth Visualization

Choose a hand activity that you can do outdoors—either gardening or an activity that you can bring outdoors. Set your intention for a visualization that you will work on during the activity. It can be from any one of the Life Arenas on your list. Wed this goal from your Life Arenas list with the intention to connect to the earth. You may want to use an affirmation to set the intention, such as "Through (your activity), I am connecting with the life force of creation. I am allowing it to flow through me. I am opening up to greater sight about (your goal)." As you work through your activity, practice staying in the now by using the five senses meditation we introduced in Chapter 11: "In this moment, I see/hear/taste/smell/touch ..."

Write about how it felt in your Creative Visualization Journal. Record any new understandings you received about yourself and your goal.

> **Affirmations**
>
> I am connected with the rhythm of life. I know that all is working together for my happiness and wholeness.

Got Rhythm? Visualize It!

Are you at a crossroads with your goal? Does it feel like you are stuck? If your vision is cloudy or you have some pent-up emotions, we recommend playing with percussion. Get some drums, some castanets, a tambourine, a triangle—whatever. You're going to bang on the drum all day!

Start by setting your intention for your visualization. Give yourself a mental snapshot of yourself as unstuck, moving forward. And get to it. Pound on that drum. Spin around the room as you play the tambourine.

Affirmations
I hear the heartbeat of life. I am dancing in the streets.

Another technique is to do drumming as a group, pulling in your collaborative visualization team you instituted in Chapter 15. Assemble everyone in your backyard, at the beach, at the park, whatever. Everyone brings a drum, and everyone dances. Take turns changing up the rhythm. Throw in some chanting. Chant your affirmations.

Tactile Tactics

Naturally, hands-on activities are tactile. As your awareness of your sense of touch increases, the two senses that you primarily use to understand and interact with your world—sight and hearing—recede. Or maybe we should say, they sharpen. When your eyes and ears bear most of the responsibility for intake of information, they often become dulled. When your sense of touch takes center stage, they can become sharper. Notice the next time you knead bread or mince garlic or prune the rosebushes if your sense of hearing becomes more acute. Take the time to notice the way the light falls through the skylight in your kitchen as you are stirring the sauce. Take the time to notice the changing light in the room as you play guitar or dance or work a jigsaw puzzle.

Essential Life Elements

One reason that tactile experiences can unlock your imagination is because they get you in touch with the elements, as defined in Chinese philosophy: wood, fire, earth, metal, water. Playing guitar means touching steel and wood. Playing violin means placing your chin on your instrument—taking it in intimately. Play an antique piano, and you are touching ivory keys. Drummers touch animal skin, or sometimes (as with Taos drums) the trunk of a tree. Bead artists touch precious stones. Mosaic makers touch ceramic or mirrored tiles. A carpenter touches wood and nails. Brainstorm the many elements you touch as you engage in your favorite hand activities.

In Chinese philosophy, each element is associated with a season. Using the metaphor of the seasons, we'll take a look at how each element shapes the progression of an idea to reality.

◆ **Wood** is connected with the beginning of spring and rising creativity. It has a sense of magic, of creating something where there was nothing before. At this stage of an idea, you are just beginning to tap into your power.

◆ **Fire** is associated with summer and creativity in full bloom: joy, laughter, radiance. It is the element of partnership. This is where your idea starts to take form. You form an alliance with your idea. You reach out and form alliances with others who can help you with your idea.

◆ **Earth** is associated with late summer moving into fall—the energy of relinquishment. Earth is about transformation, letting go of expectations, moving away from ideas to groundedness. This is the element that rules the process of moving a dream from the clouds to real life. This element is bittersweet. We'd all like to stay in that high-energy state of new ideas, but this is where we have to face the challenges that are ahead to get the idea done, to bring the idea into the material world.

◆ **Metal** is associated with fall, a time to let go, allow for change, allow for old beliefs to take new form. This element is invigorating, like a breath of fresh air. The letting go allows for new energy that moves your idea along.

◆ **Water** is associated with winter, a time to be quiet and go within for wisdom. This isn't the descent of coldness, but rather this is the strengthening of your intent. Water is connected with your emotions. At this stage, you gain the emotional assurance that your idea is right for you. This is the purification of intent. When spring comes again, you are ready to move into action.

In this next visualization, choose one of the elements that applies to the stage of your idea. Match that element for an activity you enjoy doing with your hands. We chose wood, and we chose carpentry. We chose to build shelves. Start by setting your intention. Make this intention part of the process from the beginning, as you are selecting your materials. As you plan and as you work with your element, you will weave what you are creating on the outside with your intention and your visualization on the inside. For instance, in choosing the wood, we had to imagine how the shelves would come together. We had to measure, measure again (remembering the axiom: "Measure once, cut twice; measure twice, cut once"), and cut the wood. We had to decide what kind of nails to use to hold the pieces of wood together and then we had to hammer each and every nail, one by one. This gave us a lot of time to think about our inner goal. How might it come together? What materials would we use? What would hold it together?

Watching our shelves come together in an afternoon was rewarding. It was near-instant gratification. This process affirms that we can bring into being an idea that has formed in our minds. It can be extremely valuable when you are working on a long-range goal to see something come together relatively quickly in the material world.

Imagine, See, Be

Take your affirmations to the next level and sing them. That's right—turn them into a song. Make it a folk song in which you tell the tale of a woman (or man) who created what she (or he) wanted in life. Set your affirmation to a blues beat—except you ain't got the blues about this goal, you're making it happen! Choose something triumphant: "Middle-Aged Blues" or Aretha Franklin's "R-E-S-P-E-C-T." Or try your affirmations as a rock 'n' roll football stadium chant.

Aural Meets Tactile

Making music is the convergence of the aural and tactile experience. As you play the piano or strum the guitar, you are simultaneously aware both of the physical experience of striking the key or plucking the string and the mental experience of hearing the sound.

This is a mind-body connection. You merge into an awareness of the flow of creativity through your fingertips and through the musical instrument. If you play a horn or reed instrument, the connection between your life force energy and the music is that much more direct. You are releasing your breath into the instrument.

That's why playing music can create whole-ness. You integrate the physical, mental, emo-tional, and spiritual. You create a *flow state*. This is fertile ground for the imagination—and for creative visualization.

If you play a musical instrument, the next time you play, set an intention for a visualization. Allow yourself to see in your mind's eye a pic-ture of yourself living wholly, your goal accom-plished. Send it an affirmation: "I am whole and complete. This is happening for me. It is right. It is good. I can hear the song of life flowing through me."

Deeper Meaning

A **flow state** is a state of consciousness in which you are immersed in your activity. It is marked by a sense of mastery and feelings of exhilaration. You achieve a high level of concen-tration and focus, a deep sense of enjoyment in the activity for its own sake, and a sense of time standing still.

From the Mundane to the Sublime

Did we really include "folding laundry" on our list at the beginning of this chapter? We'll wait a minute while you go back and check. So yes, we did, and were we losing our minds when we said that? What could we be thinking, grouping such a mundane task among creative activities such as drumming or knitting? Consider, too, that when Carolyn was setting her visualizations for the coming New Year, her guide word was "flourish." (More about guide words in Chapter 17.) When she broke down what "flourish" meant, it involved visualizing *no more laundry*.

Okay, so now we'll tell you what we were thinking. We included laundry on the list because we all have to do it. It's just part of taking care of the basic needs of life. But you *can* use laundry for a creative visualization. You can incorporate creative visualiza-tion into your daily chores. It's more of that "feet-in-the-mud, head-in-the-stars" thinking, anchoring us in the mundane and reaching for the sublime. Even though most of us would not list laundry as "enjoyable," it is a tactile activity that gets us in touch with real life. And it, too, can free your mind to imagine. Let yourself day-dream.

To do a laundry creative visualization session, start by setting an intention. Focus on a goal from your Life Arenas list. What do you want to see about your goal today? As you fold towels, stay mindful of how fresh they smell. Let yourself feel the softness of the terrycloth. Experience the colors. (Hopefully, you have been using color-safe bleach and you have vivid, vibrant colors to stimulate your imagination.) As you fold shirts flat, smooth your hand over the fabric. Sink into a rhythm as you fold your laundry. Take deep breaths. Become more mindful of all of your senses. Now let pictures about your Life Arena come into your mind. See yourself three months from now, one year from now, five years from now. Send some affirmations to your visualization.

Right Here, Right Now

So as you can see, creative visualization can assimilate right into your life, into some of your most enjoyable activities. By keeping your hands and your imagination active, you keep the fires of creative visualization burning. In this way, you can continue to work actively and positively to your most heartfelt desires.

The Least You Need to Know

- Hand activities bring out the dreams that are already within our minds. They stir the imagination, bring us into full aliveness, and bring us into the moment.

- Playing with percussion—drums, castanets, tambourines—can be a way to move energy, to get unstuck if you are looking for fresh ideas.

- Staying aware of our connection to the earth is another vital component of hand activities such as gardening, baking bread, sculpting, or mosaic making.

- Connecting with the essential elements of life—wood, fire, earth, metal, and water—is a way to connect with the progression of an idea from inspiration to materialization.

Chapter 17

Words Plus Images Plus Dreams

In This Chapter

- The potential of your dreams
- Creating an image bank
- The color connection
- Words in action

It was all a dream … or was it? So many of the world's great stories, from *Alice in Wonderland* to *The Wizard of Oz*, conclude with the main character waking up from a great adventure, rubbing sleep out of her eyes. It seemed too fantastical to be real, yet the character is changed forever.

Dreams, language, art—all of these are ways to use creative visualization in ways that change you indelibly. Tapping into the creative power of words, images, and dreams is to tap into your own source of imagination and creativity—your power to create what you want in your life.

The Dreaming Life

Have you ever had the experience of waking from a particularly vivid dream and not being sure of what is real and what is dream? That's how powerful our dreams are. They are a reflection of what is going on in our lives, of our stressors and joys.

Your dreaming life is your own personal wellspring of creativity. Because dreams come to us from the creative, subconscious part of our minds, it's easy to see why they can be an important tool to use with creative visualization. And if you practice creative visualization regularly, it will influence the content of your dreams. The two go hand-in-hand.

Dreams have information for us. They connect us to our subconscious, bringing some of our deepest emotions and hidden thoughts to consciousness. Sometimes, in their surreal quality, they can jolt us out of stuck thinking, presenting new ideas in ways that we wouldn't have connected in our conscious minds.

Deeper Meaning

Dream interpretation is the art of making sense of nighttime dreams and determining how they relate to your waking life. The process of understanding your dreams is the process of understanding yourself. The unique dream world you create each and every night expresses something very important about you, whether it springs from your past or your imagination.

Early sleep cycle dreams are thought to clear out daytime residue, sort of like brain housekeeping. As the night progresses, dreams become longer and more storylike. This culminates in the last dream before waking. Because at this point of the night, you are rested, these dreams often are more organized.

Many therapists, such as Shari, make *dream interpretation* an important part of their work. Even though there is a difference between daydreams and sleep dreams, one can easily influence the other. For more information about dreams, pick up Shari's other book, *The Complete Idiot's Guide to Interpreting Your Dreams, Second Edition*, with Marci Pliskin, CSW, ACSW (see Appendix B).

Setting an Intention for Dreaming

In her book *Angel Medicine: How to Heal the Body and Mind with the Help of Angels* (see Appendix B), Doreen Virtue says this about intention: "Holding crystal-clear intentions means that your whole system is geared toward the manifestation of your desire. All of your energy is placed in that direction, and positive results are inevitable."

It's quite possible to set an intention for dreaming. Ask your dreaming mind to help you with a particular problem or give you some piece of wisdom that you desire, and you will eventually be given a dream that will help you. It might take a bit of time.

Given that dreams have a powerful ability to heal, to speak to you, to enlighten you, and to help you with your goals, think about how powerful the combination of dreams and creative visualization would be.

Maximizing Your Dream Potential

Keeping a Dream Journal is the best method for remembering and working with your dreams. This way, you will be able to remember the dream and make notes about it. Even if you think it is so powerful you won't forget it, write it down (and record the date). Keep a parallel Creative Visualization Journal, noting the dates of your visualizations. Compare them. Is your subconscious dealing with similar material? How are they different? Does one balance the other, empower the other?

Both enable the expression of your deepest self. Together they may inform you of what your goals should be or help you understand why you want certain things in your life—a very powerful combination indeed.

CAUTION Don't Panic, *Focus!*

Bringing up subconscious material by stimulating our night dreaming can sometimes result in disturbing dreams. Sometimes it's a trauma buried in the past, such as moving away from friends in our school years. Spend some time thinking about these disturbing events from your adult perspective and they will probably make more sense. If the dreams are violent or emotionally wrenching, it's time to talk to a professionally licensed mental health therapist.

From Dreaming to Deciding

So how could you use one to support the other? Suppose you want to know whether you and your partner should have another child. The pros and cons tally up about even, so you both decide to use visualization (drawing on partner visualizations in Chapter 15) and your dreams to help you with the answer. Remember that most dreams come from your subconscious material—they *are* you. Here's how you could go about getting your answer:

1. Compose a visualization you and your partner can do together. Together, gaze into white candlelight as you do your visualization.

2. Practice it on a regular basis.

3. Keep separate journals on what happens as a result of your visualization sessions.

4. Ask yourself to dream about answers to your child question when you sleep.

5. Write down what comes up or who visits in your dreams.

6. Talk together about the results that you are both getting with a view to making a decision.

7. When you are ready, make the decision.

8. Be grateful that you can initiate this process. It will tell you much about yourself and your partner, and you will have accessed your deepest spiritual self.

Awakening to Images

Dreams are packed with images. They can be exhilarating, enthralling, even disconcerting. But they definitely stimulate you visually.

Using visual stimulation when you are conscious can have similar positive effects on your creative visualization sessions. Steeping yourself in the visual world can really get your imagination going. You can do it by immersing yourself in a visual activity, such as painting or sculpting. Or you can go gallery hopping to appreciate someone else's work.

In Chapter 16, we brainstormed a list of activities you can do with your hands. Many of those are visually stimulating: coloring a mandala, watercoloring, knitting, scrapbooking, or visual journaling.

Visually stimulating activities are especially useful when you have a big, wide-open goal but you aren't sure which direction to go, such as changing jobs.

Visual stimulation relaxes the active, problem-solving, evaluating side of your mind that sometimes is too "bottom-line" oriented to build the mental picture in your head. Just as something blooms in your imagination, you start evaluating it, and before you know it, you have dismissed the idea because it just doesn't seem doable.

Pursuing a big goal requires you to activate your receptive mind. This is creating for the sake of creating and no other reason. This is the part of you that says, "Why not?" when your skeptical, critical mind challenges a new idea. You need to just play for a while before you can create a vision. When you get in touch with this side, you get in touch with enough primary thought process to open your mind to infinite possibilities.

A Visual Energy Shift

When we are born, our brains contain many times the number of cells than we will ever use. So learning to live in our environment is a process of using the necessary cells and letting the rest go dormant. Laying down neural pathways along cell membranes encodes our learning so that what we have learned is available when we need to repeat a certain action. We learn when something is always the same: rain comes in the form of water. Or we learn that something may vary: sometimes parents or teachers can be in good moods; sometimes they can be in bad moods.

Here's an example: as a child of about four, Carolyn was playing outside in a white dress. On that spring day, she discovered dandelions. It was great fun to blow the puffs of seeds into the wind. There were millions of them, dotting the lawn. Only the dandelion stems stained her white dress—and that made her mother *very* unhappy. So Carolyn learned: if you play outside, you can get your clothes dirty. If you get your clothes dirty, your mother gets mad.

What are the possibilities for "unlearning" that could change the thought process?

- ◆ If you play outside, wear clothes that can get dirty.
- ◆ If you get your clothes dirty, it's okay; you can wash them.
- ◆ If your mom reacts strongly, maybe it's about her, not you.

Because most of us are collecting information verbally most of the time (by listening to or reading words)—and this is true even for the most visual among us—visual stimulation can unlock new doors to learning—and unlearning. And unlearning may be the most important of all on the path to greater creativity. Unlearning is what prompted feminist Gloria Steinem to say, "It's never to late to have a happy childhood" in her book *Revolution from Within* (see Appendix B).

Imagine, See, Be _____

Keep a clip file of photos and illustrations from magazines. Clip anything to which your eye gravitates. If it stops you, fascinates you, intrigues you, clip it. Does the image make you imagine the scene after this scene? Does it activate a dialogue in your head between the two people in the photo? Do you wonder about the town in which the photo was taken? Does the image have nothing to do with your creative visualization goal? All the better. Flash through your image bank regularly to relax into unlearning.

Color Wheel: Spinning for Fortune

Color is a vital component to visual stimulation. It sends powerful messages to the brain. Color speaks to us on a visceral level. Color evokes emotion. Color activates memories. Color awakens your cosmic connections. Because color is interconnected with emotions, with culture, and with archetypes, it connects you with your spiritual self.

That said, though many of us share interpretations and reactions to color, they are experienced in unique personal ways. Colors can be comforting, reminding us of childhood. They can be invigorating, inspiring us to imagine.

Return to Chapter 16 and the list of hand activities. Choose one, and as you do, stay mindful of your awareness of the colors involved in the activities. Maybe you are knitting a scarf with purple yarn. Purple is the color of passion, royalty, spiritual enlightenment, or transformation, just to name a few associations. What does it feel like? Compare the experience to working with pink yarn. Pink is the color of service, compassion, soothing, healing. Notice the images that come to mind. Notice the memories that come up.

We decided to brainstorm some of our associations with color. We might as well play! Add a few of your own. Which colors have positive associations for you? Which words on the list do you want more of in your life? Less of? You may want to take some notes in your Creative Visualization Journal about memories you associate with colors. (A side note: start noticing how colors appear in your dreams.) After you finish your list, make a point to be more mindful about these colors and what they mean for you as you are doing your favorite hand activity. What "scenes" came into your mind for creative visualization?

Color	Our List	Your List
White	Full enlightenment, light, reverence, purity, cleanliness, peace, innocence, winter, snow, cold, angels, marriage	
Purple	Passion, royalty, spiritual enlightenment, spiritual contentment, inspiration, mystery, transformation	
Blue	Calmness, serenity, self-expression (the sky's the limit), fidelity, truth (true blue), friendship	
Green	Blooming, creating, flourishing, outflowing, vibrant, renewal, life, triumph, growth and wisdom, hope, immortality	
Yellow	Promising, shining (like sunshine), personal power, "good as gold," solid, knowledge (particularly self-knowledge), maturity	
Orange	Change, action, vitality, earth (grounding), fruitfulness (oranges, apricots, peaches), creativity	
Red	Passion, drive, strength, fire, romance	
Pink	Service, compassion, nurturing, soothing, healing, newness, femininity	
Black	Sophistication, formality, masculinity, mystery, death, mourning	
Brown	Hearth, home, comfort, earth, reliability, endurance, stability, simplicity	

A Vision in White

Let's have some fun with the color white. You might choose a hand activity that you like. In setting up for your activity, you will want to include something visual that is white. If it's gardening, for instance, you may want to plant a moonlight garden full of white flowers, such as lilies or snow-in-summer or white peonies. If it's playing piano—well, that's easy, more than half of the keys are white! If it's knitting, choose white yarn. If you're painting, paint your wall white. Or if that seems boring, paint a white wall another color, leaving a square of white until the last. As you paint, focus on the square of white that remains. If your activity doesn't lend itself to white—after all, it doesn't make any sense to use white paint when watercoloring— then surround yourself in white. Drape yourself in white fabric. Whatever … get creative, just immerse yourself in white.

> **Affirmations**
>
> I am receiving this light, this purity of vision into my consciousness.

Set your intention for your visualization to get clearer on the Life Arena that seems the toughest to get your arms around. Choose the area in which you might have struggled to come up with concrete goals and visions. You might want to say it out loud.

As you work, meditate on white. White is made up of all colors, fused together. White balances all the energies of the other colors, each vibrating at a different level. White is purity. It is the purification from all distractions. Visualize your energy fusing in one direction. Think of the white as a beam of light, fusing all the colored light together in one band, moving forward at … well, the speed of light. See yourself as fusing together, moving at that speed.

> **Wisdom Well**
>
> One ought every day at least, to hear a little song, read a good poem, see a fine picture, and, if it were possible, to speak a few reasonable words.
>
> —Johann Wolfgang von Goethe, eighteenth-century German poet

This meditation is both calming and uplifting. We associate white with angels, clouds, the heavens, even with God.

Close with an affirmation like this: "I see myself coming together, flowing in one direction." "I see my many gifts and talents becoming part of a whole." "I am pure creativity. I am reaching for the clouds."

Words: Verbal Visualization

Words in and of themselves are images. The word "tree" is four symbols written down on a page to evoke the image of a woody perennial plant that has a trunk and branches. We associate those four letters with a picture in our minds.

Remember in Chapter 16 when we mentioned that Carolyn wrote down the word "flourish" at the top of her New Year's goals? For several years now, Carolyn has exchanged elaborate lists of New Year's goals with a network of friends. Throughout the year, they support each other with those goals. Every year, after filling in goals for each Life Arena, Carolyn tries to sum it all up in one word. This word is a theme that runs through every goal on the list. One year it was simple, "love"; another year, it was "dilate," which meant opening herself up to new experiences and giving birth to new ideas. (And yes, she wanted to conceive!) Carolyn uses her focus word when she visualizes her goals.

Let's brainstorm some verbs as focus words:

Soar	Restore	Embark
Marvel	Forgive	Surge
Flourish	Give	Trust
Laugh	Question	Triumph
Love	Purify	Build
Imagine	Cherish	Act
Transcend	Savor	Complete
Glide	Roar	Pioneer
Frolic	Splash	Master
Distill	Radiate	Conceive
Illumine	Float	Dream
Reconcile	Awaken	Emerge

Write your word on a piece of paper. Make it more powerful by getting markers or paints and drawing it on art paper. Then fill the paper with images. Use this word in your visualizations, focusing on seeing the letters before you. What other images surround it?

Here are some other ideas for using words creatively in your visualizations, many of which Carolyn uses in her writing workshops:

- **Free association.** Ideally, it's good to do this with one of your visualization groups, but it works just as well on your own. On a sheet of notebook paper, brainstorm as many words and phrases as you can think of. Just keep going without evaluating. Take whatever word or phrase pops into your mind next. If you are working with the group, you'll play off each other.

- **Free write.** Now cut up the words on strips of paper and put them in a bowl. Draw out three to five words. Using a kitchen timer, write for 10 minutes, trying to use these words. But remember, there are no rules. You aren't absolutely bound to using each word. Let them spark you. One word might stimulate an idea, and you might just run with that. You might react to a word but not actually use the word in your free-write. The only guideline is to keep writing. Don't stop. Don't evaluate. Don't cross out any words. Just keep going until the bell rings. It will lead somewhere. Trust us.

- **Deconstruct a poem.** Type or write out a favorite poem, using double-spacing. Cut the lines apart, and shuffle them in a different order. Spread them across your page, double-spaced. Under each line, write a line of your own. But again, you don't have to be a poet, just write what you feel and don't evaluate its artistic merits.

- **Write a scene.** Dialogue can be an excellent way of getting to the heart of an issue that may be key to your creative visualization. That's because dialogue by nature is external. When you read a novel, you get to read the inner thoughts of your main character. But with a screenplay or stage play, it's all dialogue. The characters have to give voice to their thoughts.

Write a dialogue between you and someone who is key to achieving your vision. Maybe this person is a helpful person, or perhaps he is a discourager. This exercise is exceptionally useful to do with someone who has undermined you or challenged you. If you feel yourself limited by judgments you perceive coming from this person, use dialogue to clear the air. Sometimes just the exercise of saying your piece is beneficial. Tell her how you really feel. Tell him why you want this goal to happen in your life. And stand in her shoes as you write her lines. Why is she against your goal? Is he really against it, or is he afraid to take that kind of risk himself? Does he just not understand? Afterward, do a visualization about him understanding your motivations better.

Here are two ways you can get into writing this dialogue:

◆ Write it to music. Because writing is left brain, rational and verbal, doing it to music can stimulate the other side of your brain. Put on some favorite music and let your writing flow. Match the rhythm and dynamics of the music as you write. What visual images come into your mind? What does the rhythm feel like? It's always interesting to see what comes out.

◆ Take some time to add affirmations to your journal. Use some of the verbs we brainstormed: "I am ready to soar." "Today I cherish all that my body can do." "Today I am gliding through my challenges with grace and serenity." "I am embarking on a new adventure with fresh eyes and an open heart." "I see a new, wiser self emerging from within."

Going Underground

The more you tap into your creativity through language, art, and dreams, the more vivid your visualizations can be. The more you access your creativity, the more you'll come to trust that your creativity is infinite. In opening up to greater creativity, you'll come to trust your subconscious mind to do the "underground" work that enhances creative visualization. Now your creative visualizations can work like a computer with a dual processor. As you continue to work with dreams, images, and words, you'll start to hone your intuition. Your intuition will become a valuable ally, something you can trust to bring about your most heartfelt desires.

The Least You Need to Know

◆ Dreams are a wellspring of personal information on which to draw for creative visualization subject matter.

◆ By setting your intention before a night's sleep, you can use dreams to solve problems.

◆ Visual stimulation can awaken your creativity and receptivity, and can be especially useful when embarking on a big picture goal.

◆ Using color stimulation to create visualizations can be invigorating and inspiring.

- Focus words, added to a creative visualization session, can assist in bringing forth the positive energy that bolsters your vision.

- Wordplay taps into your intuition.

18

Go for the Gold: Sport Sight

In This Chapter

◆ The power of the mind-body connection

◆ How top athletes visualize

◆ Develop a winning attitude

◆ Achieving peak performance

"Focus is strength," says U.S. women's soccer star Abby Wambach. She and other world-class athletes such as cyclist Lance Armstrong, Olympic marathon gold medalist Joan Benoit-Samuelson, and golfer Tiger Woods have long known the supreme edge that focused visualizing can give them in competition.

Sport sight is creative visualization applied to athletic performance. In this chapter, we'll explore how you can draw on the techniques of top athletes to enhance your performance in all arenas of life. And we'll also examine how movement, exercise, and activity can boost your ability to think big and play big.

On the Go

Sport sight is often referred to as guided imagery, mental focus, or just simply sports psychology. It involves the athlete training his (or her) mind to focus on positive mental images. Mind training is done in conjunction with body training, and then the athlete applies his mind training techniques to competition. When the pressure is on, not only does his body know what to do, his mind does, too.

Deeper Meaning

Sport sight is creative visualization in motion. By focusing on positive mental images, through guided imagery or creative visualization, athletes discipline their minds and bodies to respond under pressure.

Creative visualization in motion is taking it to a whole new level. Pair positive mental images with the well-documented mind-body benefits of exercise, and you have a potent combination.

The benefits of exercise using positive mental focus are ongoing. Positive mental imagery gets you to perform better. It gets you try harder, work a little longer. Exercise increases your sense of well-being, there's no doubt about that. In the long run, exercise increases your vitality, improving cardiovascular health, muscle tone, and strength. A regular exercise regimen can increase your self-confidence, your self-esteem and, in general, your ability to cope with life's challenges. When you have confidence in your body, you carry around with you an extra measure of competence.

Exercise provides you with a good template for setting measurable goals. You can push yourself harder, increasing resistance or more weight. You can use a heart rate monitor during an optimal workout, measuring the effectiveness of your exertion. You can go another minute longer. Or you can shave a minute off your time. For some, the measurable improvements are in body mass index or weight loss. For others, they are in competition. Perhaps, if you play team sports, you measure success by a win-loss record.

Your visualization goals with sport sight can be direct: to enhance your exercise program or increase your health and well-being. Or they can be indirect: applying the techniques of sport sight to other arenas of your life to maintain the mental focus that you hone through exercise. In this chapter, we'll explore both.

The Runner's High: Affirmations

If you regularly engage in vigorous exercise, then good for you. You have experienced what many people who exercise call the *runner's high*. All of a sudden you have twice the energy. All of a sudden you feel 10 years younger.

The next time you do your workout, notice the messages you send to yourself to keep going. It may just be, "You can do it!" Or, "Only one more lap." Or your affirmations may be more specific, directed at your biceps or hamstrings: "Biceps, you are strong" or "Hamstrings, you have the firepower." Some people send affirmations about who they are: "*I* am an athlete" or "*I* am a dancer." "Identity" affirmations can be particularly motivating if you are trying a new workout or activity. If at mid-life you are reconnecting with your desire to learn ballet or swimming or the team sport you didn't do in high school, it may feel unnatural at first. You may feel anything but graceful. You may laugh at the idea of yourself as a jock. So use those affirmations!

Deeper Meaning

Sports psychologist Michael Sachs of Temple University describes the **runner's high** as a euphoric state that athletes experience at a certain point during exercise. He describes it as characterized by an enhanced appreciation of nature and a transcendence of time and space.

Why Motion Works

When you begin to exercise, you immediately engage your mind in a struggle with your body. Initially, your mind is telling you, "You can't do this. You must stop." It continues to send signals to get you to stop: You are too tired. Your muscles are hurting. You're breathing too hard.

Pushing through this wall is the key to why motion works so effectively for positive creative visualization. Know that the mind always relinquishes and the body knows what to do. Trust in the body's wisdom. (Within reason, of course!) When the body takes over, the mind is no longer necessary. (This is why the mind fights so hard! It doesn't want to relinquish center stage.)

Many psychologists call this the flow state, which we touched on in Chapter 16. It's very similar to what we discussed in Chapter 11 about the power of the present moment. When you break through the wall and let the body take over, you are completely in the now.

What We Can Learn from Athletes

Athletes use visualization to train, to perform, or to compete. In training, athletes often visualize the course they will run, the routine they will use, or the actual competition. The value of this is explained simply by Swiss athlete Brigitte McMahon, who won the Olympic Games' first triathlon in 2000. After winning the gold, McMahon told the press she had visualized the final sprint to the finish in her mind many times. She believed she had the edge because she was prepared for the last mile, and she had already envisioned the outcome.

Athletes use sport sight during the training itself, to set their intention for that day's training. They visualize their bodies responding to what their minds want to accomplish in that day's training. They visualize their muscles being strong enough, their endurance lasting long enough.

They also use visualization to walk through the preparation before a big competition or performance: setting up, adjusting to the feel of the crowd, greeting competitors. Without visualizing these aspects, which are not present during training, the added stimuli can be a distraction. The combination of an unfamiliar setting (and perhaps unfriendly if you are the "visiting" team), the closeness of the competitors, the pressure to perform, and the noise of the crowd—any or all can rattle an athlete who doesn't have a positive mental focus.

Visualization also can be used to envision triumphing over obstacles. An athlete visualizes herself taking the steps to surmount the challenge, walking her mind through it to a positive outcome. She visualizes the outcome.

CAUTION

Don't Panic, *Focus!*

It's important to follow all the way through your visualization when focusing on surmounting an obstacle. Carry it all the way through, step by step, to the end. Often when you focus on the challenge, you give it too much energy. Realize it's natural to focus on a challenge—after all, you're trying to figure it out—but you must walk your mind all the way through, again and again, to what it feels like to come out on the other side.

The Big Psyche-Out

It is said that sports performance is just as much mental as physical. Golfer Tiger Woods, known for his uncanny concentration, has worked with a sports psychologist from an early age. And ask any free-throw shooter how she does it when the game is on the line and the opposing team's fans are waving banners and booing.

What you *believe* is crucial to how you perform. What you focus on is vital to achieving the outcome you desire. When you focus on a challenge or setback, you are giving energy to it. If the free-throw shooter notices the colorful banners or listens to the thunder of the booing crowd, she is giving energy to the negative environment. Often when an athlete "chokes," it's because he focused on what he was trying *not* to do. Maybe the last time he ran this course, he stumbled, and when he returns to this course, he replays the tape of when he stumbled. So to say an athlete choked is to say she focused on a negative visualization. Instead, when she envisions overcoming the challenge, she nails it.

In some sports, such as gymnastics or swimming, the competition is so stiff that one nanosecond of a negative visualization can be the difference in one-hundredth of a point that separates an athlete from the medal stand. Those who earn the gold are those who have positive visualizations all the time, every time. They have a vast database of positive visualizations to access, and they have rehearsed them again and again.

Affirmations
She shoots! She scores!

Ways to Use Sport Sight Techniques

Primarily, we have discussed using visual cues in sports visualization, but there are two other techniques you can use:

- **Kinetic.** You imagine what it feels like in your body as you fly down a ski run or you spin through the air above the uneven parallel bars. You visualize what your muscles feel like when you summon the final kick that gets you across the finish line. You imagine the perfect landing.

- **Auditory.** You imagine the roar of the crowd. You imagine blocking out the roar of the crowd. You listen to your breath, using that to ground yourself. You cue in to the music for your skating or gymnastics routine.

Step-by-Step: A Visualization

This visualization doesn't have to be used in an athletic setting. It can be used for any challenge you have to perform: public speaking, singing, running a meeting, going for a job interview.

1. **Training.** Training is preparing to perform. If it's public speaking, you would rehearse your speech out loud in front of a mirror or into a tape machine. If it's a job interview, you would research the company ahead of time. As you "train" for your big day, visualize yourself becoming smarter and stronger and more prepared. Develop some affirmations such as "I am training myself for the success I know is assured."

2. **Getting into gear.** Think about what "gear" you'll need to perform. What will you wear? Will you need a microphone? Will you need to carry a portfolio? A laptop to do a presentation? Plan your gear down to the last detail. Make a ritual out of assembling your gear and setting it up on location. Visualize all the steps you need to take so that it all seems familiar. Visualize that the slide projector *will* work and the microphone will not squeal with feedback. Use your setup time to send yourself affirmations. All of this "gear" is a reflection of your competence. Affirmation: "I am competent. I am prepared."

Imagine, See, Be

You can practice sport sight creative visualization with a team of collaborators, much like in Chapter 15, before facing a challenge. Brandi Chastain of the gold medal-winning U.S. women's soccer team told *Soccer Times* about the techniques she and her teammates use to visualize the outcomes of games. "I couldn't imagine it any other way," she said.

3. **Warming up.** Allow yourself enough time on your big day to arrive early and get used to your surroundings. Greet people. Actively ask them questions, showing an interest in them. Their warmth will warm you up. Affirmation: "I feel safe here. I feel comfortable."

4. **Set your intention.** The most effective visualizations are those with a specific, strong intention. What do you want to get out of your big day? How do you want to feel afterward? How do you want to view yourself? Make it an affirmation, as though it has already happened: "Today is the day I will win." "I hear applause; it's for me."

5. **Know your course.** Visualize your course. Know how you will take it. Affirmation: "This is my plan. I have a good plan."

6. **Stay in your body.** Visualize your big day kinesthetically. How does it feel to stand at the podium? How does it feel as you take the two steps up to the stage and shake the hand of the person who introduced you? How does it feel 10 minutes into your talk? Does what you're wearing feel comfortable? Attractive? Are you smiling? Can you feel the muscles on your face smiling? Affirmation: "I am presenting my best self to the world through my grace and my smile."

7. **Triumph over the obstacle.** Maybe you need to be clever. Maybe you need to be persuasive. Visualize that moment when you really nail it. See it all the way through. Affirmation: "I see myself having what it takes in the moment to overcome all obstacles."

> **Affirmations**
>
> I am comfortable. I am prepared. I know my stuff. I nail it.

Simulating Pressure: Putting It on the Line

Up until now, we have talked about ways to use creative visualization directly to improve your performance—that is, visualizing yourself performing that maneuver or task required for success.

Another technique is to visualize something else that simulates the pressure, which in turn pushes your body to perform. This is another way athletes train for competition. They have already experienced performing when everything is on the line, because they have rehearsed it in a visualization.

Another reason to use this technique goes back to the process of the mind relinquishing control to the body. You may push your mind to that point by giving your mind *something else to visualize*. Your mind wants to keep busy at all times. When you are pushing yourself, your mind is trying to protect you. When you know your body can do it, that your body holds the wisdom and strength it needs to perform, occupy your mind with a visualized quest: imagine hiking a mountain trail or walking along a beach, heading to a big rock.

Here's an example of a visualization that simulated pressure. On Halloween, the studio cycling instructor at Carolyn's gym led the class through a series of drills that took place in Roswell, New Mexico, whose claim to fame is the alien invasion in the 1950s, affectionately known as "The Roswell Incident." Being trapped with a bunch of aliens who are about to kidnap you to their spaceship is a terrific incentive to pedal faster! Through imagining escaping the spaceship and riding through the woods, knocking down branches and bumping over rocks, the class was able to simulate the adrenaline rush—and get their bodies to perform at a higher level.

The Winning Attitude

Why does rehearsing a performance in your mind better prepare you for success? When you train your mind for a successful outcome, your mind responds with

"I know what to do here." Your mind does not struggle against you, sending fight-or-flight signals as it is so prone to do when encountering unfamiliar and potentially unsafe situations. But when you have already visualized yourself doing this success-fully hundreds of times, your mind says, "Great. You've done this before. I'll just sit back and watch you do it again. I have confidence in you."

Visualizing the outcome you desire is rehearsing for success. You visualize the pre-paration. You visualize the course. You visualize training and working more purpose-fully. When you are looking for the winning edge, your best bet is to make your mind an ally. Train your mind to lead you to victory.

Peak Performing

Science suggests that a little string of amino acids, called neuropeptides, transmits emotions throughout our bodies. Every emotion, positive or negative, influences the release of neuropeptides from the brain to the body, from the body to the brain, and back again. Psychoneuroimmunologists point to these neurochemical changes as evidence of the mind's ability to influence the healing of the body. Positive emotions heal—or protect the immune system against viruses and other invaders. Negative emotions weaken the body's ability to resist disease.

Positive psychology continues to study the role that positive beliefs have on mental health. Positive emotions, thoughts, and affirmations create a new reality and form new perceptions. One recent study showed that optimists live longer because even when faced with challenges, they believe they have it in them to surmount those challenges. They believe in positive outcomes, so they pursue the assistance they need in order to achieve. For instance, the study showed that optimists who experi-enced stroke symptoms were more likely to get themselves medical care promptly.

Research is increasingly showing that mind-body exercise such as yoga, tai chi, and other focused movement activates positive emotions and perceptions. These forms of movement train the mind in the discipline of positive awareness. Practitioners often say it puts them in a state of flow, something they describe much as a runner describes the "runner's high." When you are in a state of flow, you feel you are engaged in the creative unfolding of something larger. This is peak performing.

Mihaly Csikszentmihalyi, author of *Flow: The Psychology of Optimal Experience*, pro-vides a definition of flow in telling this parable from ancient Taoist scholar Chuang Tzu. In a parable, Ting, the esteemed court butcher of Lord Wen-hui, describes the way he works: "Perception and understanding have come to a stop and spirit moves where it wants. You stop 'thinking' and just do."

Purposeful Living

Tour de France winner Lance Armstrong would certainly be in that camp. Not only has he drawn upon positive psychology for healing, he has made fear an ally. Armstrong overcame testicular cancer to come back and win the world's most rigorous cycling competition—a record seven times. He says, "To be afraid is a priceless education." He credits surviving cancer with teaching him purposeful living. From that, he learned how to train and how to win more purposefully.

"It taught me that pain has a reason," he says. "Pain and loss are great enhancers." Armstrong has used pain as a way to focus on what was essential to the core of his being. Pain makes us ask the questions we would not ordinarily ask. It makes us drop away those things that are not priorities. It distills us to our core identity. Armstrong goes on to say that, "The truth is, if you asked me to choose between winning the Tour de France and cancer, I would choose cancer. Odd as it sounds, I would rather have the title of cancer survivor than winner of the Tour, because of what it has done for me as a human being, a man, a husband, a son, and a father."

You can see why he is a winner. He knows who he is. He is willing to make difficult choices. He knows his purpose in life. He understands how to use the inevitable fears in life because he has already confronted the unthinkable. It's hard to beat someone who won't succumb to fear, but uses it as an ally. It's hard to beat someone who knows why he is here and what he is supposed to do.

> **Wisdom Well**
>
> Suffering, I was beginning to think, was essential to a good life, and as inextricable from such a life as bliss. (Suffering) … might last a minute, or a month, but eventually it subsides, and when it does, something else takes its place, and maybe that thing is a greater space for happiness.
>
> —Lance Armstrong, seven-time winner of the Tour de France

The Flame Burns Brightly

When the Olympic games returned to Athens, Greece, in 2004, the opening ceremony culminated in the lighting of the Olympic flame. The flame was on a gigantic cauldron that pivoted down as gold medal athlete Nikolaos Kaklamanakis lit it with the torch carried into the Olympic stadium. The cauldron swung up slowly and lifted the flame high above the stadium, where it burned for 17 days as the world's top athletes performed.

The Olympic flame has long served as an image for the fire burning brightly within us all. Whatever your choice for movement, exercise, or activity, let the vision of the flame burning brightly guide you in your thoughts, ideas, and plans throughout the day.

The Least You Need to Know

◆ Focusing on positive mental images, whether applied to sport, exercise, or other arenas of life, gives you performance edge.

◆ Sport sight is creative visualization in motion. It is practicing the discipline of performing under pressure, merging mind and body.

◆ Use your imagination to create your desired outcome, responding to visual, kinetic, and auditory cues.

◆ Peak performance derives from purposeful living, disciplined positive focus, and optimal flow.

Chapter 19

Visions

In This Chapter

- ◆ Visions bring messages to you
- ◆ Ordinary people, beyond-ordinary miracles
- ◆ How to use visions and dreams in creative visualization
- ◆ Sending out the invitation for a vision

Up to this point, we have largely focused on creating your own vision. But there are times when the vision comes to you—in the form of a dream, a waking vision, a voice of wisdom, a flash of brilliance, an epiphany, or an intuition.

Call it an inspiration. Call it a revelation. Call it an epiphany. Whatever you call it, it's a visionary leap of consciousness that propels you forward on the right path—with clarity and purpose. In this chapter, we'll show you how.

Becoming a Visionary for Your Own Life

We've all experienced visionary moments—a time when you know that something is coming to you, something is right for you. Perhaps you knew someone was going to speak to you and befriend you. Perhaps you knew that you were going to change careers before anything was in the works to cause that. Perhaps you knew that you would relocate. You are in touch with your intuitive knowledge when this comes to you. It seems so real that it doesn't seem like just your imagination at play, just a fantasy. It seems like a glimpse behind the curtain of the future.

So a vision isn't necessarily a movie that plays before your eyes or the experience of someone materializing in front of you and delivering a message. Sometimes it's a mental picture that comes to you so strongly that you see it as the truth. You know it's your future.

This, then, is like creative visualization in reverse. Instead of creating it—assembling a picture in your mind of where you want to go and what you want to do—you receive a picture of a new life that is revealed to you and you must act on it. When this happens, you have a jump-start on creative visualization. You already have the picture—sometimes so clearly that you already have the belief. The rest is just acting upon the information and continuing your positive focus. Continue to nurture the vision.

Seeing the Light, Feeling the Loving Hands

Once Shari read about a woman who was rock climbing alone and got into a danger-ous, life-threatening situation. She was not strong enough to continue climbing and too terrified to descend. She simply began quietly crying, believing that at some point her strength would fail and she would fall—and likely die. Just at the moment of greatest physical weakness, the moment when she knew it was all over, she felt a hand press her into the rock. And then she felt another hand under her foot. One hand held her, the other lifted her, and she was able to climb to the top of the rock.

Afterward, the woman tried to make sense of the experience. Was it not yet her time to go? Was she needed here on Earth for a while longer? She pondered why she was rescued and not others who die in car accidents or from cancer or in political vio-lence. What was important for her to know was that it wasn't possible to understand or explain her helping hands. She knew she had received a gift and she must share the account with other people. In doing so, she sent positive energy out into the world, and as we know, positive energy attracts more positive energy. Because she accepted her experience and was willing to share it, it became her gift to the world.

How Visions Work

Visions can be far stronger than visualizations you create because they come from outside. They are experienced by sight, as the apostle Paul did when he was struck by a flash of blinding white light on the road to Damascus. They can be experienced as a voice, as when the clouds parted and God spoke, when Jesus was baptized by John the Baptist. Or they can be experienced as the loving hands that helped the woman climb to the top of the rock.

Visions can give you assurance, solace, and comfort. They can bring you clarity, wisdom, and strength. They can provide you with a guiding principle for your life, as was the case for the Old Testament Jacob, when he dreamed of the ladder leading to heaven. They can give you new purpose, as with Paul—or Mohammad or Moses. Visions can be so strong that their effect lingers in your mind and heart for years—maybe the rest of your life.

Much of religious history includes accounts of visions, but the same holds true for science, as in Sir Isaac Newton's inspiration that came when an apple fell on his head. Visions can be a knock on the head, the birth of creativity and originality.

Don't Panic, *Focus!*

It's easy to dismiss accounts of visions that may have started a faith or changed society as though they could not have really happened—but don't. It's important to remember that something remarkable probably *did* happen, and it has entered the historical or mythological account to fulfill our need to explain the unexplainable. The important aspect of the account is the emotional truth of the experience that led to changes in society or the dawn of a new religion. You can trust the truth of that.

Visions can come from ordinary sources, as in Newton's apple, and they don't have to be the voice of God to gain us quantum leaps of consciousness. Sometimes they come as messages from loved ones who have passed on. Sometimes they come from our dreams and intuitions.

The three principles that are universal about visions, though, are the following:

◆ They come to you when you need them.

◆ They come to you to prepare you to act.

◆ They bring you information that you need—for now or in the future.

Ordinary People, Extraordinary Visions

Lourdes, Fatima, Medjugorje, and other shrines to the Virgen de Guadalupe became so because miracles appeared to ordinary people. You don't have to be Moses, then, to see a burning bush. And let us remember that when Moses was alone in the desert, he was just an ordinary guy tending sheep.

> **Wisdom Well**
>
> Gratitude bestows reverence, allowing us to encounter everyday epiphanies, those transcendent moments of awe that change forever how we experience life and the world.
>
> —John Milton, English poet, historian, and scholar

The book *A Course in Miracles* says there is no order in miracles. In other words, a *little* miracle is not any easier or harder to bring into fruition than a *big* one. Nor is there any distinction in the status of the person who receives the miracle. A miracle is a miracle, no matter who witnesses it, no matter who receives it.

Let's look further at what creates the conditions that bring forth a vision that can guide your life.

The Miracle of Intention

Visions come from outside you, but it is what is within you that brings the vision to you. In the case of the rock climber, what brought it to her? Was it her intention to live? Was it her willingness to tell others about her experience?

Here's a look at the qualities that bring on a vision:

♦ **Willingness to believe.** Visions most often come to those who are willing to receive them. This doesn't mean they can only come to those who make a conscious choice that they can accept, believe, and trust information, even if it originates from the supernatural. Countless accounts in history show us that visions come to doubters (such as Moses) or even enemies of the cause (Paul), who are then converted. Spiritual experiences come to us in whatever pathway we provide. And often that is related to our belief systems and our personalities. What would make sense to you? What would you be willing to accept? You don't have to be any particular religion or even have a religion or a belief in God, as we have noted before.

♦ **Willingness to let go.** The willingness to receive information from visions often is borne of desperation, as with the rock climber. When the rock climber relinquished *her* understanding of possible avenues of escape from her dire situation, other possibilities presented themselves. What remained was her life force, her will to live; what she surrendered was her knowledge and her estimation of her strength to surmount the challenge. Desperation has a way of sharpening our senses, enhancing our ability to hear information coming from our spiritual selves. Quite often, a vision springs from this humbling.

◆ **Readiness.** Visions come to those for whom the plan is uniquely right. Many of your unique qualifications to receive a vision of purpose may not be immediately apparent to you. They weren't to Moses. Moses told God he didn't have the talent to lead people, and he confessed to being terrified of speaking in public. But it turns out God was right—Moses proved to be the right guy.

Matching your unique qualifications with your singular purpose goes back to your intention. Remember in Chapter 14 when we discussed ways to make your goals life-affirming—bringing out the greatest good in yourself and those around you? When your intentions are pure, focused, and fortified, you have set the stage for the vision to find you.

You Are Not Alone

In a workshop Shari gave many years ago, a woman shared an experience she had as a young mother. She and her husband were quarreling. They had three children and not much money. They had lost touch with one another in the crush of their busy lives.

One day the woman walked toward her bedroom carrying a large basket of laundry to fold. She was praying and meditating, yet despairing about the fate of her marriage. When she rounded the corner, she saw a vision of Jesus Christ standing before her. Now this wasn't a usual part of laundry day, so needless to say, she was shocked. But she wasn't afraid. Jesus did not speak to her in the vision, but she understood that he was reassuring her that her marriage would survive. He didn't tell her how or even explain why—just that it would.

It was such a profound experience that the woman knew it was real and true. She was assured she was not alone in facing her challenges. She and her husband worked out their problems, and they have been happily married for more than 25 years.

Living in the Light of Visions

If time and time again people tell of how miraculous events occur in their lives unexpectedly, how much richer could our lives be if we work with the intent, affirmations, and rituals that go along with creative visualization? The following steps help you to capture visions and maximize them for creative visualizations.

First, record your vision in detail. Capture what it looked like and sounded like. If it needs interpretation, weave that in. What was the vision trying to tell you? Was it to give you reassurance? Was it to show you new possibilities? Was it to reveal someone who might be helpful to you? How was this vision bidding you to act? What Life Arena goal does this vision bolster?

Make your vision more concrete. Often visions come to us in surreal fashion— symbols that recur, sounds that beckon us, or people who are made of light. Try to make what came to you more tangible. Perhaps draw a picture of what happened.

Now, take your vision and send it some gratitude: "I am thankful for the reassurance that I am on the right path."

The next step is to believe. Believe that the path you have chosen has already happened. Develop some affirmations that support that. Continue to return to your vision, keeping it fresh and sending it affirmations.

Affirmations

Use these affirmations to strengthen your intent and open yourself to receiving visions:

- I am a spiritual being in a unique and positive way.
- People in all walks of life, with all sorts of belief systems have had visionary experiences.
- I can have these kinds of experiences if I open myself up to them.
- Visions may come to me through sight, hearing, touch, or imperative thought or emotion.
- What I do with these experiences is my choice, they are always for my own good and possibly the good of others.

Extending the Invitation

In the first part of this chapter, we discussed what to do when you receive the gift of a vision. But sometimes you are stuck on a problem and you need vision to move you forward. Or maybe you have enjoyed our discussion of visions but never had one, and you think it's about time you did. How do you invite a vision?

◆ **Put in the time.** Prove your intention. Woody Allen said 80 percent of success is just showing up. Likewise, Carolyn's writing professor at Arizona State University often said the published writers are the ones who stay in the room. They boot up the computer every day, strap themselves into the chair, and write. Tour de France winner Lance Armstrong, responding to a question from the press about what he was "on" that made him so unbeatable (implying drugs), said in a Nike commercial: "Everybody wants to know what I'm on. What am I on? I'm on my bike busting my ass six hours a day. What are you on?" You get the picture. Even when it seems less than productive, even when it seems there is no immediate payoff, put in the time.

◆ **Prove yourself willing.** What would you do to reach your goal? How far would you go? How flexible are you? How tireless? What would you give up? If you gave that up and were asked to give more, would you? Say, "Show me what I must do."

◆ **Ask.** Ask for it in skywriting. Ask and ask again. Ask for it to be unmistakable.

◆ **Move forward as if it has happened.** Proceed as though you are not afraid. You are not afraid it won't come. You know it will. You are not afraid that if a vision came to you, you would have to change. Proceed as though you have no doubt it will come, it will come clearly, and it will come when you need it.

◆ **Always listen.** Listen to your heart. Listen to your *messengers*.

Deeper Meaning

Messages of wisdom, insight, or comfort can come in any form, but they often come through messengers. **Messengers** are spirit guides, angels, or divine messengers. Sometimes they are loved ones who have passed on, or ancestors we have never met. Usually, your messengers come in the form that will make sense to you.

Visitations

Sometimes our dreams are infused with messages, either subtle or strong, from someone we love who has died. People describe visitation dreams as *real*, not just a dream, and in this kind of dream/visitation a message is usually delivered.

To use your dreams for creative visualization, it's best to simply "sit" with the visitation. Be gentle with yourself. Understand. Don't try to analyze it too much. It's important to continue to experience the emotional effect. Let the vision's meaning continue to come to you over the course of your life. Perhaps it will take a lifetime for your understanding of the visitation to be complete.

Altered Awareness

Essentially what we are talking about when we talk about inviting a vision is a *vision quest*. Most often, vision quests are associated with Native American traditions, but there are countless accounts through history of vision quests: Mohammad, Buddha and the bodhi tree, the Israelites' 40 years wandering the desert, Jesus Christ facing the three temptations in the desert, the Holy Grail, the Lewis and Clark expedition to find the Northwest Passage, Christopher Columbus discovering a new world, and Coronado and the search for Eldorado, the mythical city of gold.

Imagine, See, Be

A vision quest usually happens in wilderness or unknown territory. In solitude, connected to the earth, you are able to contemplate yourself and the mysteries of the universe—to see what you are made of. One commonality is deprivation of the senses—fasting or a sweat lodge, for instance—that heightens one's awareness. Think of ways to create a vision quest for yourself.

Common to a vision quest is some sort of sensory deprivation and solitude, which leads to an altered awareness. In the Native American tradition, you may fast, go to a sweat lodge, or walk across the bed of hot coals. A vision quest brings you inside yourself and in tune with the mysteries of the universe. That altered awareness creates the receptivity in you—to receive information from another dimension.

If you believe that we only operate with 10 percent of our brain capacity, you may be able to embrace the idea of other dimensions. But science is quickly trying to explain our awareness of other dimensions, other worlds. Physicist Brian Greene, who teaches at Columbia University, has postulated a new theory of energy that is meant to combine the theory of relativity developed by Albert Einstein and newer understandings of sub-atomic particles. Until now it has been impossible to combine these two theories with each other to form what physicists call the "theory of everything." Greene theorizes that energetic matter exists in the form of vibrating, circular strings. Their vibrational rate determines the dimension they are in. According to him, there are 11, and we live in one dimension, parallel to the other 10.

The string theory gave Shari pause to contemplate the spiritual implications. If we are all one, and after death we go to another dimension, couldn't this explain why we sometimes have an experience that seems to be unreal but is merely a momentary overlap of dimensions? An example is when you see a loved one who has passed on. Another is an unexplained physical phenomenon. Could this not be an overlap—or what we would call a visitation?

In her practice, Shari has heard many stories over the years about visitations from deceased relatives. Usually they come to comfort those left behind, or to leave a message, or just to reassure us they still exist, just in another form of energy.

One client's grandmother appeared in her granddaughter's car just at the moment that the grandmother died. She told the granddaughter goodbye and then was gone. Somehow the trembling granddaughter managed to keep the car on the road. At the next exit, she stopped and called home. The death was confirmed, and it occurred at the very time that grandmother was talking to granddaughter in her car. Another client lay on an operating table, having a delicate surgery with low odds of leaving the surgery suite alive. Just as she was anesthetized, she saw her brother in the corner of the room—her brother who had died of cancer the year before. Her brother assured her that no matter what—life or death—she would be fine. It's interesting to note that her brother didn't know the outcome of her surgery. In other words just because he died doesn't mean he became clairvoyant.

Shari has many more stories than we can recount, but she believes that the understanding of the existence of all 11 dimensions could explain these appearances. Perhaps the people we lose are only a dimension away and right next to us—not in some far off place. So they change their vibration form and rate (or someone shows them how), and we can see them. That also would explain why we sometimes see only part of them, upper body and head, or a very opaque image.

While writing this book, Shari was acutely missing her deceased mother. They had been really close, and Shari feels like they still are. One night as she climbed into bed, she asked her mother to let her know if she was with her. Immediately her bedside flashlight went on. It was a tremendous comfort for Shari. And she slept peacefully that night for the first time in several weeks.

Also while writing this book, Carolyn received a visit from her deceased father. She had hit a snag in her romantic relationship, and that night she was quite sad. Her father came to her in a dream. He said, "I know I've been dead for nine years, but I just had to check and see whether you were still seeing that guy. I want to know if things are okay." Later, Carolyn related the conversation to her mother, who shared that she had received a visit from Carolyn's father *that same night*, which happened to be her mother's birthday. Her mother said she had been missing Carolyn's father tremendously lately and had felt sad. That night he came and comforted her.

Unforgettable Revelations

Paranormal experiences in the form of visions, envisioning, audible voices, touch, and by other means are gifts to be cherished. These happenings may come from angels, spirit guides, deceased religious figures, deceased family members or friends. Their impact is immediate and profound. We usually don't forget them, and sometimes we are given the answer to an immediate problem. Sometimes it takes a lifetime to understand why they happened. They serve to remind us that we do not negotiate life alone.

The Least You Need to Know

◆ Visions bring you reassurance so that you will act or understand or be comforted.

◆ Ordinary people can experience extraordinary visions; you don't have to be a deity, a prophet, a psychic, or a visionary.

◆ Central to our ability to receive a vision is proving our intent.

◆ Take a vision that comes to you and use it as the beginning of a creative visualization.

◆ To create fertile ground for receiving visions, you must be willing to alter your awareness and be open to receiving information from other dimensions.

Part 6

More Visualizations You Can Do

All this wisdom, all this practice—where to apply it? The possibilities are endless.

Creative visualization can be used for love, health, and happiness. It can be used to bring prosperity into your life, and it can be used for healing. It can be used to visualize peace in your life, and peace for the world.

Imagine *that* ... world peace!

Chapter 20

Loving Visualizations

In This Chapter

- ◆ Manifesting a new love
- ◆ Building or renewing a relationship
- ◆ Resolving conflicts
- ◆ Making peace

It's Valentine's Day, and the stores are packed with arrangements of roses and baby's breath. The aisles are a swath of deep dark red, filled with heart-shaped boxes of chocolates wrapped in crimson cellophane. Over in the greeting card section, lovers and would-be lovers are pouring through the racks, searching for just the right sentiment.

For one day a year, at least, there are countless ways to express your love. And it's easy to visualize, with all those hearts and flowers delighting the senses. But what about the other 364 days of the year? How can you keep the love growing and deepening all year long? In this chapter, we'll devote some time to the one you are most devoted to. And if you don't have a Valentine, we'll show you how to visualize him or her.

Love and Its Many Splendors

Love is a many splendored thing that, try as we may, eludes an ultimate definition. From pop singers to psychologists to apostles to great sages, we have tried to pin it down, but it's a butterfly, flitting away. Love never fails, the apostle Paul tells us in the New Testament. It "bears all things, believes all things, hopes all things, endures all things" (I Corinthians 13:7). American psychologist Erich Fromm, author of *The Art of Loving*, described love as the only sane and satisfactory answer to the problem of human existence. St. Thomas Aquinas said, "Love takes up where knowledge leaves off." (Love, then, is sanity and insanity at the same time!)

In the first section of this chapter, we have included three visualizations: to attract a new relationship, to build on a nascent relationship, and to renew an ongoing relationship. In the second half of this chapter, we'll show you how to use visualization to resolve conflicts in relationships and make peace with relationships that have ended.

This chapter and the three that follow offer some ways to apply visualizations to your life, but by this time, you are surely ready to develop your own. Remember the following key steps, and you can apply your visualization to any topic you can dream of:

- Write out a goal. Make it a simple statement, such as "I want a new love."

- Set your intention for the visualization. Example: "I want this new love to enrich my sense of myself as a woman (or man)."

- Choose a setting.

- If you believe it will help you, choose an object or symbol that will help you visualize your goal.

- If you believe it will help you, choose an activity that will help you visualize your goal and focus your intentions on it (much like the activities we covered in Chapters 16–18).

- If you are visualizing with a partner, set your intention together. (But even with a partner, set your individual intentions before coming together for a visualization session.)

- If you are visualizing with a partner or a group, establish the setting, protocol, and ground rules for your visualization.

- Start with relaxation breathing.

- Create your vision.

◆ Meditate on your vision.

◆ Affirm your vision.

◆ Continue, outside of the visualization session, to send it positive energy. (In the upcoming sample visualizations, you'll see there are many creative ways to do this!)

Attracting a New Love

Our ideas about romantic love derive from the days of chivalry when a princess pined away in a tower, looking to the horizon for her prince returning on a white steed. The prince, too, must have spent hours visualizing the princess as he embarked on his quest across the land to seek his love and his fortune. What does she look like? When will I hear her voice, see her face for the first time? Or if off on a quest: when will I hold her in my arms again? With princes off on chivalric quests for decades at a time, there was plenty of time for the imagination to take hold. (Back home, chastity belts infused the imagination with longing, we might add.)

To set up a visualization to attract a new love, first get clear about what kind of relationship you want to attract. Make a practical list of "must have," "would be nice to have," and "can live without." Okay, now throw it away. This visualization isn't about a quest or looking outside of yourself for the answers. It's not a shopping list. Ah, but you knew that already, didn't you?

It's more about looking at yourself to see what traits you are attracting. You must know what you are sending out into the great unknown—to that distant horizon where you wait for the prince and his steed (or, if you are a man, the castle tower and the princess) to materialize. What is intentional? What is not? And what is blocking the new love? *A Course in Miracles* says, "Your task is not to seek for love, but to seek and find within yourself all the barriers you have set against it." Hmmm … so it's not a process of addition so much as subtraction. Implied in that line of wisdom is that *love is always trying to find you.*

Love is always coming toward you. Forget the news magazine reports that say that a woman over the age of 35 has more likelihood of being killed by a terrorist than ever getting married. We are meant to love and be loved.

Before this visualization, in your Creative Visualization Journal, write about how a relationship would enhance your life. What parts of your personality would you like to be able to express that you are not expressing now? How would you be a better person for having this "someone" in your life?

Examine the goals you have made in your Life Arenas. Beside each one, write the value behind it. Examine where you are putting your energies. What like-minded soul energy might be attracted to that energy?

Deeper Meaning

In *The Art of Loving,* Erich Fromm defines healthy love as the "union with somebody, or something, outside oneself, under the condition of retaining the separateness and integrity of one's own self." He writes that immature love says, "I love you because I need you." But mature love says, "I need you because I love you."

Ask yourself where this "someone" fits into your life. Where are you able to receive? What parts of your life are closed off? What are you willing to change?

Now, you are ready to visualize. Imagine yourself imbued in white light. If it is useful to you to use the images of chivalry, see yourself standing in the castle tower that can see to the horizon, or as the knight cresting each hill, looking for the tower to appear on the horizon. From that vantage point, see yourself emanating this white light out into the world. The light spreads out into the world, drawing to it light of similar quality. Send this an affirmation that is active and in the present tense, such as this one:

I am a pure white light, and I am attracting all the love I know is intended for me, right here, right now.

Building a Relationship

Okay, you snagged one. Now what do you do with him (or her)? Seriously, the first steps you take in a relationship often define the patterns you will develop together. This visualization can help you build a healthy, vital relationship. Use this one, and maybe you won't have to do the next one! (We are just kidding here: any rewarding relationship deserves the devotion that we describe in the subsequent exercise on renewal.)

For this one, we turn to the food of love: chocolate. Blindfold your partner. Yes, you heard us. Ask him to lie on his back on a bed or sofa. As you feed him a chocolate, he visualizes a mental picture of what lays the foundation for a good relationship. He visualizes himself taking those steps to build the relationship as he savors the chocolate.

The receiving partner chooses from this list of statements (or makes up some of his own):

I am seeing a relationship in which there is a balance of giving and receiving over time.

I am seeing a relationship in which both partners are healthy and whole.

I am seeing us taking the first steps toward building trust.

I am seeing a relationship in which I am able to express my best self.

I am seeing a relationship in which I can be honest and forthright, loyal and true.

Get specific in your vision about how you define "a balance of giving and receiving" or "building trust."

Close the visualization with this affirmation:

I am tasting this relationship and all of its magnificence right now.

Now, switch roles.

> **Wisdom Well**
>
> Love takes off the masks that we fear we cannot live without and know we cannot live within.
>
> —James Baldwin, American author

Renewing a Relationship

This visualization is aimed at renewing a relationship that might have gotten off track. But many of the steps in this visualization can be used to attract a new relationship or make peace with an old one. We use water as a symbol in this visualization because it is often associated with the realm of one's emotions. Water is vital for our sustenance; water continually flows; water refreshes us. And so it is with love.

1. Individually set your intention for this visualization, writing in your Creative Visualization Journal. Steer away from what you don't want. If the relationship has gotten in a rut, it may be hard to think out of the box. You may only be able to think of your partner's irritating habits.

   Start with this question: if you could build a relationship that was all you wanted it to be, starting from scratch, what would it be? What would it look like? Even if you know you can't afford a trip to the Greek islands, write down that you want to go with your soul mate to Patmos. There's a value behind that desire, and it will be useful to share it with your partner.

2. Exchange lists with your partner and discuss them. Remember to keep it positive. Say what you *do* want, not what you haven't liked.

3. Sitting down together, take a few moments to write about how this relationship enhances your life, much as you did in Chapter 15. Read one positive statement at a time and discuss it.

4. Now you are ready to create your visualization together. Sit across from one another, on the floor or in two cozy chairs pulled together. Sit so that you are nearly touching and so that you can easily look into your partner's eyes. Many people find it helps to clasp their hands together.

   Close your eyes. Breathe deeply three times to calm your mind. Many people find that visualizing together, especially with a lover, is much more creative with their eyes closed. It allows you to explore your own mind and your own mental pictures. It anchors the individuals more in their own intuition while at the same time maintaining the connection through physical touch.

   Using one or two of the examples you crafted with your partner, paint a mental picture of a mutual desire, filling in the details. It's helpful if one partner begins, speaking about three sentences to describe this picture of a renewing relationship. Then the other adds to the vision. Flip back and forth, adding to the vision and deepening it until it feels complete.

5. Close it by speaking two or three affirmations each, out loud, taking turns. Afterward, record the visualization in your journals.

6. Agree to spend five to seven minutes a day together meditating silently on your visualization.

7. Keep your visualization dynamic by placing a symbol in your bedroom (or another shared space) that reminds you of your commitment to renewal. A fountain with water trickling over smooth stones is a gentle yet constant reminder of renewal. Focus on it daily, repeating a fresh affirmation to yourself. Use it to visualize a cycle of renewal, a continual, unbroken flow.

It's important to use a fresh affirmation every day, lest it become rote. It's important to keep your mind active and alive with possibilities. Many couples find that placing an affirmation box by the fountain spurs them to practice fresh affirmations. Write your daily affirmation and leave it in the box. Make them specific. If you say, for instance, "I derive true joy from listening to my partner," write about something fascinating your partner said. Share them with your partner at the close of the week. Share what surprised you about yourself.

Here are some other affirmations you might try:

When my partner experiences happiness, it is my happiness, too.

I am increasingly aware of the skills I bring to this relationship. I watch with wonder as my skills improve, day by day.

I feel empowered in this relationship.

I am getting my needs met in this relationship.

I am exhilarated when I know I am speaking my needs in this relationship in a loving, respectful way.

Tools for Love: Making Peace

Conflicts inevitably arise in relationships. Carolyn once heard a minister say, "Everyone's incompatible." His point was that incompatibility was no excuse for not trying to work it out. Sure, there are plenty of "deal breakers" when it comes to long-term relationships, but different personalities and different viewpoints are built in to the picture. Eventually, live with someone long enough, and you'll surely find that person irritating. It's human nature to experience—and ultimately focus on—the differences. Just to make it more of a challenge, we also have a deep inborn desire to be *right*.

But we also want to be happy. We want someone who will not find us quite so irritating. We don't want to be alone. We want to be with someone who, most of the time, sees our light and not our darkness.

Don't Panic, *Focus!*

If you are in a physically or emotionally abusive relationship, you are not playing on a level playing field. The techniques we suggest here for renewing a relationship or resolving conflict in a relationship cannot work when partners do not come together as equals. A pattern of ongoing abuse, often identified as the cycle of violence by psychologists, is a dangerous power-and-control dynamic where allowing yourself to be vulnerable, as in these exercises, is setting yourself up for more abuse. Seek professional help for yourself and your children to protect yourself, stay intact emotionally, and end the violence.

In her work as a psychologist Shari has helped many couples learn how to resolve conflicts. She doesn't solve their problems; she teaches them the tools to use themselves. In the following sections we look at some strategies that she has used.

Setting the Ground Rules

The first step to resolving conflicts with your partner is to agree on ground rules:

- No verbal attacks.

- Keep statements positive.

- Avoid beginning a sentence with "you," especially when you are angry. A "you" statement is an accusation. A "you" statement is essentially the opening statement of an argument. An "I" statement is about how you are experiencing the relationship. When you say, "you always leave your socks on the floor," you are setting up the other person to deny and defend. A better approach would be, "It really bothers me when I see your socks on the floor. It's important to me that we keep the house we share together neat. It would mean a lot to me if you could pay more attention to this small thing." See the difference?

- Avoid the words "never" or "always." Again, this sets up an argument. The other person will almost always (there's that word again!) defend herself, rehashing the 1 percent of the time when she does not do this thing, and then you end up having a petty, unproductive argument. But also remember with compassion that when you do slip, or when you hear your partner say "always" or "never" (as in "you always leave your socks on the floor"), what you're really hearing (or saying) is that this is something that's important to you.

- Either person may call for a time out when they are overwhelmed by what is being said.

- Agree never to argue in front of the children.

How to Listen

Here are some guidelines for listening:

- Allow for different styles. Remember that no two people think or process alike. One may know what to say or how she feels immediately; the other may have to process for a few days.

- Use empathetic listening. Empathetic listening is a deepening of the reflexive listening techniques that you'll find in many marriage counseling books. In reflexive listening, the other partner plays back, nearly verbatim, what the speaker said, as in, "You are telling me that you do not like it when you see my socks on the floor."

Empathetic listening means putting yourself in the other person's skin *for a moment.* As you listen to him speak, feel the unspoken emotions behind it. Think: why is this person sharing this with me? It's not: to make me feel guilty or inadequate. It's not: to get my goat. It is, however, usually one of these: It's important to him. It upsets him. It makes him feel uneasy.

Keep your empathetic listening response to "I" statements, too: "I am hearing that when your father's business associate died, it was important to you that we attend the funeral as a family." You may not have thought it was important. As you are listening, you become your partner. So you forget, for a moment, that it would never occur to you to accompany your spouse to his father's business associate's funeral. You resist the urge to say, "No one ever does that!" or "It would have cost us $1,000!" When you sit inside your partner's head, you are trying to answer the question: why would this be important to him?

♦ Jot down some quick notes when you are listening to your partner so that you may continue listening. Make a note that you want to respond to something, and get back to listening. Also use the paper to write statements when you become too confused or overwhelmed to speak.

♦ Set a time limit for each person to speak, and agree on a time limit for the other person to respond. Keep it short at first—say 10 minutes—if the conflict is emotionally charged. You can go longer when you have gone through the steps a few times and have had some shared successes and built some trust in each other and the process. Most people find 1 to 1½ hours about right.

♦ Agree on a number of sessions. It is good to establish a limit. Both of you will find comfort in knowing it won't be an endless process. Both of you will find security in knowing the other partner has committed to the effort. Six is a good number for major conflicts. One is adequate if you can keep it small. But if you are just starting out, don't limit it to one. You'll find that your first issue is generally fraught with some additional complexities, and you are learning a new process.

As you go through the process you may need to negotiate new rules. You may also find that it's best to start out with a trusted therapist. Many couples have let a lot of issues build up before they get to the point of creating a formal conflict resolution process. If that's the case for you, you may need a third, unbiased professional to get you back on track.

Imagine, See, Be

Pretend to be an anthropologist. Never stop seeking to know your partner as though he or she is an exotic creature you have just discovered living alone in the jungle, wearing nothing but an animal skin. Never think you can fill in your partner's sentences (even if 90 percent of the time you can). Resist the temptation to judge. Try to figure out his or her essential nature, using the analytical detachment of a scientist collecting data sets. "Really? What's your thinking behind that?" Ask why. The answers may surprise you.

Of course, some relationships cannot be resolved, and we are called upon to make peace with them. In Chapter 22, we will explore some ways you can use visualizations to make peace with a relationship that has ended.

Two by Two

Sharing your life with someone can be one of the most gratifying experiences in life. A relationship is a dance of togetherness and separateness, intimacy and solitude, rock-solid commitment, and new discoveries. It is a weaving together of two hearts. Use these visualizations and make up some visualizations of your own and you'll undoubtedly have all the love you need.

The Least You Need to Know

- Use the examples in this chapter to create visualizations on any topic.

- To use visualization to manifest a new love, first get clear on what you want, who you are, and how much you are willing to give.

- You can make your relationship a continually renewing entity by practicing visualizations and affirmations together.

- Combine visualization with conflict resolution skills to restore harmony to your relationship.

21

Prosperity Visualizations

In This Chapter

- Attracting abundance
- Imagining infinite possibilities
- Defining your beautiful, secure world
- Cultivating your capacity to thrive

To live long and prosper means more than having plenty of money. It means living with much love and good health. It may mean you have a lot of money, or it may mean that you have exactly what you need without undue struggle. For some, prosperity means that you have work that you love to do and creates better lives for yourself and others. The monetary rewards are immaterial.

In this chapter, we'll explore ways to use creative visualization for material and emotional prosperity. You'll learn to use visualizations to create abundance in your life, enhance your capacity to create, and manifest those little coincidences that bring you good fortune.

Attracting Prosperity

The word prosper derives from the Latin word *prosperus*, which means favorable, and the word stem *spes*, which means hope. It means to nourish, to succeed, to thrive, or to grow in a vigorous way. But the words we want to highlight are *hope* and *favorable conditions*. You must believe, or hope—and that combination creates the favorable conditions that allow you to thrive.

Prosperity consciousness is a metaphysical term that means changing how you think and believe about prosperity. You attract a higher level of abundance in your life because you believe you already have it, right here, right now. You believe that what you need in order to thrive is out there and *will always be available*. Not only that, you live as though you already have it. *Your positive energy attracts the very thing you need.* Essentially, it works on the same principles as creative visualization.

Wisdom Well

Abundance is not something we acquire. It is something we tune into.

—Wayne W. Dyer, American author and self-motivation lecturer

The consciousness breaks down into three key components:

1. Believing in abundance

2. Believing in limitless replenishment

3. Connecting to the source of your creativity

This series of visualizations is designed to give you a blueprint for creating prosperity visualizations of your own.

Cornucopia: An Abundant Universe

What defines abundance for you? For many, images of abundance derive from nature, from plentiful food to a lush garden. Or maybe you think of fertility—making babies. Abundance suggests there are no limitations, that the world is constantly creating more and more—or, as Carolyn's father was fond of saying, "There's more where that came from."

In the area you have set up for creative visualization sessions, set up a symbol that represents abundance to you, such as a bowl of fruit or a vase of flowers. Take in the details of it: the dimples in the oranges, the waxy red-gold skin of the apples, the contours of the bananas, the brown speckles on the pears. Spend two to three minutes observing with a sharp awareness of detail—as though you might have to describe this bowl of fruit to someone else. Some people find it helpful to make notes because it prompts them to notice more.

Now close your eyes and breathe deeply. Hold this picture in your mind as you imagine what abundance would look like in your life. See your life as full of texture and color, rich with a variety of tastes and smells.

Pulling one of the Life Arena goals from your list, fill in this sentence: "Because I have (name your goal: meaningful work, a thriving business), my life is filled with much texture and color. I am tasting life in its fullness."

As you continue over the next week or so to work with this visualization, place symbols in your home, in your car, or on your desk that spark your imagination for abundance. Move the bowl of fruit to the center of your dining room table. Put a vase of flowers on your desk at work. Hang a garland of rosemary from your rear view mirror.

> ### Affirmations
>
> The universe is abundant and alive.
>
> I live in a world that is constantly creating. This source of creation abides in me and thrives.
>
> There is plenty. I am drinking from all the riches life has offered me.

Flying to Infinity

"To infinity and beyond!" proclaims the astronaut toy hero Buzz Lightyear in the movie *Toy Story*, each time he leaps into the air. Infinity—how grand is that? *Infinity* is defined as limitless space, time, and distance. In mathematics, it is the number that represents an ever-increasing quantity. It is out there on the line that stretches out into the beyond and has no end. At a certain point, the number becomes so high that it takes on a life of its own. The symbol for infinity is: ∞.

Because we tend to measure prosperity in numbers, infinity can be a good way to visualize it. The infinity symbol itself looks like a figure eight lying on its side and is called a *lemniscate*. It was invented in 1655 by mathematician John Wallis. About 40 years afterward, the mathematician Bernoulli named it, using the Latin *lemniscus*, which means ribbon. This ribbon is continuous. It has no end. One end flows into the other.

When you visualize the infinity symbol in your mind's eye, animate it. Light it up. Electrify it. Imagine it as a neon tube, glowing pink or blue or purple. Or see it as water, continually flowing. Sit and stay with this active vision, and let yourself feel the constant renewal.

You may wish to strengthen this visualization by hooking one of your Life Arena goals to it. Envision within the infinity symbol the swirl of limitless jobs, money, lovers—whatever it is, it's yours, and it's continuously replenishing.

Jobs end, money gets spent, lovers leave. But better jobs come, more money arrives (just in time!), and new lovers appear to teach us deeper love. We must remember: Love is always seeking us. Prosperity, too. Trust that when you are aligned with self- and life-affirming purpose, the universe will give you the means to express it.

Lilies of the Field

This visualization centers on beauty, because beauty opens our hearts to abundance. The way Matthew Fox says it in *Creativity: Where the Divine and the Human Meet* (see Appendix B) is "all who tap into beauty and put it in the world are in a conversation with God, the author of beauty in nature." Becoming aware of the beauty that surrounds you lifts you outside of yourself and connects you with something larger than yourself, by whatever name you call it. That means connecting to the limitless possibilities that allow you to prosper.

> **Wisdom Well**
>
> When you have only two pennies left in the world, buy a loaf of bread with one, and a lily with the other.
>
> —Chinese proverb

Take note today of 10 beautiful things you experience—and fully experience them. Let yourself be seduced by them: the sweet songs of the first birds of spring. The magnificent scent of roses, the velvet touch of their petals. The salty sea breeze stinging your nostrils as you inhale deeply, gulping it in. The gentle tinkling of the wind chimes in the caressing breeze. Take the time to consider the lilies of the field, how they delight you.

Here are some affirmations to use with your beauty visualizations:

Magnificent things are going on all around me.

Magnificent things are coming through me.

Magnificent things are unfolding within me.

I am participating in Divine beauty.

I am tapping into the fountain of total beauty.

I am luminous, reflecting the beauty that created me and surrounds me.

The Color of Security

For the inspiration for this visualization, we turn back to Chapter 17, where we used the color white in a visualization. But this time we will use purple because it is the color of prosperity. It is considered the royal color as well as the color of spiritual enlightenment. Purple suggests passion, fertility, and creativity.

We will combine that with the advice from Chapter 16, about the power of tactile (or "hands-on") visualization to activate the imagination and positive energy.

Drape yourself in a rich purple fabric (velvet, chenille, satin, silk). It can be a blanket, a quilt or throw, a coat, or a length of fabric you get from a fabric store. The richer the texture, the richer your visualization will be.

Close your eyes and breathe deeply, staying fully aware of the sensation of the purple fabric that embraces you. Visualize yourself sinking into this fabric, sinking into infinite abundance.

Your visualization will focus on security. Assess what security means to you. Quantify each item you list as specifically as possible. For instance, using the first item on our sample list, define how much money in the bank feels like enough for you. Eight months' income? What feels secure for you—the money market? How liquid does it need to be?

- Money in the bank
- Affordable mortgage (or rent)
- Reliable car
- Health insurance
- 401(k) matching
- A growing retirement account
- Working for a stable company
- Owning an established business

What defines wealth for you? Remember to be specific. Describe something you can see in your mind's eye. Here's a sample list to spark your imagination:

- Driving a car with heated leather seats
- Owning a painting by an artist with some renown

- A hand-knit sweater you bought in Italy

- Fine crystal

- A plasma TV

We'll point out now that the items on both lists are external. They are all outside of you—something you seek to acquire. Now let's take inventory of the wealth you have within. That is already in your control. Here's a sample list:

- I am wise with money.

- I am hard-working.

- I am sharp.

- I am talented.

- I am good at motivating people to do their best.

- I am resourceful.

- I have many friends I can rely on. They are just as loyal to me as I am to them.

- I am in good health because I eat right and exercise regularly.

Continue to brainstorm this list. Write them down so you may refer to them. This is your intangible wealth. These items form the basis of your security.

Now, you are ready to create a visualization. Choosing one or two items from the third list, create a mental picture around it—something tangible that illustrates that trait in your life. For instance, with "I am talented," if you have created something, whether it be a gallery painting or a technical training manual, create a visualization around the material result of your talent.

Wisdom Well

The psychic task which a person can and must set for himself is not to feel secure, but to be able to tolerate insecurity.

—Erich Fromm, American psychologist and author

Use these affirmations and develop some of your own:

I am secure because I know that perfect abundance imbues my life in every way.

I am resting in the richness of all this life has to offer me.

I am secure because I am attracting into my life all that I need and ever will need.

As you go into the next week, notice where the color purple turns up in your surroundings. Use it to stay aware of the ways prosperity is manifesting in your life.

Taking Care of Your Prosperity

When we think of prosperity, we tend to think of what we are bringing into our lives. But just as vital to prosperity is development of our capacity to prosper. By tending to your talents and resourcefulness, you undeniably will prosper.

Remember the Aesop's fable about the goose that laid the golden egg? A farmer and his wife had the good fortune to have a goose that produced an egg of gold every morning. Every day they sold an egg, and quickly they became rich. But they decided they weren't getting rich fast enough. They wondered if they could get to the stash of gold inside the goose and be richer than rich. So they killed the goose, only to discover that inside, it was just an ordinary goose.

When we say we are protecting the goose that laid the golden egg, we are saying we are taking care of our capacity to produce. The golden egg is what you need and desire, but the way to get it is to take care of the goose. Or, as motivational lecturer Wayne W. Dyer reminds us about the law of attraction, it's not that people who make money become successful, but that successful people attract money. "They bring success to what they do," he says. When you take care of your capacities, you have the golden touch.

The Capacity for Success

We brainstormed this capacities list, but feel free to add your own:

Health _____

_____

Skills _____

_____

Knowledge _____

_____

Alliances _____

_____

Love _____

_____

Family _____

_____

Creativity _____

_____

Integrity _____

_____

Faith _____

_____

Imagine, See, Be

Make it a regular practice to send out affirmations for each area of your capacities. These affirmations help you recognize your talents and resourcefulness. They help you stay in a state of gratitude for the attributes that enable you to manifest abundance in your life. Here's one example: *I am happy and healthy. In my radiant health, I attract all the light and vitality that is in this world.*

When you have health, you are productive. When you have love, you are like a knight in shining armor—invincible.

Take a moment to write a two- to three-sentence visualization to match each word on your list, describing the optimum. What does the picture of perfect health look like for you? Write a scene from your life in which your skills and knowledge really shine. After you go through the list, look back over it. All of this adds up to the picture of prosperity. Are there any areas in which you are not flourishing? Strengthen that area with a visualization that is more fleshed out. Write affirmations for that area.

Well-Deserved Success

It's important to examine your beliefs about what you deserve. Ask yourself if you may be creating pitfalls for yourself. Examine the attitudes about abundance in your family of origin. What beliefs do you agree with? Disagree with? Which ones do you need to shed? What do you believe about people who are successful? Do you see them as different from you, or do you see the similarities? Ask yourself this hard question. Do you subconsciously believe that you must be a martyr to have abundance? Do you place high stock in self-sacrifice? Do you value pretending not to have abundance, lest others envy you? You may be surprised by your answers.

Examine what came up for you when you asked these questions. Explore them in your Creative Visualization Journal.

Choose from these affirmations, or write some of your own:

All that I need exists within me.

I believe that I deserve prosperity and abundance.

Abundance is a spiritual as well as physical manifestation.

I have the capacity to share the steps to abundance with others.

I will live in abundance for the rest of my life no matter what is going on around me.

Don't Panic, *Focus!*

How much is enough? How do you know? In the myth of Midas, he asked that everything he touched would turn to gold. This worked until he touched his food and wine, and it turned to solid gold before he could partake of it. Then he realized he did not need that much gold. Once you can answer this question for yourself, you have captured the abundance that is meant for you. Or as psychologist Erich Fromm said, "The only truly affluent are those who do not want more than they have."

True Thriving

To prosper means not to struggle. Sure, it may take some hard work and sacrifice to get to where you want to go. There's a lot to be said for a healthy work ethic. You may have to make some tough choices to get established or make dramatic changes in your life. No doubt you have heard the term "taking the path of least resistance." We say this sometimes when we see someone take the easy way out, settling for substandard because no one was blocking the way. But with creative visualization, you *use* the energy of resistance to move you ahead on the right path.

When you use the magical combination of seeing it, believing it, and living it, you'll find those tough choices almost make themselves. You feel you are so near to your goal—you are living as though you already have it—and you believe there is more, so much more, manifesting in your life. Creative visualization can make the difference between the work to get there being a struggle or being a continuing unfolding of opportunities, insights, and right action. In this scenario, you can only thrive.

Thriving is the goal, too. Often when Carolyn does a visualization about something that presents a struggle, she augments the visualization with something like, "and let this unfold in my life with grace and dignity" or "and allow me flourish as I manifest this in my life."

Thriving is not achieved through sheer willpower or mere positive thinking. Focus instead on creating an outward flow of all that is good coming through you. Focus on staying in alignment with your vision. (This doesn't mean you are inflexible, by the way. It means you keep your awareness focused on the values behind your goal and stay open to what might unfold.) And use movement—that's right, exercise—to increase the vitality that allows you to grow luxuriantly.

What follows are two visualizations to get you started.

Let It Flow

Doreen Virtue, a psychologist and author of many books on healing with angels, says that we *deserve* to give. By that, she is saying that we all deserve the deep satisfaction that comes with contributing to the well-being of others. Virtue (her real name!) urges us to not allow any negativity on the part of someone else to prompt us to shut down the wellspring of giving that lives within each of us.

This visualization focuses on giving to others in a way that increases your abundance and theirs. To develop the vision, check in with yourself with these questions:

- ♦ In what ways does your giving style feel as though it takes too much from you?

- ♦ In what ways do you restrain yourself from gestures of good will out of concern it will lead to too much involvement in others' lives?

- ♦ In what ways do you feel your capabilities are limited to help others' spiritual development in abundance and prosperity?

- ♦ In what ways do you give out of obligation—as a parent, child, sibling, role model, professional, volunteer?

- ♦ Whose approval do you seek in your professional roles? In your interpersonal roles (as parent, spouse, adult child)? What are those expectations?

Now let's create a shift. Write a new vision of what it would look like to give in ways that are congruent with who you are. What would it look like for you to step outside the expectations and obligations? In what ways would you be able to give—and give more—if you were leading the life you have envisioned? These are big questions. The answers may not come immediately. Expect that your spiritual self will show you what you need to do in these areas.

Prosperity in Motion

The sense of well-being that results from exercise and movement is a close cousin to prosperity. Physical health is vital to your capacities. It is vital to your emotional prosperity. Use your regular workouts to create more prosperity visualizations, drawing on the techniques we introduced in Chapter 18. Almost any form of exercise will create this sense of well-being, but some focus on the flow of the life-force energy and abundance. Ashtanga yoga, which emphasizes synchronizing the breath as you flow from one pose to the next, is one. Others include martial arts such as Tai Chi or Nia, a dance technique that borrows from martial arts. We encourage you to find a form of exercise that emphasizes flow and use it to develop prosperity visualizations in motion.

Prosperous in Body, Mind, and Spirit

Keep working at these visualizations, and you are bound to thrive. A prosperous body creates a prosperous mind, and a prosperous mind creates a prosperous spirit. You may find the rewards are infinite, that they stretch beyond your wildest dreams. You may find that you have the golden touch.

The Least You Need to Know

◆ Turn to nature for symbols of abundance to use in your visualizations, using a bowl of fruit or vase of flowers.

◆ Use the infinity symbol in your visualizations to imagine limitless possibilities.

◆ Beauty opens your mind to abundance and prosperity and connects you with something larger than yourself.

◆ Protect your ability to prosper by maintaining your capacities and sending affirmations of gratitude for your talents and resources.

◆ Continue to thrive by practicing ways to give of your spirit generously.

◆ Use movement to create the vitality that allows you to prosper.

Chapter 22

Healing Visualizations

In This Chapter

- ◆ Visualizations to stay healthy
- ◆ Affirmations for chronic health problems
- ◆ Emotional healing
- ◆ The cure for multitasking
- ◆ Reconnecting spiritually

Health and well-being are the currency of happiness. When you are healed in body, mind, and spirit, you have the optimum conditions for creating a life brimming with vitality and serenity.

But try as we might to achieve the perfect state, there are times when our bodies fail us, our minds are overloaded, and we feel disconnected from the ones we love and our Creator. In this chapter, we will show you how you can use visualizations to get on track for healing in every area of your life.

Visualize Vitality and Serenity: The Building Blocks of Health

The first part of this chapter is about physical health and how visualizations can help us reach our optimum health—as well as be at peace with optimum, as we define it. Some of what we discuss here concerns illnesses that all of us are subject to, such as colds, flu, and stomach viruses. Visualizing good health covers a broad spectrum of circumstances. Perhaps you are in good health, but how do you maintain that, be thankful for that, visualize that for others?

Or suppose you were born with a chronic illness or develop one. Remember you are whole, just as you are. Visualizations are important so that you can reach and maintain peace. Peace means understanding yourself from a whole and spiritual perspective and that perspective is as individual as you are.

Perhaps you have come to a chronic health condition as you aged or as the result of an accident. Peace is yours, too. Use these techniques to understand that you have all you need and that yours is a pathway of serenity and discovery. Remember all you have accomplished in spite of your physical problems and rejoice in that.

Make each suggestion, each visualization about who you are—not any false perception of who you are not. Give yourself to peace, serenity, and wellness as it is defined in *your* life.

 Don't Panic, *Focus!*

Some health visualizations may be difficult if you deal with a chronic condition. If you can do them yourself, that is fine. If you need to have someone else perform these activities, do that. Shari is disabled and is no longer active in private practice. Most of these visualizations require help from someone else. But she adapts them as she wishes so that they are meaningful for her and so that they contribute to peacefulness in her life. Remember that it is both the *intent* and *focus* that are important, not just the physical labor.

Visualizations to Ward Off Illness

"There's something going around," we often say when we notice a slew of people around us coming down with colds or the flu. But you don't have to join them. Just because the germs have you in their sights doesn't mean it's inevitable that you have to be the unsuspecting prey.

Use any or all of the following visualizations to ward off ill health and increase your *vitality*. Carolyn tried using healing visualizations starting once cold weather set in and used them all through the winter, successfully avoiding getting her yearly up-close-and-personal visit from the flu, which typically coincided with post-holiday air travel.

Deeper Meaning

Vitality is defined as the power to live. It is what is necessary to manifest life. It concerns all things that support life. Vitality comprises all that is essential to existing, knowing, and understanding. The definition of vitality begins at home—with you.

Hearth and Home

In the Chinese art of feng shui, the gua in the center of your home rules health. It's easy to figure out which area of your home is health. When you enter the front door of your home, the foyer or first room is your career gua. Straight ahead, in the center, is your health gua. In some homes, this is the living room; in others, it's the kitchen. It's the heart of your home. Look back to Chapter 13 for a diagram of the guas.

To develop a visualization around your health, start with your space. Spend some time cleaning and straightening this area of your home (or have someone do this as you watch) as you visualize yourself at optimum health. To enhance this area, using feng shui principles, add plants that you change with the season (to keep the ch'i, or life energy, fresh). Light red or yellow candles with the intention of staying in perfect health, as you define it.

From this, you will have a picture of a physical space that you can use in a creative visualization session. Maintain your positive focus on this vision and use your affirmations. And the extra benefit is that you'll automatically feel better when you see how neat and organized your space is.

Purification

The kitchen is the place you gather with family and friends to prepare your sustenance. It may be the room where you spend the most of your waking hours. Take some extra time to scrub down your kitchen. Pull everything off the counters and get back in there to the places you miss when you do the daily once-over. Get serious about those burners on the stove. Suds up the sink and scrub it down. Mop the floor. (Again, this visualization works just as well if you have someone else do the cleaning.) As you work, set your intention to purify, purging all germs. Use the image of purifying in your next creative visualization session, focusing on activating all those healthy white blood cells, your body's natural defense against viruses and bacteria. Send this picture affirmations.

Not only is this an active visualization (much like the hands-on laundry visualization we did in Chapter 16), it's practical. Think of all those germs you killed. Make sure you disinfect all the doorknobs and phones in your house while you're at it.

Nurturing

There's nothing like the nurturing love of a mother, father, or someone close to you when you are sick. You can be well into the middle years of life, but when you get sick, it can still cross your mind that it sure would be nice to have your mother near, bringing you chicken soup and hot tea, saying, "Dear, dear."

Summon that nurturing energy by collecting images of nurturing mothers:

- Madonna and child
- Greek mother/fertility goddess Demeter
- American impressionist painter Mary Cassatt's images of mothers and children
- Egyptian mother goddess Isis

Or find an image at mothergoddess.com and use it as inspiration to make one of your own. A good, searchable source for art can be found at artcyclopedia.com or the images search on Google.com. (Conversely, you may find father or friend or animal images more nurturing than mother images.)

Centrally position pictures of those who nurtured you in the past or who continue to do that now. If you love animals, search for images of animal fathers or mothers nurturing their young. Sometimes these images touch us in ways that art images of people cannot. Use the image to create a visualization of healing. Write some affirmations just for this visualization.

Nourishment

Bread is the staff of life, providing nourishment. Taking a cue from our chapter on hands-on visualization (see Chapter 16), bake bread. Now we realize that baking bread may not be your thing, or you may simply not have time for it. This visualization is very powerful if you bake the bread, but it can be just as powerful if someone does it for you (as in, walking into a Great Harvest bakery). You may also use the image of baking bread in a creative visualization session, imagining all the steps. If you do not wish to bake, buy a freshly baked loaf of bread and make it central on your altar as you do this visualization. You can also imagine the steps you took to obtain the bread. Going to your favorite bakery, taking in the wonderful aromas, picking out your choice, smelling it all the way home in your car. Imagining how your partner and children or parents, whoever your family is, will react to this wonderful scent.

Imagine kneading the bread, your fingers laced through the dough. Imagine the bread in the oven, the dough rising. Imagine the scent of bread wafting through the house. Imagine taking the bread from the oven, with a crisp crust and a soft center. Visualize the nourishment that the bread offers for you and your family. Imagine biting into the warm bread, nourishing your body and soul.

Imagine, See, Be

Cooking with love is another way to develop a nourishment visualization. With a partner, prepare a multi-course dinner or one special dish. Set your intention beforehand to prepare every ingredient with love. Set aside plenty of time so you can cook slowly. When you serve your partner, serve him lovingly. Savor every bite. It's made from love. Another approach is for each person to prepare a dish for the other. You may also go to your favorite restaurant together or have friends in and tell them to each bring a "love" dish.

Fortification

Many products on the market help you fortify yourself from colds, from vitamin C to echinacea. Everyone, it seems, has a secret weapon against cold germs, whether it's Daily Chi Builder or grapefruit extract. We encourage you to research the market thoroughly—not just to take the advice of a friend. Ask your doctor about herbs. Check the news reports and official publications from the Federal Drug Administration, National Institutes of Health, and medical journals. Once you are convinced that an herbal supplement is appropriate and safe for you, begin to visualize that fortification is spreading through you as you take it. Use this affirmation: "I am strong. I am healthy. I am a fortress of vitality."

More Purification

Make a visualization ritual of washing your hands. Doctors recommend washing your hands more often during cold and flu season, as one of the best ways to prevent illness. So if you are following doctor's orders, you'll have plenty of opportunities to visualize good health. If you like, use scented soaps. That makes each hand-washing a pleasant little break in the day.

Each time you wash your hands, stop and take deep breaths. Get centered and hold a picture in your mind's eye of good health. Slowly rub the soap over your palms, fingers, and tops of your hands. Rub the soap between your fingers and up and down each one. Take it slow. Say this affirmation out loud or in your mind: "I am healthy. I am whole."

Visualization for Chronic Conditions

Here are some affirmations that may be helpful to use if you are dealing with chronic health problems:

I live my life in the light of who I am, not who I am not.

I affirm the wisdom that I have obtained from dealing with this illness.

I am serene.

I am wise about what treatments to pursue and which medical professionals I am to see.

I know all that I need to know now and I am open to what others may suggest to me.

I am able to make my own decisions and owe no one an explanation.

I am spiritually perfect.

Here is an example of a visualization that you might use if you live with compromised health. Do this visualization in your quiet meditation space. Sometimes being outside for meditation is quite healing and affirming—perhaps at the foot of a tree or a quiet place in a park.

1. Set up your altar with items that signify the peace, serenity, and wisdom that you have acquired. If you are outside, your altar might be at the base of a tree.

2. Spend time being thankful for all that you are and for your unique contributions to others around you. Visualize giving to someone.

3. Spend time being thankful for your perfect spirituality and your ability to access it. Ask to be reminded to do this more often during your busy day.

4. Spend time being thankful for those who share your life. Visualize those for whom you are most thankful.

5. Spend time being thankful for the understanding and peace that you have claimed for yourself about your physical condition. Visualize yourself being wrapped in a rainbow of colors and those colors staying with you always. This is your peace blanket. Take this image with you.

6. Visualize the soft, white, living light of perfect health. It surrounds you. It is unique to you. Perfection is defined by this light, and it belongs to you.

7. End your visualization by rereading your affirmations, and any that you have added to the list above.

8. Leave your meditation space remembering that you carry the rainbow colors of your peace blanket and the white light of perfection in regard to health.

Healing the Heart

Our hearts can carry wounds that change the course and the quality of our lives. A broken heart, distance between you and a friend, the stain of unforgiveness—these things can imbue our lives to where we are living with our hearts muffled, protected against further pain. But as Canadian-American chemist and author Orlando A. Battista said, "An error doesn't become a mistake until you refuse to correct it." To take that another step: a heartbreak doesn't become a wound unless you neglect to heal it.

Of course, many relationships have a season. Or they continue, but in another form, as when a couple with children divorces but continue to have a relationship in a parenting alliance. Even friendships ebb and flow over time. Some conflicts that seemed irreconcilable can be resolved

 Wisdom Well

One of the most lasting pleasures you can experience is the feeling that comes over you when you genuinely forgive an enemy—whether he knows it or not.

—Orlando A. Battista, Canadian-American chemist and author

with time and distance. Some conflicts persist, but the relationship must continue. Both must forgive and make peace with the things they could not change.

To come to peace with a relationship that has ended or changed form can take much effort, but the rewards of forgiveness are boundless. Integral to forgiveness is healing yourself. When you say you forgive someone but are still poignantly aware of the harm she caused you, you still have not completely forgiven. True forgiveness comes when you can present to the "someone" a picture of a healed, restored, thriving person. You are no longer a living reminder of the pain she caused. You can present to her a whole person.

In some cases, the wound may not completely heal. You may still have children together and know you are never going to be a married couple again, for instance. It's important that, while you cannot restore life to the way things were, you learn to live, healed, with the way things are. You must heal emotionally around this wound. You may carry it around with you as part of who you are, but it no longer dominates your actions and thoughts. This is true forgiveness.

Wisdom Well

The root of your life problems becomes nonexistent when you start to cherish others.

—Lama Zopa Rinpoche, Buddhist monk

If this is the case for you, begin by making the focus of your visualizations on healing your own wound. How does the emotional pain of the loss of this relationship affect the way you live your life? Look at your Life Arenas. Examine the choices you make. Notice the people you allow in, the people you shut out. Build a series of visualizations around each of these issues. Take it step by step. At the end of each one, add to the picture of yourself as whole, intact, and thriving. Begin each day, to live and breathe that picture.

Healing of the Mind

American author and self-motivation lecturer Wayne W. Dyer says, "if we are to have magical bodies, we must have magical minds." Healing of the mind is necessary when we overtax our minds. Our culture demands more and more of our brainpower, requiring multitasking to get any job done. A 2001 study conducted at the University of Michigan showed that our minds are less effective when we are multitasking. Indeed, the study even suggested that too much multitasking over time may result in a cumulative effect: the death of brain cells. It calls up the words of those drug abuse prevention announcements: This is your brain. This is your brain on multitasking.

If you feel tasked out, try these prompts for visualizations:

♦ **Keep the bowl empty.** Set an empty bowl in a place in your house where you will encounter it several times during the week. Each time you see the bowl, let it be a reminder to you to keep the bowl empty. Discard thoughts that keep you out of the now. Get rid of any clutter in your mind.

In your next creative visualization session, envision this empty bowl, directing your focus to it. Visualize peace in its emptiness.

♦ **Make the bowl sing.** Buy a Tibetan singing bowl at a metaphysical store or off the Internet. Play this metal bowl by rubbing a playing stick in a circle above the rim, letting the vibration create a calming hum. This is called making the bowl sing. Use playing the bowl as a way to anchor you in a visualization about achieving a clear mind.

♦ **Travel light.** Don't hold on to judgments about yourself and others. Set an intention in your next creative visualization session to release all judgments as they come up. Develop an affirmation that can cue you to release them when you notice them coming up, one that goes something like this: "I now release this judgment, committing it to the strong hands and wise mind of my spiritual self."

♦ **Embrace the present moment.** Use some of the techniques we outlined in Chapter 11 to bring yourself back into the present.

♦ **Practice preparation.** So much of the clutter in our minds results from rushing about, not having enough time to prepare for the day ahead. We don't have enough time to do the laundry, pay the bills, or make the meals, so we rush through all of these things frantically, doing them only half as well. Allow time in your schedule for preparation. Devote creative visualization sessions to envisioning yourself going through your day prepared, having the wisdom to eliminate anything that is not necessary from your day.

♦ **Practice completion.** It sounds simple, but life is more serene when you finish one task before you start another. If you have two or three big deadlines coming at once, you might be tempted to work on one for a chunk of time, then switch to the other for a little while. Instead, take one task all the way to completion, including delivering the document in person if that's what it takes. The physical act of completing the task all the way to the end means that you leave a wide open, uncluttered chunk of your mind for the next task. Notice how much more effective you are when you do this. Use your creative visualizations to imagine

---

Affirmations
I am at perfect peace each moment of the day.

the first task completely done and out the door. Imagine yourself turning to the next deadline with focus and precision. Use affirmations: "I am effective and focused in each task I complete today."

Connecting to Spirit

The book *A Course in Miracles* (see Appendix B), a psychological spiritual belief system, says there is only one problem: it is our belief that we are separated from our Higher Being. These visualizations provide a template for you to get back to that state. Again, we leave them open for you to interpret "Higher Being" for yourself.

Seeking Definition

Perhaps you have muddled your way through these chapters without quite knowing how you define your Higher Being. It may be that you have a few definitions overlaying each other in your life—your beliefs from childhood underlying new, half-formed beliefs of adulthood. Use this visualization to come up with a much more clearly focused definition of that Power in your life.

For the moment, let's throw out all the names we have for God. Instead, take a look at this list we have brainstormed of attributes that God might have. Circle the ones that fit your individual understanding and *your* experience.

Loving	Wise	Unknown	Free
Kind	Strong	Compassionate	Perfect
Generous	Merciful	Just	Immense
Gracious	Omnipresent	Dynamic	Incomprehensible
Good	Infinite	Pure	Light
Forgiving	Omniscient	Personal	Within
Powerful	Eternal	Immutable	All-encompassing
Magnificent	Transcendent	Part of a trinity	Comprising all matter
Peaceful	Creative	Simple	
Calm	Omnipotent	Complex	Undefinable
Awe-inspiring	Mysterious	Intelligent	

Take five or six words from your list and focus on them in your visualization session. Set your intention to further define this presence in your life—in all life. Visualize this answer coming to you clearer and clearer with each passing day. Visualize people coming into your life who can help you give the vision shape and definition. Visualize it as an ongoing quest.

Reconnecting

Visualize your spirituality as being all around, within, part of you. You are a part of it, indistinguishable; we are all one. Imagine an infinite glowing white cloud of light and pure love. Realize that you are a part of that cloud, not separate from it. It is where you are, who you are, all of the time. It is from that you were created. Ask to be reminded of this in waking hours and in dreams. You have never been apart from this love and light; you have merely sometimes been unaware of it.

Remember that spiritual living means ongoing conversation with your higher power or higher self, which is in truth inseparable from you. This conversation may include confessions of difficulties or problems, requests for answers, requests for ways to reconcile with those you have offended and restoration to harmony. Remember your breath prayer from Chapter 11.

Speak it each minute of the day, consciously or unconsciously.

Purifying

Spiritual wisdom from many traditions teaches us that one reason we believe that we are separate from God is because we look at ourselves and see we are not worthy. Turn back to some of the visualization rituals we have used in this chapter for purification and forgiveness. Use them, and use affirmations to see yourself as someone deeply loved by your Creator, just as you are.

Perfect Peace

No matter your circumstances in life, perfect peace and serenity are possible. You and your higher self or higher power have all that you need to live in this state perpetually. You can never really be separated from your Creator. Physical circumstances notwithstanding, perfect peace is only a whisper away.

The Least You Need to Know

◆ Use visualizations about nurturing, nourishment, home, love, and fortification to build good health.

◆ If you have a chronic health condition, you may use these techniques to understand that you have all you need and create the pathway to serenity and acceptance.

◆ Heal your heart by using visualization to build bridges with others and practice forgiveness.

◆ Calm your mind by keeping the bowl empty, traveling light, embracing the present, and practicing preparation and completion.

◆ Heal your spiritual wounds by using visualization to define your Creator and reconnect.

Chapter 23

Imagine the World You Want to Live In

In This Chapter

- ◆ Active visualizations that make a difference
- ◆ Collaborative visualizations that build community
- ◆ Taking prosperity universal
- ◆ Ever-expanding enlightenment

Imagine a world with no suffering. Imagine a world without poverty or war. Imagine all six billion of us with the same vision—peace, healing, prosperity, and love.

This chapter links creative visualization to its highest and ultimate outcome. Imagine if all of us saw the same vision for the world and poured our energy into it. In the sentiments of John Lennon's classic song, *Imagine*, we hope you'll join us, and someday the world will live as one.

Beyond Wishing: Active Visualizing

Let us imagine for a moment that if you asked every person on the planet, one by one, if they desired peace, personal contentment, security, and spiritual enlightenment, each person would probably say, "Of course." If you asked each person if they wanted to end poverty, racism, hunger, terrorism, you would assuredly get an almost unanimous, "Yes!"

To get started, make a list, being as specific as possible, about the change that you would want to see in the world. Ahead in this chapter, we will lead you through sample visualizations for these topics:

◆ Peace

◆ Building community

◆ Embracing diversity

◆ Healing the earth

◆ World prosperity

◆ Spiritual enlightenment

Before we dive in, take this list and brainstorm your own list of ways you want to change the world. Beside each one, make a specific goal, much as you did with the Life Arenas list in Chapter 1.

Many of the sample visualizations in this chapter use specific applications, but the techniques you use to prepare for the visualization can be applied to any issue. Refer to the list of techniques we used in the beginning of Chapter 20 to develop visualizations of your own. And read on to gain some inspiration for some powerful global visioning.

May Peace Prevail on Earth

No more war. No more poverty. An end to racism, hunger, and terrorism. These afflictions persist in our world. Most of us, most of the time, feel we cannot make much difference against the larger forces that create them. The first step is to see our individual power to turn the tide. It is said that peace begins at home, and that is where we will start.

The Peace Pole is a four-sided obelisk monument that displays the message, "may peace prevail on earth," in multiple languages. There are more than 200,000 Peace Poles in 180 countries, and many people use them as a way to visualize and pray for world peace. There is one in the meditation garden at the U.S. Pentagon. There are Peace Poles at the pyramids in Giza, Egypt; at the United Nations, at the site of the 2002 Winter Olympics in Salt Lake City, and the Magnetic North Pole in Canada. Quietly all over the world, these obelisks with a message of peace have been planted in gardens, parks, and churches. (Go to worldpeace.org/peacepoles to find out about getting one for your community or your private garden.)

The Peace Pole is a specific way to visualize world peace—and do it in a community. But there are many other ways to begin. Let's start right here at home. What creates peace within, and how can creative visualization bolster that?

- **Inner contentment.** If you experience inner contentment, then you are not striving or competing in the world. You are not focused on taking something from the world. You visualize yourself as intact and content, so you don't need to take. You know that whatever you need is coming to you, coming to you perfectly as it is meant to come, in just the right timing. Use your visualizations to bolster your contentment.

- **Healthy view of self.** You see yourself as part of a greater whole. You see your beliefs and actions as interconnected with others. You do not see yourself as "better than" or "less than" others.

- **Accepting of your shortcomings.** In accepting your own mistakes, you are more compassionate about others' miscues.

- **Seek first to understand, then to be understood.** When you find yourself thinking someone is "acting crazy," stop and try to understand the thoughts, feelings, or illness that could have created that behavior. The people who outrage us—from terrorists to crazy drivers—have valuable lessons for us about peace.

Many of the visualizations we have done so far have set the stage for creating inner peace. The bulk of this book has focused on creating inner happiness by manifesting your most heartfelt desires in life. When you see your life's purpose clearly and you are secure in the continuing unfolding of that purpose, you have achieved step one.

Building the Bonds of Community

We have used creative visualizations to enhance and even heal some of your crucial interpersonal relationships. Now we can use the same techniques to heal your relationship with the world. (Remember the visualization we used for metta, creating compassion, in Chapter 14? You can use that visualization in this context.)

Lebanese poet and philosopher Kahlil Gibran sets us up for this visualization. He wrote, "Your neighbor is your other self dwelling behind a wall. In understanding, all walls shall fall down. Who knows but your neighbor is your better self wearing another body? See that you love him as you would yourself. He too is a manifestation of the most high."

For this visualization, your goal is to see your neighbor as your better self wearing another body. One first step for understanding and dealing with what scares, disgusts, or bothers you is to study that very factor in yourself. Is there any of that trait in you? More than likely there is a small residue of that trait, and you may be consciously disciplining yourself not to develop that trait or give into pressure from our culture to allow that trait to flourish. So when you see it in another, often your energy is highly charged around it—for two reasons: one, you carry a little of it yourself. Two, you have made a judgment about it. You want to distance yourself from it. Build a visualization around this.

The second step is compassion. Try to understand how that trait manifests in the people you dislike. This doesn't mean that if you empathize, you agree with it. Building the bridge to empathy and compassion ends discrimination for many people.

Learning leads to tolerance. Psychologists study mental and emotional illnesses to foster healing in their patients. But a good bit of their training is in learning about themselves, looking inward. Physicians must learn the way an illness attaches itself to the body in order to promote healing. Journalists interview people to understand how they think. Engineers study the internal logic of a machine to understand how it works.

Think about ways you can educate yourself about people of the world who you perceive are against what you believe in. Use the steps we just outlined to create a visualization.

Imagine, See, Be _____

In traditional martial arts, students are taught to use self-mastery, discipline, mental focus, and inner tranquility to defend themselves. Rather than seeing an attacker as a threat, the practitioner of martial arts uses the force of his opponent to gain mastery. Serious martial arts students believe the discipline is not about learning how to fight, but how to live—not to dominate, but how to fulfill your purpose. Apply this philosophy to your visualizations about peace, tolerance, and diversity.

Diversity: So Much Talent

Every person is unique, which led to Martin Luther King Jr. saying that we live in a world in which our diversity will either create "chaos or community." In *Where Do We Go From Here: Chaos or Community* (Beacon Press, 1968), he reflected on the problems of the world, including nuclear weapons, poverty, and the riots of the times. He described rioting as not revolutionary—bringing about change—but reactionary, because it "invites defeat."

Our diversity—our differences—can either create divisiveness or strength, King said. With divisiveness, only the talents of the few contribute to solutions to world problems. When we embrace diversity, we accept the talents of many. What would the world be like if everyone was given an opportunity to fully contribute his or her talents? How long would it take to find a cure for cancer? Take a topic near and dear to your heart, and create a vision around it. Envision all the great minds and hearts of the planet contributing their knowledge and skills to solving this problem.

Don't Panic, *Focus!* _____

Discouraged? Do the world's problems seem too big? Increase the power of your visualizations by collaborating. American anthropologist Margaret Mead said: "Never doubt that a small group of thoughtful, committed citizens can change the world. Indeed, it is the only thing that ever has." See it, believe it, do it—and not only will you change your world, you'll likely gain a new understanding about the power of community.

Heal the Earth, Heal Ourselves

On average, the food we eat travels 1,200 miles before it reaches us. Many of us give hardly a thought to the techniques required to grow anything more than a beefsteak tomato in the backyard garden. This is fine. Somewhere at some point in human history, we figured out that the people who were good at agriculture, who owned the equipment and the fertile soil should grow food for the rest of the world. Then the rest of us went off to invent cell phones and manufacture silicon chips.

But twenty-first century life means that many of us live in cities, cut off from a direct awareness of our dependence on a healthy environment. Yet the environment itself offers healing properties that are just now being rediscovered. Ward Chaney discovered that many of the people who populated the inner city of Boston rarely ate or could hardly find a fresh, locally grown vegetable, so he started the Food Project. The experiment led to some of the city's toughest neighborhoods producing more than 60,000 pounds of organically grown vegetables in five years, just by converting vacant lots into vegetable gardens. The result was not just a flourishing of fresh produce, but healthier and happier people. Tending to vegetable gardens gave inner city kids a sense of empowerment.

We'll use that as a jumping off point for a visualization about environmental healing. First, to heal the environment, we must revere it. We must connect with it and others who cherish it.

- ◆ **Cherish the environment.** One weekend afternoon, take a stroll through the farmer's market in your community. Make a point of taking it in slowly, so allow enough time that you don't feel you have to rush off somewhere else. As you fill up your basket with produce, make the effort to connect with the growers. Chat with them about their vegetables and how they grow them. Take your basket home, full of flavor and stories, and prepare a meal for yourself and your family. As you do, visualize the connection that you have to the earth. Your affirmation: "I am connected to all life."

- ◆ **Make good choices.** Next assignment: find out how you are connected into the many ways we are polluting our environment. This requires a real gut-check and some substantial research. There's a lot of misinformation out there, and some of it can be overwhelming. Make a commitment to make small changes, little by little, in your buying habits. Each week, choose one, such as recycling your cardboard. It may be as simple as buying a separate trash receptacle so that you can sort it out as you go. As you instill this habit in your life, empower it by visualizing the impact your small change will have on the world at large. Visualize it rippling out, growing larger and larger. Your affirmation: "I am doing my part. My good choices and positive energy are spreading through the world."

♦ **Make your voice heard.** Find a way that your voice can be heard. Again, there are a myriad of causes out there, and it can be confusing and overwhelming to sort it out. How can one person make a difference in global warming or saving the rain forest or preserving the habitats of the tiger? All of these causes seem so worthy, but there is only so much of you.

Discard those thoughts, and use this visualization, and we assure you, you'll feel better about the whole thing. Pick a cause that really resonates with you. Now you need to make your vision less abstract. Oil drilling off the shore of an Alaskan wildlife habitat or deforestation in the remote rain forests of South America are so far away. You'll need to inhabit your vision. Fill it with wildlife, with plants, with insects. Insects that bite will really make it seem real! Gather pictures off the Internet (again, go to google.com and do an image search) or get a book from your community library. Find an account of someone who has explored the region, in a book or a movie or on a website. It's even better if you start corresponding with someone involved in the cause through e-mail. The more directly you can get to the human experience, the closer you get to compassion.

Build your visualization around all the images and information you have collected. In each visualization session, send positive energy to this visualization, creating positive images in your mind. Imagine many, many others on the planet doing the same. Know that you are not alone. Envision yourself as connected with other like-minded people. Imagine all of you collected on a hill overlooking the site of your environmental cause, holding hands, united in your effort. Your affirmation: "I, and many other strong individuals, are preserving this rain forest. Together, we are a healing force."

♦ **Make waves.** Take the power of your visualization to the next level by making waves with your local politicians. Use visualization to prepare yourself for positive, effective action in letting your opinions be known to the people who represent you in government. Your affirmation: "I, and many other strong individuals, believe that this person has the power to vote for the world I am envisioning."

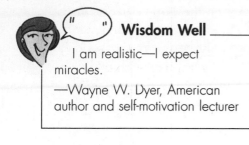

Finally, use this visualization of Mother Earth healing the world. Envision her holding the earth in her arms. Imagine her embracing all the people, plants, and animals, every ocean, every mountain, every forest, whispering soothing words to the earth. Summon this energy from within yourself. Your affirmation: "Together, we are all nurturing the earth that sustains us."

World Prosperity

As you prosper, so does the world. How can you draw on the visualizations from Chapter 21 to create visions for world prosperity? Simple. The techniques we used in Chapter 21 can be broadened to apply globally.

- ◆ Visualize an abundant world.

- ◆ Visualize a continually replenishing Earth. Visualize the continually replenishing talents and skills of all people of Earth.

- ◆ Visualize the beauty of the world.

- ◆ Visualize a secure world, where all believe they have enough. Visualize a safe world, where all people are free from danger.

- ◆ Visualize a world that nurtures the capacities of all individuals. Visualize a world that doesn't use them up, but instead sustains and enriches each individual's capacity to produce.

- ◆ Visualize a world in which there is no struggle—effort, yes. Desire, yes. But there is no struggle because we do not have to take from another person to create our own happiness. Visualize a world in which all experience vitality and grow luxuriantly.

Sound lofty? It is. Bring it down to a level where you can see the differences unfolding in your life. Practice generosity. Practice compassion. Get closer to your family and your community. Visualize the impact of your small pebbles rippling out into the world.

The Light of the World

For our closing visualization, we will end on a note of hope. It's easy to get discouraged when we think about the challenges we face as a global population in the twenty-first century. It can sometimes feel like we are so alone in desiring a better world. This visualization focuses on an ever-expanding sense of spiritual *enlightenment*, a world waking up to its own healing.

The song *From a Distance*, recorded by Bette Midler and Nanci Griffith and written by Julie Gold, comes to mind. The song talks about the way Earth's Creator must see us as we sleep at night. At night, a measure of peacefulness descends upon Earth. From a distance, we have plenty. We look the same. We live as one.

On the Internet, it's fairly easy to find satellite photos of Earth taken at night. (Go to google.com and do an image search of "Earth at night".) Generally, they show clusters of lights around the centers of population, such as the eastern and western seaboards of the United States, western Europe, India, China, and Japan.

Deeper Meaning

To **enlighten** is to give the light of fact and knowledge, to reveal those beliefs we know to be truths. It is also to be free from ignorance, prejudice, or superstition. To enlighten is to share with another your intentions, to give meaning and clarification to your actions, to promote understanding and joining together.

Use one of these images to create a visualization of a world waking up to a deeper knowledge of peace, prosperity, and compassion.

As you take in the image, dwell on the individual clusters of lights, envisioning each cluster as one more individual awakening to the infinite possibilities for what this world can be.

It helps to be specific, so use these steps, coupled with affirmations, imagining each light as an individual waking up to:

◆ Inner contentment

◆ Freedom from danger

◆ Freedom from hate

◆ Freedom from doubt

- ◆ Freedom from despair

- ◆ Dignity

- ◆ Clarity

- ◆ Purpose

Activate the image in your mind, adding more and more clusters of lights, coming on one by one. Imagine them twinkling as more and more lights come on. When it feels complete, watch the lights glimmer. Feel the strengthening of this energy. Feel it building. Your affirmation: "I am living in a world that is awakening to the power of the Infinite, the compassion of our Creator. I am seeing that happening now."

The Wellspring for Change

So as you can see, if you take care of yourself, get yourself in alignment with your purpose and become clear on your unique contribution, you can have a great impact on your world. The techniques of creative visualization and the exercises we have developed here are just a start. Awaken to your own power through creative visualization. Open your mind and your heart to the way intention can create miracles in your life—and in the world. Be the change you want to see in the world.

The Least You Need to Know

- ◆ Make your global visualizations active by imagining steps you can take that directly impact your world.

- ◆ To achieve peace in the world, create peace within.

- ◆ Practice tolerance by seeing your neighbor as "your better self wearing another body," and embrace the diversity of others' talents by committing to understanding them.

- ◆ To create change, use your visualizations to connect with the heart of your cause, make good choices in your daily life, and make your voice heard.

- ◆ Hold the vision of a world waking up to enlightenment and cherish it, sending it affirmations.

Creative Visualization Journal

Here's a guide to setting up a Creative Visualization Journal that will help you make the most of this book. We recommend setting up your journal in four sections.

Life Arenas

The first section should be the goals you set in Chapter 1, corresponding to your 10 Life Arenas:

Love _____

_____

Family _____

_____

Work _____

_____

Money _____

_____

Health _____

_____

Home _____

_____

Personal growth _____

_____

Spirituality _____

_____

Leisure/rejuvenation _____

_____

Creative self-expression _____

_____

Visualizations

The second section will be where you keep a summary of each visualization. We recommend setting them up based on the essential components of creative visualization:

Goal

Pick up the first line from your Life Arenas list.

_____

The Vision

Imagine your dream. What would it look like? Use your other senses, too. What would it sound like? Taste like? Set it in dialogue. Make it a movie, a series of moving pictures. Inhabit it. Fully envision it.

_____

_____

_____

_____

Believe

Write why this dream is right for you. How would your life be better for achieving this goal?

_____

_____

_____

Focus

Make a list of cues that will help you focus on this vision.

_____

_____

_____

Affirm

Keep a list of two or three essential affirmations specific to this dream.

_____

_____

_____

Progress Report

The third section of your Creative Visualization Journal will be where you keep track of your progress week by week. Use these prompts:

This week I faced these challenges ...

This week I had these doubts ...

This week I experienced these triumphs ...

This week I learned ...

This week I met/contacted ...

In the week ahead, I will take these steps ...

In the week ahead, my allies are ...

My affirmation for the week is ...

As you develop your Creative Visualization Journal, you may find you want to break down your goal into smaller steps. If you remember in Chapter 12, we talked about building a bridge to a big picture goal. So you may start out with a big dream: find meaningful work. Then you start to break it down. Create a visualization entry in your journal for each step. Set up a new page for each one. Link your visualizations with cross-referencing.

Affirmations

In the fourth section, record affirmations as you collect them. Some people like to do them by categories, aligning them with Life Arenas, for instance. Or you can just collect them as you develop them.

Make It Your Own

These are just guidelines to get you started well down the road of creative visualization. Your Creative Visualization Journal should be uniquely you. Once you start practicing, you'll find you want to customize your journal to fit your needs. After all, the best Creative Visualization Journal is a journal that you will use.

Appendix B

Resources

Here's a guide to further reading:

Adamson, Eve, and Gary R. McClain, Ph.D. *Empowering Your Life with Joy.* Indianapolis: Alpha Books, 2003.

Berkowitz, Rita, and Deborah S. Romaine. *Empowering Your Life with Angels.* Indianapolis: Alpha Books, 2004.

Chodron, Pema. *The Places That Scare You: A Guide to Fearlessness in Difficult Times.* Boston: Shambala Publications, 2001.

Csikszentmihalyi, Mihaly. *Flow: The Psychology of Optimal Experience.* New York: Perennial, 1991.

Domar, Alice D., Ph.D., and Henry Dreher. *Self-Nurture: Learning to Care for Yourself As Effectively As You Care for Everyone Else.* New York: Penguin Books, 2000.

Dyer, Wayne W. *The Power of Intention: Learning to Co-Create Your World Your Way.* Santa Monica, CA: Hay House, 2004.

Flynn, Carolyn, and Erica Tismer. *Empowering Your Life with Massage.* Indianapolis: Alpha Books, 2004.

Foundation of Inner Peace. *A Course in Miracles*. Mill Valley, CA: 1975.

Fox, Matthew. *Creativity: Where the Divine and Human Meet*. New York: Tarcher Putnam, 2002.

Gawain, Shakti. *Creative Visualization: Use the Power of Your Imagination to Create What You Want in Your Life*. Novato, CA: New World Library, 2002.

Gibran, Kahlil. *The Prophet*. New York: Knopf, 1923.

Grabhorn, Lynn. *Excuse Me, Your Life is Waiting: The Astonishing Power of Feelings*. Charlottesville, VA: Hampton Roads, 2003.

Greene, Brian. *The Elegant Universe: Superstring, Hidden Dimensions, and the Quest for the Ultimate Theory*. New York: Vintage, 2000.

Hanh, Thich Nhat. *Anger: Wisdom for Cooling the Flames*. New York: Riverhead Books, 2002.

Hay, Louise L. *You Can Heal Your Life*. Santa Monica, CA: Hay House, 1984.

Hicks, Esther and Jerry, and Wayne W. Dyer. *Ask and It is Given: Learning to Manifest Your Desires*. Santa Monica, CA: Hay House, 2004.

Myss, Caroline. *Anatomy of the Spirit: The Seven Stages and of Power and Healing*. New York: Three Rivers Press, 1996.

———. *Invisible Acts of Power: Personal Choices That Create Miracles*. New York: Free Press, 2004.

———. *Sacred Contracts: Awakening Your Divine Potential*. New York: Harmony Books, 2001.

———. *Why People Don't Heal and How They Can*. New York: Three Rivers Press, 1998.

Piver, Susan. *Joyful Mind*. New York: Rodale, 2002.

Pliskin, Marci, CSW, ACSW, and Shari L. Just, Ph.D. *The Complete Idiot's Guide to Interpreting Your Dreams, Second Edition*. Indianapolis: Alpha Books, 2003.

Ruiz, Don Miguel. *The Four Agreements: A Practical Guide to Personal Freedom*. San Rafael, CA: Amber-Allen Publishing, 1997.

———. *The Mastery of Love: A Practical Guide to the Art of Relationship, a Toltec Wisdom Book*. San Rafael, CA: Amber-Allen Publishing, 1999.

Sher, Barbara. *Wishcraft: How to Get What You Really Want*. New York: Ballantine Books, 1979.

Spangler, David. *Everyday Miracles: The Inner Art of Manifestation*. New York: Bantam, 1995.

———. *Laws of Manifestation*. Forres, Scotland: Findhorn, 1981.

Steinem, Gloria. *Revolution from Within: A Book of Self-Esteem*. New York: Little Brown and Company, 1992

Tolle, Eckhart. *The Power of Now: A Gateway to Spiritual Enlightenment*. Novato, CA: New World Library, 1999.

———. *Stillness Speaks*. Novato, CA: New World Library, 2003.

Virtue, Doreen. *Angel Medicine: How to Heal the Body and Mind with the Help of Angels*. Santa Monica, CA: Hay House, 2004.

———. *Healing with Angels: How the Angels Can Assist You in Every Area of Your Life*. Santa Monica, CA: Hay House, 1999.

———. *Messages from Your Angels: What Your Angels Want You to Know*. Santa Monica, CA: Hay House, 2002.

Williamson, Marianne. *A Return to Love*. New York: HarperCollins, 1996.

———. *A Woman's Worth*. New York: Random House, 1993.

———. *Enchanted Love: The Mystical Power of Intimate Relationships*. New York: Simon and Schuster, 2001.

Glossary

collaboration   The process of coordinating effort, sharing knowledge, and refining ideas with a group of two or more people. In a collaborative group, people work together to encourage creative ideas, achieve shared goals, and solve challenging problems. With collaboration, the whole is greater, stronger, and more effective than any individual working alone would be.

consciousness   The state of being aware of your own feelings. It is the process of examining your motivations in a deep and conscious way and allows you to clarify your vision.

creative visualization   The technique of using your imagination, intention, positive focus, and affirmations to manifest what you want in your life. By directing positive energy to that mental picture, you can make that vision a reality.

dream interpretation   This involves recording your dreams and understanding how they relate to your waking life. The process of understanding your dreams is the process of understanding yourself.

epiphany   A profound realization that often results in dramatic new understanding and significant changes on the inner and outer paths. Author Caroline Myss defines epiphany as "a sudden illumination of our intimate union with the Divine." The Greek root of the word means, "to manifest." Myss says that during an epiphany, your relationship to the Divine is transformed from doubt to deep trust. When you trust that your path is right, you are able to manifest.

enlightenment   This means receiving the light of fact and knowledge, to reveal those beliefs we know to be truths. When you are enlightened, you free yourself from ignorance, prejudice, or superstition.

flow   To move gently, smoothly, easily; to glide. Tapping into flow is a way to align yourself with the positive energy of the universe. Flow is the natural way to achieve your truest desires and highest goals.

flow state   Flow is when you achieve a high level of concentration and focus, a deep sense of enjoyment in the activity for its own sake. Many people say they have the sense of time standing still.

healthy self-esteem   This means having a positive, fairly accurate vision of yourself. You consider yourself to have mostly positive attributes, though you are aware of your flaws.

imagination   The power of forming mental images of what is not actually present. Your imagination allows you to picture what you have yet to create in your life.

infinity   A number in mathematics that is an unimaginably large number. It represents endless, unlimited space, time, distance, or quantity. The mathematical symbol for infinity is a figure eight lying on its side. The symbol is called a *lemniscate*.

integrity   The quality of being complete. To be integrated is to hold all facets of yourself consciously in your mind and in harmony. Integrating your conscious and subconscious beliefs and motivations allows you to function unimpaired—at optimum levels.

intention   An aim, a plan, or a purpose. Intention moves wishing into action. Intention is a complex, magical mix of determination, strong desire, belief, and clarity. It is an annunciation to yourself—and to the Universe—that you want it.

introspection   Looking inward to know yourself. It is reflecting on what dominates your thoughts and examining your attitudes about yourself, others, and the world. It helps you gain self-knowledge.

intuition   A way of knowing something without conscious reasoning. Intuition draws upon information and knowledge you may already have received but have not yet processed in a conscious way.

love   When it is healthy, love is something that American psychologist Erich Fromm, author of *The Art of Loving*, defines as the "union with somebody, or something, outside oneself, under the condition of retaining the separateness and integrity of one's own self." The distinction between immature love and mature love is that immature love says, "I love you because I need you" but mature love says, "I need you because I love you."

manifestation   To make something apparent to the senses so that it is clear and evident, most particularly to the sense of sight. Manifestation is breathing life into an idea until it takes form.

messengers   Entities that bring messages of wisdom, insight, or comfort. They can be spirit guides, angels, or divine messengers. Or they can be loved ones who have passed on, or ancestors we have never met.

mindfulness   Staying aware of something, holding it in your mind. Often mindfulness means keeping your mind on what you are experiencing in the present moment. Mindfulness engages all the senses.

nonintentionality   Being unaware of intentions that result in outcomes you don't want.

runner's high   The term sports psychologists use to describe a mental and physical phenomenon that occurs during exercise. It is a euphoric state characterized by an enhanced appreciation of nature and a transcendence of time and space.

sanctuary   A place of refuge or protection. In a religious context, it's a building set aside for worship, a holy place. In other contexts, it's simply a place where you can practice spiritual introspection.

self-actualization   The process of achieving personal fulfillment and inner harmony. Humanistic psychologist Abraham Maslow identified self-actualization in a hierarchy of human needs.

soul clarity   The recognition of your highest purpose. This recognition is a convergence of the inner and outer paths, when you see clearly that the material world and your relationships are methods by which you may find, know, and have your best and brightest life.

spiritual self-knowledge   Awareness of a deeper meaning for your life, something beyond yourself. When you practice spiritual self-knowledge, you see how you fit with others, with nature, with the animating force of the universe. This awareness connects you with creation, and you see more meaning in your life.

sport sight   Using focused visualization to discipline an athletic endeavor. The technique uses positive mental images, guided imagery, or creative visualization to help athletes train their minds and bodies to respond under pressure.

synchronicity   A meaningful coincidence. Two events occur by different causes at the same moment in time, but they are linked. Often the perception of a coincidence as being meaningful allows you to see a transcendent truth.

vitality   The power to live. It includes everything that is necessary to manifest life. It concerns all things that support life.

Index

D

J